T0210993

Lecture Notes in Computer Science 10566

Commenced Publication in 1973
Founding and Former Series Editors:
Gerhard Goos, Juris Hartmanis, and Jan van Leeuwen

More information about this series at http://www.springer.com/series/7411

Samia Bouzefrane · Soumya Banerjee
Françoise Sailhan · Selma Boumerdassi
Eric Renault (Eds.)

Mobile, Secure, and Programmable Networking

Third International Conference, MSPN 2017
Paris, France, June 29–30, 2017
Revised Selected Papers

 Springer

Editors
Samia Bouzefrane
Conservatoire National des Arts et Métiers
Paris
France

Selma Boumerdassi
Conservatoire National des Arts et Métiers
Paris
France

Soumya Banerjee
Birla Institute of Technology
Mesra
India

Eric Renault
Institut Mines-Télécom
Evry
France

Françoise Sailhan
Conservatoire National des Arts et Métiers
Paris
France

ISSN 0302-9743   ISSN 1611-3349 (electronic)
Lecture Notes in Computer Science
ISBN 978-3-319-67806-1   ISBN 978-3-319-67807-8 (eBook)
DOI 10.1007/978-3-319-67807-8

Library of Congress Control Number: 2017953431

LNCS Sublibrary: SL5 – Computer Communication Networks and Telecommunications

Printed on acid-free paper

This Springer imprint is published by Springer Nature
The registered company is Springer International Publishing AG
The registered company address is: Gewerbestrasse 11, 6330 Cham, Switzerland

Preface

The rapid deployment of new infrastructures based on network virtualization and cloud computing triggers new applications and services that in turn generate new constraints such as security and/or mobility. The International Conference on Mobile, Secure and Programmable Networking aims at providing a top forum for researchers and practitioners to present the future networking infrastructures, services and applications and their security.

MSPN 2017 was hosted by CNAM (Conservatoire National des Arts et Métiers) a French public institute created in 1794 and dedicated to long-life education. CNAM is based in the heart of Paris and is associated with the museum of arts and crafts.

We had 35 submissions and the Program Committee accepted 17 papers. Every submission was assigned to three members of the Program Committee for review. The accepted papers originate from: Algeria, Australia, China, Colombia, France, Germany, India, South Korea, Luxembourg, Morocco, Norway, Tunisia, and United Kingdom. Two brilliant invited speakers completed the technical program. The first speaker was Dr. Hanène Maupas from OT-Morpho, who presented the vision of industry in terms of identity and security in the Internet of Things. The second speaker was Dr. Nikolaos Georgantas, the head of the MIMOVE team at Inria, which is the best research institute in computer science in France.

We would like to thank the authors for their high-quality paper contributions, the chairs and the members of the Technical Program Committee (and the additional reviewers) for reviewing the submitted papers and selecting a high-quality program, and the general chairs for their support. Our special thanks go also to the Organizing Committee members for their great help and to the sponsoring institutions.

We hope that all the participants enjoyed this successful conference, made a lot of new contacts, and had a pleasant stay in Paris.

June 2017

Soumya Banerjee
Selma Boumerdassi
Samia Bouzefrane
Eric Renault
Françoise Sailhan

Organization

MSPN 2017 was organized by CEDRIC Lab of CNAM Paris and the University of Limoges with the cooperation of IFIP WG 11.2 Pervasive Systems Security.

General Chairs

Samia Bouzefrane	CNAM, France
Mehammed Daoui	University Mouloud Mammeri of Tizi-Ouzou, Algeria
Damien Sauveron	University of Limoges, France

Steering Committee

Selma Boumerdassi	CNAM, France
Eric Renault	Institut Mines-Télécom, Télécom SudParis, France
Samia Bouzefrane	CNAM, France

Program Chairs

Soumya Banerjee	Birla Institute of Technology, Mesra, India
Françoise Sailhan	CNAM, France

Organizing Committee

Amar Abane	CNAM, France
Lyes Bouali	CNAM, France
Habiba Chelah	CNAM, France
Jean-Marc Farinone	CNAM, France
Thinh Le Vinh	CNAM, France
Sarra Mehamel	CNAM, France
Lynda Saad	CNAM, France

Technical Program Committee

Emad Abd-Elrahman	National Telecommunication Institute, Cairo, Egypt
Nitin Agarwal	University of Arkansas at Little Rock, USA
Hanifa Boucheneb	Ecole polytechnique of Montreal, Canada
Mohand-Cherif Boukala	USTHB, Algeria
Shampa Chakrabarty	NSIT, New Delhi, India
Emmanuel Conchon	University of Limoges, France
Alan Devy	TSSG, Ireland
Yuhui Deng	Jinan University, China

Filippo Gaudenzi	Università degli Studi di Milano, Italy
Cherif Ghazel	ENSI/University of Manouba, Tunisia
Lorenza Gonzalez Manzano	Carlos III University of Madrid, Spain
Hanen Idoudi	ENSI/Manouba University, Tunisia
Milena Janakova	Silesian University in Opava, Czech Republic
Bouabdellah Kechar	University of Oran 1 Ahmed Ben Bella, Algeria
Selma Khebbache	Telecom SudParis, France
Frank Alexander Kraemer	NTNU Trondheim, Norway
Sjouke Mauw	University of Luxembourg, Luxembourg
Alessio Merlo	University of Genoa, Italy
Hassnaa Moustafa	Intel, USA
Paul Mühlethaler	Inria, France
Abdelkader Outtagarts	NOKIA Bell Labs, Villarceaux, France
Karima Oukfif	University Mouloud Mammeri of Tizi-Ouzou, Algeria
Vasile Palade	Coventry University, UK
Georgios Skourletopoulos	University of Nicosia, Cyprus
Nicolas Trèves	CNAM, France
Neil Yen	University of Aizu, Japan
Stefano Zanero	Politecnico di Milano, Italy
Gongxuan Zhang	Nanjing University of Science and Technology, China
Weishan Zhang	University of Petroleum, China
Peiyi Zhao	Chapman University, USA

Additional Reviewers

Amar Abane	CNAM, France
Kiran Kumar Bandeli	University of Arkansas at Little Rock, USA
Zahia Bidai	University of Oran, Algeria
Hend Fourati	ENSI/Manouba University, Tunisia
Hamza Khemissa	CERIST, Algeria
Duc-Hung Luong	NOKIA Bell Labs, Villarceaux, France
Youcef Ould-Yahia	CNAM, France
Radha Krishna Reddy Pallavali	Inria, France
Loic Perennou	CNAM, France
Arindom Roy	IBM Research, USA and India
Longbo Santa	University of Osaka, Japan

Sponsoring Institutions

Conservatoire National des Arts et Métiers, Paris, France
University of Limoges, France
OT-MORPHO, France

Contents

Efficient Implementation of Pedersen Commitments
Using Twisted Edwards Curves 1
  Christian Franck and Johann Großschädl

Enhanced Sinkhole System: Collecting System Details to Support
Investigations 18
  Martin Ussath, Feng Cheng, and Christoph Meinel

An Autonomous System Based Security Mechanism for Network
Coding Applications in Content-Centric Networking 34
  Li Xu, Hui Li, Jiawei Hu, Yunmin Wang, and Huayu Zhang

An Ultra-Lightweight Authentication Scheme for Heterogeneous Wireless
Sensor Networks in the Context of Internet of Things 49
  Hamza Khemissa, Djamel Tandjaoui, and Samia Bouzefrane

Authentication Based Elliptic Curves Digital Signature for ZigBee
Networks 63
  Ouassila Hoceini, Hossam Afifi, and Rachida Aoudjit

Formal Modeling and Performance Evaluation of Network's Server
Under SYN/TCP Attack.. 74
  Naouel Ouroua, Wassila Bouzegza, and Malika Ioualalen

Empirical Evaluation of a Distributed Deployment Strategy
for Virtual Networks 88
  Carsten Hahn, Stephan Holzner, Lenz Belzner,
  and Michael Till Beck

Identifying Service Contexts for QoS Support in IoT Service Oriented
Software Defined Networks 99
  Hong Jin Kim, Moon Yong Jung, Won Sang Chin,
  and Ju Wook Jang

A Fast Bit-Level MPLS-Based Source Routing Scheme in Software
Defined Networks: SD-{W,L}AN..................................... 109
  Ali El Kamel, Manel Majdoub, and Habib Youssef

Requirements and Complexity Analysis of Cross-Layer Design
Optimization for Adaptive Inter-vehicle DSRC 122
  Keyvan Ansari, Hannaneh Sadat Naghavi, Yu-Chu Tian,
  and Yanming Feng

Technique Stages for Efficient Wideband Spectrum Sensing
Based on Compressive Sensing.................................... 138
    Evelio Astaiza, Héctor Bermudez, and Octavio J. Salcedo Parra

Predicting Response Time-Related Quality-of-Service Outages
of PaaS Cloud Applications by Machine Learning.................. 155
    Angela Schedel and Philipp Brune

Intelligent Road Design Using Artificial Intelligence Techniques........... 166
    Camilo Isaza Fonseca, Octavio J. Salcedo Parra,
    and Brayan S. Reyes Daza

Mobility Prediction in Vehicular Networks: An Approach Through Hybrid
Neural Networks Under Uncertainty 178
    Soumya Banerjee, Samia Bouzefrane, and Paul Mühlethaler

Building of an Information Retrieval System Based
on Genetic Algorithms... 195
    Badr Hssina, Soukaina Lamkhantar, Mohammed Erritali,
    Abdelkrim Merbouha, and Youness Madani

A GRC-Centric Approach for Enhancing Management Process
of IoT-Based Health Institution................................. 207
    Fouzi Lezzar, Djamel Benmerzoug, Kitouni Ilham,
    and Aomar Osmani

Energy Consumption Estimation for Energy-Aware, Adaptive Sensing
Applications.. 222
    Nattachart Tamkittikhun, Amen Hussain, and Frank Alexander Kraemer

Author Index 237

Efficient Implementation of Pedersen Commitments Using Twisted Edwards Curves

Christian Franck$^{(\boxtimes)}$ and Johann Großschädl

Computer Science and Communications Research Unit,
University of Luxembourg, 6, Avenue de la Fonte, L–4364,
Esch-sur-Alzette, Luxembourg
{christian.franck,johann.groszschaedl}@uni.lu

Abstract. Cryptographic commitment schemes are used in many contexts, whereby the size of the secret data and the security requirements depend on the target application. Using a software library that has been designed for other purposes (e.g., key-exchange or digital signatures) to compute commitments can be complicated or inefficient. We present in this paper a flexible implementation of Pedersen commitments based on elliptic curves in twisted Edwards form. The implementation supports a set of five curves of varying cryptographic strength, which are defined over 127, 159, 191, 223, and 255-bit pseudo-Mersenne prime fields. One can dynamically (i.e., at runtime) choose one of the curves according to the required level of security, and it is also possible to adapt to the size of the data to be committed by varying the number of base points. The point arithmetic is performed with optimized formulas using extended coordinates and dynamically pre-computed tables are utilized to speed up the scalar multiplication. Our implementation is written in ANSI C (with optional x86 assembler optimizations for the field arithmetic) and was compiled and tested successfully with Visual C on Windows, gcc on Linux, and clang on macOS. We present detailed benchmarking results for the field and point arithmetic on all five curves. When using an Intel Core i7 processor clocked at 2.7 GHz as test platform, we can compute more than 38,000 commitments per second on a twisted Edwards curve over a 127-bit field.

1 Introduction

Traditional coin-flipping, where Alice calls either 'heads' or 'tails' and then Bob flips a coin, is not secure when it is done online. The problem is that Alice does not see the coin toss and Bob could simply cheat and pretend the outcome was 'tails' if Alice has called 'heads'. To prevent Bob from such cheating, Alice can compute a cryptographic commitment for either 'heads' or 'tails' and send it to Bob, instead of sending her choice directly. This commitment is binding Alice to her choice, but does not actually reveal it to Bob [9]. Alice will then only open the commitment and let Bob learn her choice once he has flipped the coin and announced the result. Opening the commitment discloses her choice and proves to Bob that it is authentic.

© Springer International Publishing AG 2017
S. Bouzefrane et al. (Eds.): MSPN 2017, LNCS 10566, pp. 1–17, 2017.
DOI: 10.1007/978-3-319-67807-8_1

What differentiates cryptographic commitment schemes from other crypto-graphic primitives like digital signatures is that commitments often have to be secure only for a relatively short period of time. Taking the coin-flipping from above as example, the commitment needs to be secure for just the few seconds until Bob has flipped the coin. Therefore, the orders of common multiplicative groups and elliptic curves used by classical signature schemes (e.g., 256 bits in ECDSA [21]) are unnecessarily large for short-time commitments, which makes the computation of such commitments unnecessarily costly. Various short-lived applications could profit from more "lightweight" alternatives.

A well-known commitment scheme based on the complexity of the Discrete Logarithm Problem (DLP) was introduced by Pedersen in 1991 [22]. Pedersen commitments are especially interesting since they are computationally binding and unconditionally hiding. The latter means for the above example that even when Bob had unlimited computational power, he would not be able to obtain Alice's choice from the commitment [9]. On the other hand, the computational binding property implies that it is not possible for Alice to change her mind and open the commitment to a different choice, unless she has the ability to solve the DLP. Interestingly, it has also been shown that one can prolong the lifetime of a Pedersen commitment, which means that it is possible to securely replace a Pedersen commitment with a weak security parameter by a Pedersen commitment with a stronger security parameter if the need arises [10]. Hence, one can start with lightweight commitments and switch to stronger ones later on.

In this paper, we introduce a software library that was specifically designed for the computation of Pedersen commitments [5, 22] so that they can easily be adapted to meet different requirements. The library features:

- *Adjustable security level (commitment size).* The library can be configured to use elliptic curves of different strength (i.e., different cardinality) in steps of 32 bits, ranging from 127 to 255 bits. In this way, the library is capable to generate commitments of different length and can be adapted for various security requirements.
- *Adaptable to the size of the secret data.* In order to generate commitments for secret data of "large" size, the library supports extended Pedersen commitments [5] on elliptic curves, which require a multi-scalar multiplication $C = s_1 P_1 + s_2 P_2 + \cdots + rQ$ with an arbitrary number of base points. This allows to maintain the homomorphic properties of Pedersen commitments even if the size of the secret data is large.
- *State-of-the-art elliptic curves.* A collection of five elliptic curves in twisted Edwards form [3], defined over 127, 159, 191, 223, and 255-bit pseudo-Mersenne prime fields, comes with the library. These curves satisfy all common security and efficiency requirements. In particular, the parameter a of these curves is -1, which facilitates the use Hisil et al's optimized point addition formulas for extended coordinates introduced in [16].
- *Fast fixed-base scalar multiplication with pre-computation.* The library uses the fixed-base windowing method described in [4], which employs pre-computed tables containing multiples of the base point in order to speed

up the scalar multiplication. It is possible to dynamically pre-compute such tables for any number of base points, and also the number of table entries can be adapted to allow for trade-offs between speed and RAM footprint.

- *Pre-computation of affine or extended affine coordinates.* One can choose to pre-compute either two or three coordinates per point in the table, and the corresponding optimized formulas will be used for the point addition. The two-coordinate variant is a bit slower, but reduces the table size by 33%.

- *Generic C and optimized x86 assembler code.* For maximal compatibility the library was written in ANSI C99, and performance-critical field-arithmetic operations were additionally implemented in x86 assembler to minimize the execution time. The source code was successfully compiled (and tested) on three different operating systems using three different compilers.

- *Resistance against timing attacks.* All arithmetic operations (with only one exception, namely inversion in the prime field) as well as the table look-ups have constant (i.e. operand-independent) execution time. The field inversion adopts the extended Euclidean algorithm [15] in combination with a simple multiplicative masking technique to thwart timing attacks.

The rest of the paper is organized as follows. In Sect. 2, we review the basics of Pedersen commitments and elliptic curve cryptography. Then, in Sect. 3, we motivate and describe the details of our implementation. In Sect. 4, we present benchmarking results for some selected curves, and in Sect. 5, we discuss some possible applications of our library. We conclude with remarks in Sect. 6.

2 Background

2.1 Commitment Schemes

Cryptographic commitment schemes allow one to commit to some secret value without having to reveal it (at the time of making the commitment), but it is possible to reveal the value later and to prove that the revealed value is indeed the correct value [9]. In general, a commitment protocol is performed between a committer and a verifier, and consists of the two following steps:

1. *Commit:* In order to commit to a secret value s, the committer chooses a random value r and sends the commitment

$$C = \text{commit}(s, r)$$

   to the verifier. The knowledge of C does not provide the verifier with any information about the secret value s.

2. *Open:* In order to open the commitment, the committer sends (s, r) to the verifier. The committer is bound to the value s, which means it is hard to create another pair of values (s', r') such that

$$C = \text{commit}(s', r').$$

As explained in [9], a commitment scheme can be either computationally binding and unconditionally hiding, or it can be unconditionally binding and computationally hiding. However, it can never be unconditionally hiding and unconditionally binding at the same time.

Pedersen Commitments. The Pedersen commitment scheme, in its original form as described in [22], uses a prime-order subgroup of $\mathbb{Z}_p^*$ as basic algebraic structure. However, it is also possible to embed the computation of Pedersen commitments into an elliptic-curve group $E(\mathbb{F}_p)$. Assume $E(\mathbb{F}_p)$ contains two points P and $Q = \alpha P$, both having prime order q, whereby the scalar $\alpha < q$ is unknown. In this setting, the commitments are of the form

$$C = \text{commit}(s, r) = sP + rQ.$$

Similar to "classical" Pedersen commitments operating in $\mathbb{Z}_p^*$, the elliptic-curve variants are *unconditionally hiding* since every possible value of the secret s is equally likely to be committed in C. More precisely, for any $s' \neq s$, there exists an $r' \neq r$ such that $\text{commit}(s', r') = C = \text{commit}(s, r)$; this r' can be obtained by computing $r' = (s - s')/\alpha + r \bmod q$. Therefore, the verifier can not learn anything about s from C, even if she had unlimited computing power. Furthermore, elliptic-curve Pedersen commitments are *computationally binding* since the committer can not open a commitment to s as $s' \neq s$, unless she is able to solve the Elliptic Curve Discrete Logarithm Problem (ECDLP). Namely, if the committer could find a pair (s', r') that commits to the same C as (s, r), then it would be easy for her to get $\alpha = (s - s')/(r' - r) \bmod q$, which contradicts the hardness assumption for the ECDLP.

The idea of Pedersen commitments can also be extended to multiple values $s_1, \ldots, s_n$, as shown in [5]. The commitments are then of the form

$$C = s_1 P_1 + s_2 P_2 + \cdots + s_n P_n + rQ. \tag{1}$$

As a consequence, one can use Pedersen commitments to commit to messages of arbitrary length. We assume the points $P_1, P_2, \ldots, Q$ are chosen at random and their respective discrete logarithms are unknown.

Pedersen commitments also have homomorphic properties. Given the commitments

$$C_1 = s_1 P + r_1 Q \text{ and } C_2 = s_2 P + r_2 Q$$

for the values s_1 and s_2, one can compute a commitment C_{12} corresponding to the secret value $s_1 + s_2$ and the random value $r_1 + r_2$, with

$$C_{12} = (s_1 + s_2)P + (r_1 + r_2)Q = (s_1 P + r_1 Q) + (s_2 P + r_2 Q) = C_1 + C_2.$$

In order to preserve this homomorphic property for longer messages, one can not just use a hash function $\mathcal{H}$ and compute $C = \mathcal{H}(s_1|\cdots|s_n)P + rQ$, but it is necessary to compute a commitment as in Eq. (1).

2.2   Twisted Edwards Curves

Twisted Edwards (TE) curves were introduced in 2008 by Bernstein et al. [3] as a generalization of Edwards curves [11]. Formally, a TE curve is defined by an equation of the form

$$E : ax^2 + y^2 = 1 + dx^2 y^2 \tag{2}$$

over a non-binary finite field $\mathbb{F}_q$, where a and d are distinct, non-zero elements of $\mathbb{F}_q$. Every TE curve is birationally-equivalent over $\mathbb{F}_q$ to a Montgomery curve and, thus, also to an elliptic curve in Weierstraß form. The order of a TE curve is divisible by 4 (i.e. TE curves have a co-factor of $h \geq 4$), and every TE curve contains a point of order 2, namely $(0, -1)$. Given two points $P_1 \in E(\mathbb{F}_q)$ and $P_2 \in E(\mathbb{F}_q)$, their sum $P_3 = P_1 + P_2$ can be computed as

$$(x_3, y_3) = (x_1, y_1) + (x_2, y_2) = \left(\frac{x_1 y_2 + y_1 x_2}{1 + d x_1 x_2 y_1 y_2}, \frac{y_1 y_2 - a x_1 x_2}{1 - d x_1 x_2 y_1 y_2} \right).$$

The point $\mathcal{O} = (0, 1)$ serves as neutral element of the addition, and the negative of a point (x_1, y_1) is $(-x_1, y_1)$. Note that the addition formula specified above is *unified*, which means it can also be used for point doubling. Furthermore, as shown in [3], the given addition formula is *complete* (i.e. yields the correct sum for any pair of points, including corner cases like $P_1 = \mathcal{O}$, $P_2 = \mathcal{O}$, $P_2 = -P_1$) when the curve parameter a is a square and d a non-square in $\mathbb{F}_q$. In order to avoid costly inversions in the point arithmetic, one normally uses a projective coordinate system. A well-known example are the so-called extended projective coordinates from [16], which allow for particularly efficient point addition when $a = -1$. A point in extended project coordinates is represented by a quadruple $(X : Y : T : Z)$ where $T = XY/Z$. The projective curve equation is

$$(aX^2 + Y^2)Z^2 = Z^4 + dX^2 Y^2, \tag{3}$$

which can be simplified to $aX^2 + Y^2 = Z^2 + dT^2$. The TE curves we use for the implementation of Pedersen commitments feature a fast and complete addition law, meaning that $a = -1$ is a square in the underlying prime field.

3 Implementation Details

In this section, we give an overview of our software implementation of Pedersen commitments using TE curves. We aimed to reach three main goals, namely (i) high performance, (ii) high scalability, and (iii) support for a wide range of x86 platforms. In order to achieve fast execution times, we decided to implement all performance-critical operations, in particular the multiplication and squaring in the underlying field, not just in C but also in Assembly language. Our software is scalable because it supports Pedersen commitments of varying cryptographic "strength" (using TE curves of different order) without the need to recompile the source code. Finally, to support many platforms, we developed our software for the standard x86 architecture and refrained from using 64-bit instructions or SIMD extensions such as SSE. In this way, our implementation of Pedersen commitments can run on a plethora of x86-compatible platforms, ranging from high-end 64-bit Intel Core processors down to embedded 32-bit variants like the Intel Quark [18] for systems on chip. As part of our future research, we plan to extend the software with an optimized 64-bit Assembler implementation of the field arithmetic so that it can reach peak performance on 64-bit processors.

3.1 Prime-Field Arithmetic

The arithmetic operations in the underlying field, especially multiplication and squaring, have a massive impact on the overall execution time of elliptic curve cryptosystems, and our TE-based Pedersen commitments are no exception. It is common practice to adopt finite fields defined by primes of a "special" form in order to maximize the efficiency of the modular reduction operation. As will be explained in Subsect. 3.4, the TE curves we use are defined over fields based on *pseudo-Mersenne primes*, which are primes of the form $p = 2^k - c$, where c is small in relation to 2^k [15]. The elements of $\mathbb{F}_p$ are integers with a length of up to k bits, and the product z of two such integers a, b is at most $2k$ bits long. To reduce z modulo p, one can exploit $2^k \equiv c \bmod p$, which results in a reduction technique with linear complexity. More concretely, in order to reduce z modulo p, the product z is first split up into an upper part z_H and a lower part z_L so that $z = z_H 2^k + z_L$; then, z_H is multiplied by c and $z_H c$ is added to z_L. These steps are repeated with the obtained result and, finally, subtractions of p have to be performed to get a fully reduced result (see e.g. [20] for details).

As will be specified in full detail in Subsect. 3.4, the prime fields we use are defined by pseudo-Mersenne primes of the form $p = 2^k - c$ where k is a multiple of 32 minus 1 (e.g. $k = 255$) and c is at most 29 bits long (i.e. c fits in a single x86 register). We represent the field elements by arrays of 32-bit words of type uint32_t, which means in the case of $k = 255$ that an array has eight words. In the beginning of this section we mentioned already that our software contains two implementations of the field arithmetic, one written in C and the other in x86 Assembly language. The C implementation is generic in the sense that the arithmetic functions can process operands of any length. Every function of the C arithmetic library gets besides the arrays for the operands and the result an extra parameter that specifies the number of words the arrays consist of. On the other hand, the x86 Assembler library comes with a dedicated implementation for each supported operand length, which means, for example, that it contains five functions for modular multiplication, optimized for 127, 159, 191, 223, and 255-bit fields. Each of these functions was carefully hand-tuned and loops were fully unrolled to maximize performance.

A multiplication in a pseudo-Mersenne prime field is normally performed in two steps: first, the field elements are multiplied, yielding a double-length product, and thereafter a modular reduction is carried out, taking into account the special form of the prime. Our Assembler implementation applies the so-called *product-scanning method*, which means the 64-bit word-products resulting from multiplying pairs of 32-bit words are summed up in a column-wise fashion (see [15, Algorithm 2.10] and [20, Algorithm 1] for a more formal description). The biggest challenge one has to tackle when implementing the this technique on an x86 processor is the small register file, consisting of just eight general-purpose registers, one of which is the stack pointer register ESP. The MUL instruction in x86 reads one operand from the EAX register, while the second operand can be either in a register or in memory. It executes an unsigned 32-bit multiplication and places the 64-bit product in the EDX:EAX register pair. Our implementation of the modular multiplication stores the double-length product of the two field elements in a temporary array on the stack, which is accessed via ESP. Of the remaining seven registers, three hold the column sum, two contain the pointers to the operand arrays, and EAX/EDX are used to execute MUL instructions.

The square of a field element can be computed using fewer MUL instructions than the product of two distinct field elements. Our implementation is based on the optimized squaring technique described in [20].

3.2 Point Arithmetic

The to date most efficient way of performing point arithmetic on a TE curve is to use the extended coordinates proposed by Hişil et al. [16]. In this coordinate system, a point $P = (x, y)$ is represented by a quadruple $(X : Y : T : Z)$ where $x = X/Z$, $y = Y/Z$, $xy = T/Z$, and $Z \neq 0$. Such extended coordinates can be seen as homogenous projective coordinates of the form $(X : Y : Z)$, augmented by a fourth coordinate $T = XY/Z$ that corresponds to the product xy in affine coordinates. The neutral element $\mathcal{O}$ is given by $(0 : 1 : 0 : 1)$, and the negative of a point in extended coordinates is $(-X : Y : -T : Z)$. A point represented in standard affine coordinates as (x, y) can be converted to extended coordinates by simply setting $X = x$, $Y = y$, $T = xy$, and $Z = 1$. The re-conversion is done in the same way as for homogenous projective coordinates through calculation of $x = X/Z$ and $y = Y/Z$, which costs an inversion in the underlying field.

In the following, we roughly explain the unified addition/doubling formulae using extended coordinates as given by Hişil et al. in [16, Sect. 3.1]. Let P_1 and P_2 be two arbitrary points on a TE curve represented in extended coordinates of the form $(X_1 : Y_1 : T_1 : Z_1)$ and $(X_2 : Y_2 : T_2 : Z_2)$ where $Z_1, Z_2 \neq 0$. When $a = -1$ (as is the case for all our curves from Subsect. 3.4), a unified addition $P_3 = P_1 + P_2 = (X_3 : Y_3 : T_3 : Z_3)$ consists of the following operations.

$$A \leftarrow (Y_1 - X_1) \cdot (Y_2 - X_2), \quad B \leftarrow (Y_1 + X_1) \cdot (Y_2 + X_2), \quad C \leftarrow k \cdot T_1 \cdot T_2,$$
$$D \leftarrow 2Z_1 \cdot Z_2, \quad E \leftarrow B - A, \quad F \leftarrow D - C, \quad G \leftarrow D + C, \quad H \leftarrow B + A,$$
$$X_3 \leftarrow E \cdot F, \quad Y_3 \leftarrow G \cdot H, \quad T_3 \leftarrow E \cdot H, \quad Z_3 \leftarrow F \cdot G$$

$$(4)$$

The factor k used in the computation of C is $-2d/a$, which means in our case $k = 2d$ since the parameter $a = -1$ for all our TE curves. It is easy to observe that computational cost of the point addition amounts to nine multiplications (9M) in the underlying prime field, plus a few "cheaper" field operations like additions. When P_2 is given in affine coordinates (i.e. $Z_2 = 1$), the addition is a so-called "mixed addition" and requires only eight multiplications (8M). Hişil et al. also introduced a formula for doubling a point $P_1 = (X_1 : Y_1 : T_1 : Z_1)$ so that the result $P_3 = 2P_1$ is also given in extended coordinates. For TE curves with parameter $a = -1$, the sequence of operations to double a point is

$$A \leftarrow X_1^2, \quad B \leftarrow Y_1^2, \quad C \leftarrow 2Z_1^2, \quad D \leftarrow -A, \quad E \leftarrow (X_1 + Y_1)^2 - A - B,$$
$$G \leftarrow D + B, \quad F \leftarrow G - C, \quad H \leftarrow D - B,$$
$$X_3 \leftarrow E \cdot F, \quad Y_3 \leftarrow G \cdot H, \quad T_3 \leftarrow E \cdot H, \quad Z_3 \leftarrow F \cdot G.$$

$$(5)$$

A doubling carried out via Eq. (5) requires four multiplications (4M) as well as four squarings (4S) in the underlying field. Unlike the addition formula given in Eq. (4), the doubling operation does not use the auxiliary coordinate T_1 of the point P_1. Therefore, the computation of T_3 in Eq. (5) could be simply omitted whenever a doubling is followed by another doubling. A similar observation can be made for the addition because the coordinate T_3 in Eq. (4) does not need to be computed when the subsequent operation is a point doubling.

In order to accelerate the point doubling operation, we do not compute the auxiliary coordinate T_3 as in Eq. (5) but output the two factors E and H it is composed of instead. In this way, the resulting point $P_3 = 2P_1$ consists of five coordinates instead of four, which means P_3 is actually represented in the form of a quintuple $(X_3 : Y_3 : E_3 : H_3 : Z_3)$. The coordinate T_3 is split up into factors E_3 and H_3 such that $E_3 H_3 = T_3 = X_3 Y_3 / Z_3$, thereby saving a multiplication in the point doubling. The subsequently-executed operation can recover T_3, when needed, by simply multiplying E_3 by H_3. Of course, such a modification of the doubling requires to adapt the point addition accordingly [8]. We modified the addition formula specified in Eq. (4) to output the two factors $E = B - A$ and $H = B + A$ instead of $T_3 = EH$. In this case, when the addition is performed with P_1 represented by $(X_1 : Y_1 : E_1 : H_1 : Z_1)$ as input, the auxiliary coordinate $T_1 = E_1 H_1$ has to be computed first since it is used as operand. However, this modification has no impact on the overall cost of the point addition since the computation of the coordinate $T_3 = EH$ is simply replaced by computing the coordinate $T_1 = E_1 H_1$. On the other hand, the cost of the point doubling gets reduced from 4M + 4S to 3M + 4S thanks to this optimization.

Our software for Pedersen commitments actually computes so-called mixed additions, which means point P_1 is given in projective coordinates (in our case extended projective coordinates in the form of a quintuple, see above), whereas P_2 is represented using affine coordinates. We implemented two variants of the mixed addition; the first expects P_2 in standard affine (x, y) coordinates, while in the other variant, P_2 must be provided in extended affine coordinates of the form (u, v, w) where $u = (x - y)/2$, $v = (x + y)/2$, and $w = dxy$, similar to the mixed addition in e.g. [4,20]. The exact formula for the former variant is specified in Appendix A (Algorithm 1) and has a cost of 8M plus a multiplication by the parameter d, which is fast for all our TE curves since d is small. On the other hand, the latter variant takes only 7M (because the product dxy is pre-computed), but this performance gain comes at the expense of requiring three coordinates for P_2, which can be undesirable on certain platforms or for certain scalar multiplication techniques that pre-compute and store many points.

3.3   Computation of Pedersen Commitments

The high-level strategy we use to compute the commitments is a generalization of the fast fixed-base exponentiation techniques described in [6,19,23], which is also used by Bernstein et al. in [4]. The basic idea is that a scalar multiplication with a fixed base point, i.e. an operation of the form $S = \kappa P$ where P is known a priori (e.g. it is the generator of an elliptic-curve subgroup), can be computed faster using a (possibly small) table with pre-computed points. To avoid cache attacks, we use constant-time table look-ups as described in e.g. [4]. In order to accelerate the scalar multiplication, we write the k-bit scalar κ as

$$\kappa = \sum_{i=0}^{\lceil k/4 \rceil} \kappa_i \cdot 16^i$$

with $0 \leq \kappa_i \leq 15$ for $i \in \{0, 1, \ldots, \lceil k/4 \rceil\}$ and pre-compute 15 multiples of the base point P, namely the set $\{16^i P, (2 \cdot 16^i)P, \ldots, (15 \cdot 16^i)P\}$ for every i from 0 to $\lceil k/4 \rceil$. This reduces the computation of S to $\lceil k/4 \rceil$ point additions since

$$S = \sum_{i=0}^{\lceil k/4 \rceil} (\kappa_i \cdot 16^i)P.$$

As will be detailed in Subsect. 3.4, we use primes of the form $p = 2^k - c$, where k is a multiple of 32 minus 1, and also the bitlength of our scalars is a multiple of 32 minus 1, similar to [2]. Thus, we can assume $0 \leq \kappa_{\lceil k/4 \rceil} \leq 7$, which means we can also utilize signed coefficients κ_i' with $-8 \leq \kappa_i' < 8$, so that

$$S = \sum_{i=0}^{\lceil k/4 \rceil} (\kappa_i' \cdot 16^i)P.$$

Signed coefficients have the big advantage that only eight pre-computed points (namely $\{16^i P, (2 \cdot 16^i)P, \ldots, (8 \cdot 16^i)P\}$) are needed for every i. They have no impact on performance because the negative of a point (x, y) on a TE curve is simply $(-x, y)$. To further reduce the number of pre-computed points, we write

$$S = \sum_{i=0}^{\lceil k/8 \rceil} (\kappa_{2i}' \cdot 16^{2i})P + 16 \cdot \sum_{i=0}^{\lceil k/8 \rceil} (\kappa_{2i+1}' \cdot 16^{2i})P.$$

Hence, at the cost of four point doublings (since $16 = 2^4 = 2 \cdot 2 \cdot 2 \cdot 2$), we can halve the number of necessary pre-computed points, and the pre-computations need to be done only for $i \in \{0, \ldots, \lceil k/8 \rceil\}$ instead of $i \in \{0, \ldots, \lceil k/4 \rceil\}$. In the context of Pedersen commitments, we can have expressions of the form

$$C = s_1 P_1 + s_2 P_2 + \cdots + s_n P_n + rQ,$$

which have several base points. We "integrate" these computations according to

$$C = \sum_{i=0}^{\lceil k/8 \rceil} \kappa_{2i}^{(1)} 16^{2i} P_1 + \cdots + r_{2i} 16^{2i} Q + 16 \sum_{i=0}^{\lceil k/8 \rceil} \kappa_{2i+1}^{(1)} 16^{2i} P_1 + \cdots + r_{2i+1} 16^{2i} Q^{16}$$

so that we have to do the four point doublings of the second term only once. As the number of base points gets larger, the relative cost of these four doublings decreases, and it can make sense to do some further modifications to obtain an expression of the form

$$
C = \sum_{i=0}^{\lceil k/16 \rceil} \cdots + 16 \left(\sum_{i=0}^{\lceil k/16 \rceil} \cdots + 16 \left(\sum_{i=0}^{\lceil k/16 \rceil} \cdots + 16 \sum_{i=0}^{\lceil k/16 \rceil} \cdots \right) \right),
$$

which again reduces the number of pre-computed points at the expense of eight point doublings (i.e. we have to perform 12 doublings altogether).

Our software for Pedersen commitments supports all these possibilities; it is up to the user to choose which trade-off between the amount of pre-computed points and number of point doublings suits best for a certain application. The amount of memory m (in bytes) required to store the pre-computed points can be calculated using the formula

$$
m = b \cdot \frac{(k+1)^2}{4(t+1)},
$$

where b is the number of base points, $t \in \{2, 4, 8, 16, 32\}$ is the number of times that the four point doublings are performed, and k denotes the bitlength of the scalar (which is, in our case, the same as the bitlength of the underlying prime field and is always a multiple of 32 minus 1). The factor $(k+1)^2$ in the above formula implies that choosing a smaller prime p whenever possible will reduce the memory requirements significantly.

The high-level API of our x86 software for the computation and verification of Pedersen commitments supports the following six functions:

- *Pre-computation:* $\Omega = \mathrm{precomp}(\Gamma, (P_1, P_2, \ldots), \tau)$. Pre-computes points to speed up a fixed-base scalar multiplication using the TE curve parameters $\Gamma = (k, c, d)$, a set of base points $(P_1, P_2, \ldots)$, and a parameter τ to trade memory usage for speed.
- *Commitment:* $C = \mathrm{commit}(\Gamma, (s_1, \ldots, s_n), r, \Omega)$. Computes a commitment for the set of secret values $(s_1, \ldots, s_n)$ using the random number r and the pre-computed points Ω. The output is compressed as described in [4].
- *Verification:* $\{0, 1\} = \mathrm{verify}(C, \Gamma, (s_1, \ldots, s_n), r, \Omega)$. Verifies whether the set $(s_1, \ldots, s_n)$ and number r correspond to the commitment C.
- *Compression:* $C = \mathrm{compress}(\Gamma, A)$. Converts the point A in standard affine to a commitment C (in compressed representation).
- *Decompression:* $A = \mathrm{decompress}(\Gamma, C)$. Decompresses a commitment C to recover the x and y coordinate of the corresponding affine point A.
- *Addition:* $A = \mathrm{add}(\Gamma, A_1, A_2)$. Adds the two affine points A_1 and A_2.

3.4   Supported TE Curves

A TE curve needs to meet several security and efficiency criteria in order to be suitable for cryptography applications. A discussion of these criteria is outside the scope of this paper; we refer the interested reader to [14] and the references given therein. Our software for Pedersen commitments comes with a set of five TE curves, which are defined over pseudo-Mersenne prime fields having lengths of 127, 159, 191, 223, and 255 bits. The co-factor of the curves is $h = 8$, and so they provide security levels of 62, 78, 94, 110, and 126 bits. Concretely, the five TE curves we use are specified by the following equations.

$$-x^2 + y^2 = 1 + 182146x^2y^2 \bmod 2^{127} - 507$$
$$-x^2 + y^2 = 1 + 49445x^2y^2 \bmod 2^{159} - 91$$
$$-x^2 + y^2 = 1 + 141087x^2y^2 \bmod 2^{191} - 19$$
$$-x^2 + y^2 = 1 + 987514x^2y^2 \bmod 2^{223} - 235$$
$$-x^2 + y^2 = 1 + 4998299x^2y^2 \bmod 2^{255} - 19$$

The latter four curves are taken from [14], where it is described how they were generated and what security properties they meet. We generated the first curve (i.e. the curve based on the 127-bit field) from scratch, following the guidelines in [14]. However, it must be noted that solving the ECDLP in a 124-bit elliptic curve subgroup is well within reach for a well-funded adversary; therefore, this curve is only suitable for commitments with short-time security requirements in the area of a few seconds. Also the adequacy of the curve over the 159-bit field (providing a security level of roughly 78 bits) must be carefully evaluated. The main characteristics of all five curves are summarized in Table 2.

Our software is not restricted to these curves and can be easily extended to support other pseudo-Mersenne prime fields and TE curves, provided that the following conditions are fulfilled. First, the constant c of the pseudo-Mersenne prime $p = 2^k - c$ is at most 29 bits long and k is a multiple of 32 minus 1. The resulting prime p must be congruent to 5 modulo 8 so that $a = -1$ is a square in $\mathbb{F}_p$ (and the TE addition law can be complete [3]) and square roots modulo p (which are needed for the decompression of compressed curve points [4]) can be computed efficiently via Atkin's method [1]. Second, the parameter d of the TE curve is at most 32 bits long and a is fixed to -1 so that the fast addition formula proposed by Hişil et al. [16] can be used. The resulting TE curve needs to have a co-factor of $h = 8$ and meet all other requirements listed in [14].

4   Benchmarking Results

In this section, we present some benchmarks for the field arithmetic operations and the computation of commitments for five different security levels using the curves given above. We made an effort to ensure the C and Assembler source codes can be compiled (and execute correctly) with three different compilers on three different operating systems, namely Microsoft Visual C on Window 7, gcc

Table 1. Computation time of field operations on a 2.7 GHz Core i7 CPU.

Prime p	$2^{127} - 507$	$2^{159} - 91$	$2^{191} - 19$	$2^{223} - 235$	$2^{255} - 19$
C99					
Multiplication	95 cycles	123 cycles	165 cycles	200 cycles	256 cycles
Squaring	89 cycles	120 cycles	156 cycles	191 cycles	230 cycles
Assembler					
Multiplication	51 cycles	68 cycles	85 cycles	111 cycles	140 cycles
Squaring	48 cycles	59 cycles	71 cycles	87 cycles	108 cycles

on Linux, and clang on macOS. All timings were collected with a test program that was compiled with clang version 3.9.0 (using -O2 optimization level) and executed on an Intel Core i7 CPU clocked at 2.7 GHz. We measured the cycle counts of the different operations following the approach described in [17].

4.1 Field Operations

As explained in Subsect. 3.1, our software contains two implementations of the field arithmetic: one is speed-optimized (i.e. written in x86 Assembly language) and supports 127, 159, 191, 223, and 255-bit primes, whereas the second aims for high flexibility and is "generic" so that it can be used for pseudo-Mersenne primes of arbitrary length (in steps of 32 bits). This second implementation is written in ANSI C99 and not particularly optimized in any way. Table 1 shows the cycle counts of multiplication and squaring (including modular reduction) on an Intel Core i7 processor. We can observe that the field operations become significantly more expensive as the bitlength of the prime increases. For example, multiplication and squaring for 255-bit operands is roughly 2.5 times more costly as the same operations for operands of a length of 127 bits. Squaring is about 23% faster than multiplication (for 255-bit operands), but the difference decreases for shorter operands or when the operations are written in C. While the assembler implementations of multiplication are nearly two times as fast as their C counterparts, the speed-up factor due to Assembly programming grows even above two for squaring.

The performance of the field arithmetic on an Intel Core processor could be much improved by using 64-bit instructions or the SSE extensions. However, as stated in the previous section, we aimed to support a wide range of x86 platforms, and hence we restricted ourselves to the standard 32-bit x86 instruction set. In this way, the software can also run on embedded x86 processors like the Intel Quark [18], which features neither 64-bit instructions nor SSE.

4.2 Commitments

As mentioned in Subsect. 3.3, we use tables with pre-computed points to speed up the computation of the Pedersen commitments. These tables are generated dynamically for the chosen TE curve, taking into account the number of base points. It is possible to trade performance for RAM requirements by choosing between standard affine and extended affine coordinates, and by increasing the number of point doublings as described in Subsect. 3.3.

The results in Table 2 show that the size of the pre-computed tables grows rapidly as the elliptic-curve groups (and underlying fields) become larger. When the size of the underlying field doubles from 127 to 255 bits, the table size and computation time increases by a factor of roughly between three and four. The time spent for the pre-computation of tables grows by even larger factors. This confirms that committing to a secret value through two 128-bit commitments is much cheaper in terms of table size and computation time than using a single 256-bit commitment instead. However, as stated in Subsect. 3.4, commitments generated using a TE curve of such small order can only be considered secure for a very short period of time (e.g. a few seconds).

We can further see in Table 2 that for the TE curve over the 255-bit prime field, the computation of a commitment using pre-computed points in extended affine coordinates is only marginally faster than when using conventional affine coordinates. However, the tables holding points in extended affine coordinates are 50% larger than the tables containing conventional affine coordinates. It is remarkable that the advantage of pre-computing three coordinates vanishes the smaller the order of the curve becomes. For example, for the TE curve over the 127-bit field, the variant using standard affine coordinates turns out to be even faster than the approach based on extended affine coordinates.

The verification of a commitment consists in using the revealed value(s) to accomplish the same computations that were made when the commitment was created. Therefore, the computational cost of a verification is the same as the cost of computing a commitment.

5   Applications

Since Pedersen commitments are used in an increasing number of contexts, we believe that our software can be useful in many application domains. To give concrete examples, we discuss potential usage scenarios in two areas.

First, we look at the field of untraceable communication where two variants of the dining cryptographers protocol [7] have been introduced that both make extensive use of Pedersen commitments. The dining cryptographers protocol is multiparty protocol in which all participants first establish pairwise secret keys and then later they publish random-looking values derived from said keys. The sum of all the published values can reveal the message, but it is impossible to determine which participant was the sender. For many years, this protocol was considered to be impractical because a malicious participant could disrupt the communication by publishing wrong values and remain undetected. In the two more recent approaches [12,13], this problem has been tackled using Pederson commitments. During the initialization phase, the n participants are required to compute n or n^2 Pedersen commitments for each subsequent transmission

Table 2. Parameters and benchmark results for selected twisted Edwards curves on a 2.7 GHz Core i7 CPU.

Prime p	$2^{127}-507$	$2^{191}-19$	$2^{223}-235$	$2^{255}-19$
Curve par. d	182146	141087	987514	4998299
Security (Safe curves)				
subgr. order n	2^{124}	2^{188}	2^{220}	2^{252}
pollard-rho	$2^{61.83}$	$2^{93.83}$	$2^{109.83}$	$2^{125.83}$
embed. degree	$n/4$	n	$n/2$	$n/9$
tr. Frobenius	$-2^{63.17}$	$-2^{96.00}$	$-2^{112.19}$	$-2^{127.40}$
CM field discr	$-2^{126.75}$	$-2^{189.99}$	$-2^{221.46}$	$-2^{254.64}$
twist secure	yes	yes	yes	yes
rigid design	yes	yes	yes	yes
Size				
commit. size	128 bit	192 bit	224 bit	256 bit
Precomputed affine coordinates				
Simple commitment with 2 base points				
computation	71158 cycles	152229 cycles	204995 cycles	253231 cycles
precomp.	3892328 cycles	10658120 cycles	14830488 cycles	21045653 cycles
table size	8192 bytes	18432 bytes	25088 bytes	32768 bytes
Multiple commitment with 10 base points				
computation	307827 cycles	676167 cycles	928502 cycles	1117830 cycles
precomp.	19696098 cycles	50817550 cycles	74457348 cycles	104493723 cycles
table size	40960 bytes	92160 bytes	125440 bytes	163840 bytes
Multiple commitment with 25 base points				
computation	758717 cycles	1651434 cycles	2284449 cycles	2797713 cycles
precomp.	49074094 cycles	127289535 cycles	186253419 cycles	260234216 cycles
table size	102400 bytes	230400 bytes	313600 bytes	409600 bytes
Precomputed extended affine coordinates				
Simple commitment with 2 base points				
computation	71912 cycles	150958 cycles	204109 cycles	235712 cycles
precomp.	3949639 cycles	10222641 cycles	14974472 cycles	21170345 cycles
table size	12288 bytes	27648 bytes	37632 bytes	49152 bytes
Multiple commitment with 10 base points				
computation	311964 cycles	670083 cycles	923140 cycles	1099020 cycles
precomp.	19833071 cycles	51258665 cycles	74953927 cycles	107634723 cycles
table size	61440 bytes	138240 bytes	188160 bytes	245760 bytes
Multiple commitment with 25 base points				
computation	774411 cycles	1651590 cycles	2257933 cycles	2633260 cycles
precomp.	49852794 cycles	128884006 cycles	188669593 cycles	263449068 cycles
table size	153600 bytes	345600 bytes	470400 bytes	614400 bytes

round. This makes a large number of commitments to pre-compute during the initialization and many commitments to verify in each transmission round. In settings where the expected lifetime of commitments is in the range of seconds to minutes, an elliptic curve of small order can be used, e.g. our curve over the 127-bit field). The number of bases depends on the size of the messages; when only short signalling messages are transmitted, a few bases will suffice.

Another field in which Pedersen commitments can be used is the long-time archiving of digital documents containing sensitive data [10]. Certain countries like Estonia require hospitals to store large amounts of medical data, and there are also lots of sensible government data that has to be kept secure for several decades. To guarantee the privacy and authenticity of the data without having to reveal it, one may opt to generate Pedersen commitments. In this case, the expected lifetime and the required security level of the commitments has to be much higher than in the previous example, and so one may decide to utilize an elliptic curve providing a security level of 128 bits (e.g. our TE curve over the 255-bit field) or even above. The data can be longer, so one might chose to go for a larger number of bases. It is possible to replace a commitment after some time by an equivalent commitment with stronger security parameters [10].

These two examples clearly illustrate that different usage scenarios require different kinds of Pedersen commitments. While in the first scenario there is a need for "lightweight" commitments for small messages, the second scenario is about long-term security for large(r) documents. Our software was designed in such a way that it can easily be configured for any of these use cases.

6   Concluding Remarks

We presented an x86 software library specifically aimed at computing Pedersen commitment based on TE curves with optimized formulae for the addition and doubling of points. The arithmetic functions in the underlying pseudo-Mersenne prime fields have been implemented in both ANSI C and x86 Assembly. On the higher level it is possible to dynamically pre-compute points for fast fixed-base scalar multiplication with a variable number of base points.

The results of the benchmark tests confirm that the stronger commitments based on large-order curves are much more expensive in terms of computation time and memory requirements than their more "lightweight" counterparts. To provide a concrete example, a 256-bit commitment can be three to four times more expensive than a 128-bit commitment. It makes therefore sense to have a software that allows to adjust the commitments to their expected lifetime, the size of the secret data, and the available memory for pre-computed points.

Finally, we discussed possible application scenarios for the software, but we believe there are many more. We hope that the software will prove to be useful to researchers who plan to implement protocols using Pedersen commitments.

A   Algorithms for Point Arithmetic

Algorithm 1. Point addition on a twisted Edwards curve with $a = -1$

Input: Point P_1 in extended projective
coordinates $(X_1 : Y_1 : E_1 : H_1 : Z_1)$ sat-
isfying $E_1H_1 = T_1 = X_1Y_1/Z_1$, point
P_2 in affine coordinates (x_2, y_2), curve
parameter d

Output: Sum $P_3 = P_1 + P_2$ in ext. proj.
coordinates $(X_3 : Y_3 : E_3 : H_3 : Z_3)$

1: $T_1 \leftarrow E_1 \cdot H_1$
2: $E_3 \leftarrow Y_1 - X_1$
3: $H_3 \leftarrow Y_1 + X_1$
4: $U_2 \leftarrow y_2 - x_2$
5: $V_2 \leftarrow y_2 + x_2$
6: $X_3 \leftarrow E_3 \cdot U_2$

7: $Y_3 \leftarrow H_3 \cdot V_2$
8: $E_3 \leftarrow Y_3 - X_3$
9: $H_3 \leftarrow Y_3 + X_3$
10: $U_2 \leftarrow x_2 \cdot y_2$
11: $V_2 \leftarrow 2d \cdot U_2$
12: $X_3 \leftarrow T_1 \cdot V_2$
13: $Y_3 \leftarrow 2Z_1$
14: $U_2 \leftarrow Y_3 - X_3$
15: $V_2 \leftarrow Y_3 + X_3$
16: $X_3 \leftarrow E_3 \cdot U_2$
17: $Y_3 \leftarrow V_2 \cdot H_3$
18: $Z_3 \leftarrow U_2 \cdot V_2$
19: **return** $(X_3 : Y_3 : E_3 : H_3 : Z_3)$

Algorithm 2. Point doubling on a twisted Edwards curve with $a = -1$

Input: Point P_1 in extended projective
coordinates $(X_1 : Y_1 : E_1 : H_1 : Z_1)$ sat-
isfying $E_1H_1 = T_1 = X_1Y_1/Z_1$

Output: Double $P_3 = 2 \cdot P_1$ in ext. proj.
coordinates $(X_3 : Y_3 : E_3 : H_3 : Z_3)$

1: $E_3 \leftarrow X_1^2$
2: $H_3 \leftarrow Y_1^2$
3: $T_1 \leftarrow E_3 - H_3$
4: $H_3 \leftarrow E_3 + H_3$
5: $X_3 \leftarrow X_1 + Y_1$

6: $E_3 \leftarrow X_3^2$
7: $E_3 \leftarrow H_3 - E_3$
8: $Y_3 \leftarrow Z_1^2$
9: $Y_3 \leftarrow 2Y_3$
10: $Y_3 \leftarrow T_1 + Y_3$
11: $X_3 \leftarrow E_3 \cdot Y_3$
12: $Z_3 \leftarrow Y_3 \cdot T_1$
13: $Y_3 \leftarrow T_1 \cdot H_3$
14: **return** $(X_3 : Y_3 : E_3 : H_3 : Z_3)$

References

1. Atkin, A.O.: Probabilistic primality testing (summary by F. Morain). In: INRIA Research Report 1779, pp. 159–163 (1992.) http://algo.inria.fr/seminars/sem91-92/atkin.pdf
2. Bernstein, D.J.: Curve25519: new diffie-hellman speed records. In: Yung, M., Dodis, Y., Kiayias, A., Malkin, T. (eds.) PKC 2006. LNCS, vol. 3958, pp. 207–228. Springer, Heidelberg (2006). doi:10.1007/11745853_14
3. Bernstein, D.J., Birkner, P., Joye, M., Lange, T., Peters, C.: Twisted edwards curves. In: Vaudenay, S. (ed.) AFRICACRYPT 2008. LNCS, vol. 5023, pp. 389–405. Springer, Heidelberg (2008). doi:10.1007/978-3-540-68164-9_26
4. Bernstein, D.J., Duif, N., Lange, T., Schwabe, P., Yang, B.-Y.: High-speed high-security signatures. J. Cryptographic Eng. 1–13 (2012)
5. Brands, S.: Rapid demonstration of linear relations connected by boolean operators. In: Fumy, W. (ed.) EUROCRYPT 1997. LNCS, vol. 1233, pp. 318–333. Springer, Heidelberg (1997). doi:10.1007/3-540-69053-0_22

6. Brickell, E.F., Gordon, D.M., McCurley, K.S., Wilson, D.B.: Fast exponentiation with precomputation. In: Rueppel, R.A. (ed.) EUROCRYPT 1992. LNCS, vol. 658, pp. 200–207. Springer, Heidelberg (1993). doi:10.1007/3-540-47555-9_18

7. Chaum, D.: The dining cryptographers problem: unconditional sender and recipient untraceability. J. Cryptol. 1(1), 65–75 (1988)

8. Chu, D., Großschädl, J., Liu, Z., Müller, V., Zhang, Y.: Twisted Edwards-form elliptic curve cryptography for 8-bit AVR-based sensor nodes. In: Xu, S., Zhao, Y. (eds.) Proceedings of the 1st ACM Workshop on Asia Public-Key Cryptography (AsiaPKC 2013), pp. 39–44. ACM Press (2013)

9. Damgård, I.: Commitment schemes and zero-knowledge protocols. In: Damgård, I.B. (ed.) EEF School 1998. LNCS, vol. 1561, pp. 63–86. Springer, Heidelberg (1999). doi:10.1007/3-540-48969-X_3

10. Demirel, D., Lancrenon, J.: How to securely prolong the computational bindingness of pedersen commitments. IACR Cryptology ePrint Archive 2015:584 (2015)

11. Edwards, H.M.: A normal form for elliptic curves. Bull. Am. Math. Soc. 44(3), 393–422 (2007)

12. Franck, C., Sorger, U.K.: Untraceable voip communication based on dc-nets. CoRR, abs/1610.06549 (2016)

13. Franck, C., van de Graaf, J.: Dining cryptographers are practical (preliminary version). CoRR, abs/1402.2269 (2014)

14. Ghatpande, S., Großschädl, J., Liu, Z.: A family of lightweight twisted Edwards curves for the Internet of things. Preprint, submitted for publication (2017)

15. Hankerson, D.R., Menezes, A.J., Vanstone, S.A.: Guide to Elliptic Curve Cryptography. Springer, New York (2004)

16. Hisil, H., Wong, K.K.-H., Carter, G., Dawson, E.: Twisted edwards curves revisited. In: Pieprzyk, J. (ed.) ASIACRYPT 2008. LNCS, vol. 5350, pp. 326–343. Springer, Heidelberg (2008). doi:10.1007/978-3-540-89255-7_20

17. Intel Corporation: How to Benchmark Code Execution Times on Intel® IA-32 and IA-64 Instruction Set Architectures (2010). White paper http://www.intel.com/content/dam/www/public/us/en/documents/white-papers/ia-32-ia-64-benchmark-code-execution-paper.pdf

18. Intel Corporation: Intel® Quark™ SoC X1000 (2015). Product specification http://ark.intel.com/products/79084/Intel-Quark-SoC-X1000-16K-Cache-400-MHz

19. Lim, C.H., Lee, P.J.: More flexible exponentiation with precomputation. In: Desmedt, Y.G. (ed.) CRYPTO 1994. LNCS, vol. 839, pp. 95–107. Springer, Heidelberg (1994). doi:10.1007/3-540-48658-5_11

20. Liu, Z., Großschädl, J., Li, L., Xu, Q.: Energy-efficient elliptic curve cryptography for msp430-based wireless sensor nodes. In: Liu, J.K.K., Steinfeld, R. (eds.) ACISP 2016. LNCS, vol. 9722, pp. 94–112. Springer, Cham (2016). doi:10.1007/978-3-319-40253-6_6

21. National Institute of Standards and Technology (NIST): Digital Signature Standard (DSS), July 2013. FIPS Publication 186-4, http://nvlpubs.nist.gov/nistpubs/FIPS/NIST.FIPS.186-4.pdf

22. Pedersen, T.P.: Non-interactive and information-theoretic secure verifiable secret sharing. In: Feigenbaum, J. (ed.) CRYPTO 1991. LNCS, vol. 576, pp. 129–140. Springer, Heidelberg (1992). doi:10.1007/3-540-46766-1_9

23. Pippenger, N.: On the evaluation of powers and related problems. In: Proceedings of the 17th Annual Symposium on Foundations of Computer Science, pp. 258–263. IEEE Computer Society (1976)

Enhanced Sinkhole System: Collecting System Details to Support Investigations

Martin Ussath[✉], Feng Cheng, and Christoph Meinel

Hasso Plattner Institute (HPI), University of Potsdam, 14482 Potsdam, Germany
{martin.ussath,feng.cheng,christoph.meinel}@hpi.de

Abstract. Adversaries use increasingly complex and sophisticated tactics, techniques and procedures to compromise single computer systems and complete IT environments. Most of the standard detection and prevention systems are not able to provide a decent level of protection against sophisticated attacks, because adversaries are able to bypass various detection approaches. Therefore, additional solutions are needed to improve the prevention and detection of complex attacks. DNS sinkholing is one approach that can be used to redirect known malicious connections to dedicated sinkhole systems. The objective of these sinkhole systems is to interrupt the communication of the malware and to gather details about it. Due to the fact that current sinkhole systems focus on the collection of network related information, the gathered details cannot be used to support investigations in a comprehensive way and to improve detection and prevention capabilities.

In this paper, we propose a new approach for an enhanced sinkhole system that is able collect detailed information about potentially infected systems and the corresponding malware that is executed. This system is able to gather details, such as open network connections, running processes and process memory, to provide relevant information about the malware behavior and the used methods. The approach makes use of built-in remote management capabilities and standard commands as well as functions of the operating system to gather the details. This also ensures that the footprint of the collection approach is small and therefore also difficult to recognize by a malware. For the evaluation of the proposed approach, we executed real-world malware and collected details from the infected system with a prototypically implemented enhanced sinkhole system. The gathered information shows that these details can be used to support investigations and to improve security solutions.

Keywords: DNS sinkholing · Malware analysis · Malware behavior · Threat intelligence

1 Introduction

Nowadays, companies have to defend their self against an increasing number of attacks that try to comprise single computers systems or complete IT infrastructures. Therefore, different prevention and detection systems, such as firewalls,

© Springer International Publishing AG 2017
S. Bouzefrane et al. (Eds.): MSPN 2017, LNCS 10566, pp. 18–33, 2017.
DOI: 10.1007/978-3-319-67807-8_2

Intrusion Detection Systems (IDSs) and anti-virus solutions, are deployed. These systems use various signature- and anomaly-based detection approaches to identify and block attacks. Although, these detection approaches provide a decent level of protection against some attacks, different adversaries are still able to bypass these approaches and compromise different companies, such as ThyssenKrupp [15], Lockheed Martin [21], RSA [14] and Bit9 [13]. The reason for this is that attackers are constantly evolving and improving their tactics, techniques and procedures. This is especially true for sophisticated attackers, but also standard attacks use more and more complex approaches, such as polymorphic malware, encrypted communication and runtime decryption, to hinder or prevent detection. Therefore, it is necessary to improve the general detection and investigation capabilities to keep up with the increased number of complex attacks.

Compromised systems have to communicate with other systems that are under the control of the attacker to receive commands, download additional malware or upload extracted information. Before such a communication channel can be established, the compromised systems often use the Domain Name System (DNS) to resolve domains to get the corresponding IP address of the external system. To interrupt the external communication and to prevent further malicious activities of the compromised system, DNS sinkholing can be used to modify DNS responses. This allows to redirect the communication to a dedicated sinkhole system. If a sinkhole receives a connection request from another system, it is very likely that this system is compromised. For this approach, it is crucial that only known malicious domains are sinkholed, otherwise legitimate connections will be interrupted and uninfected systems are wrongly classified as compromised. To improve the defense capabilities and for further investigations, sinkhole systems try to gather as much information as possible about the compromised system and the corresponding malware that initiated the DNS request as well as the connection to the sinkhole. Due to the fact that malware often use encrypted and custom protocols to communicate, current sinkhole systems can only collect very few details. The reason for this is that the compromised system usually closes the connection to the sinkhole, as soon as it recognizes that the communication partner it not able to use the intended protocol. Especially for sophisticated malware, which is difficult to analyze, it is necessary to gather more detailed information to support investigation efforts and to improve prevention as well as detection systems. Therefore, additional methods should be used within sinkhole systems to collect reasonable information about the compromised systems and the corresponding malware.

In this paper, we propose a new approach for an enhanced sinkhole system that allows to automatically gather detailed information from potentially compromised systems that try to connect to a sinkholed domain. With the collected information and further analyses, it is possible to reveal additional details about the used malware that can be used to improve prevention and detection capabilities. Our approach only relies on built-in functionalities of the operating system to extract relevant details. Therefore, the footprint is very small and attackers are probably not able to recognize the information gathering. Although, our approach is able to collect various different details about the potentially compromised system, we will focus on information that provides relevant insights into the behavior of the malware. Furthermore, we show that it is possible to extract details from potentially infected systems, which are otherwise difficult to gather. With the collected information it should be possible to support investigations and decide if further analyses, such as forensic investigations, are needed.

The remainder of this paper is structure as follows. In Sect. 2 we describe the work that is related to the topics malware analysis and sinkhole systems. In the following section, we explain the concept of DNS sinkholing and how it can be implemented, including the different requirements. In Sect. 4 we describe the proposed approach of an enhanced sinkhole system and the characteristics of such a system. Afterwards, in Sect. 5 we explain the prototypically implemented enhanced sinkhole system and evaluate the proposed approach by executing real-world malware in a lab environment. Finally, Sect. 6 concludes our paper and proposes future work.

2   Related Work

It is necessary to identify and analyze compromised systems as well as the corresponding malware to improve prevention and detection approaches. Due to the high number of new malware samples and families [6,22] it is relevant to use dynamic analysis methods that can scale with the increasing number of threats.

Different sandbox systems [4,10,23] were proposed to automatically analyze malware and to record the relevant behavior. Based on the analysis reports, it is possible to extract crucial details about the malware and identify potentially compromised systems. Malware authors are aware of the capabilities of sandboxes and therefore they try to bypass or detect these analysis systems [5], by checking the execution environment. If a malware recognizes a sandbox, it changes the behavior [3], so that the analysis report does not reveal any relevant details. Although, sandbox systems employ various methods to make the execution environment undistinguishable to a usual system [12,24], it cannot be ensured that the analysis report contains all relevant details about the malware.

DNS sinkholing is another approach to gather details about the behavior of malware. It relies on the fact that malware often uses DNS to resolve the domain names of external systems [19]. To sinkhole a connection, a specifically configured DNS server is used to redirect the communication to a dedicated sinkhole system. The enhanced sinkhole system (ESS) was proposed [11], to overcome the limitations of legacy sinkhole systems and to gather more detailed information about the malware and the infected system. The sinkhole system supports different protocols, such as IRC, HTTP and other TCP-based protocols, and is able to gather various details, such as source IP, source port, protocol type, user agent, host and request info. Furthermore, the ESS tries to verify if the incoming connections are related to a malware activity or not. The so-called rule checker module uses signatures to identify malicious communication attempts and allows to provide additional details about the malware. A limitation of the

ESS is that encrypted and heavily obfuscated network packets are excluded from the analysis procedure, which lowers the usefulness of the system. Furthermore, the information that is gathered about the malware and the infected system cannot support investigations in a comprehensive way.

Another sinkhole system [9] focuses on capturing the raw network packets for later analysis. Due to improvements, such as a more resilient sinkhole system and the monitoring of all network interfaces, the system is able to capture five times more network packets than "conventional" systems. Next to this, the proposed sinkhole system also gathers transmitted data and stores it in a database. Although, the collection of network packets and the transmitted data can reveal some insights about the infected system and the behavior of the malware, it still provides only limit details if the malware uses encrypted communication protocols. Due to the fact that more and more malware families use obfuscated or encrypted communication protocols [20], the described approach can only provide limited details in such cases.

3   DNS Sinkholing

DNS sinkholing is used to prevent further malicious activities of malware and detect already infected systems. This approach is not only applied by security vendors and researchers, such as Microsoft [16], Kaspersky [17] and ShadowServer [1], but also by companies to protect their own infrastructure against malware.

3.1   Concept

The general concept of DNS sinkholing is to change the DNS response in such a way that the potentially infected systems do not connect to a system of the attacker, such as a command and control server, but instead connect to a dedicated sinkhole system. Through the redirection of the communication, the malware is not able to reach the intended system of the attacker and therefore further malicious activities can be blocked, such as uploading of data or receiving of new commands.

For the implementation of DNS sinkholing, it is necessary to adapt the configuration of the local DNS server so that responses to certain domains are changed and point to a sinkhole system. If the objective is just to block the potentially malicious connections, it is possible to use for example localhost (127.0.0.1) as DNS sinkholing destination. Most often, it is the objective to use special sinkhole systems to record or gather details about the infected systems, so that it is possible to trigger additional activities, such as reinstallation of the system or clean up. Therefore, we will focus on such type of sinkholes, because they can provide valuable information for later investigations.

One advantage of the DNS sinkholing approach is that newly infected systems automatically connect to the sinkhole system, if the corresponding domains are sinkholed. Thus, new infections can be identified relatively easy and the initial communication of the malware is already blocked. This means, it is no longer necessary to trigger scheduled searches with all known malicious domains on recorded log events to identify newly infected systems.

Nevertheless, it needs to be considered that not all infected systems can be identified through the sinkholing of malicious domains. First of all, if a malware uses IP addresses to communicate with external systems of an attacker, no domain name is resolved and therefore it is not possible to change the response and redirect the communication to a sinkhole system. Due to the fact that domain names offer an additional layer of abstraction and further ways to obfuscate the destination, for example through the usage of the (double) fast-flux approach [8], a majority of the malware uses domain names to determine the address of external systems [19]. Another possibility for infected systems is to bypass DNS sinkholing by using external DNS servers to resolve domain names. In such cases the local DNS server does not receive a corresponding request and cannot change the response. To prevent the usage of external DNS servers, all outgoing DNS requests, except from the local DNS server, should be blocked.

3.2 Implementation

For the implementation of DNS sinkholing the local DNS server needs to support Response Policy Zones (RPZs). This feature is available in different DNS server implementations [2], such as BIND 9 or BlueCat DNS. In the following, we will briefly describe the necessary configurations to implement DNS sinkholing within a BIND 9.10 DNS server.

Initially, it is required to specify a zone file with the corresponding domains that should be sinkholed. One example for such a zone file is shown in Listing 1.1. This zone description is similar to an authoritative zone, but it is possible to specify arbitrary domains and corresponding resource records, which should be used from the DNS server to change the original response. In the example, the domain malicious.com will be resolved to a local IP address (10.13.37.42), which could be the address of a sinkhole system.

Listing 1.1. Response Policy Zone File for BIND

```
$TTL 60
$ORIGIN sinkhole.rpz.
@    IN   SOA ns1.sinkhole.rpz. root.sinkhole.rpz. (
                2
          604800
           86400
         2419200
          604800 )

@      IN    A    10.13.37.42
@      IN    NS   ns1.sinkhole.rpz.
ns1    IN    A    10.13.37.42

malicious.com   IN   CNAME   @
```

Afterwards, the `response-policy` statement is used to specify that the zone file is used as Response Policy Zone. Furthermore, it is possible to disable the recursive resolution of sinkholed domains with the `qname-wait-recurse` statement. Otherwise, the DNS server will try to resolve the potentially malicious domain, which might be recognized by the attackers. This part of the configuration is shown in Listing 1.2.

Listing 1.2. BIND Configuration Options

```
options {
  [...]
  response-policy {
    zone"sinkhole.rpz";
  }
  qname-wait-recurse no;
};
```

To monitor the RPZ activities, it is possible to configure a dedicated log file that records when the DNS server changes a response according to the specified response policy zone file.

3.3   Malicious Domains

The most crucial part of an effective DNS sinkholing is the selection of the domains that should be sinkholed. It needs to be considered that usually all services offered by the systems behind these domains are no longer accessible. Therefore, the blocking of all not well known domains could have a significant impact on the users of the network. Nevertheless, it is necessary to sinkhole malicious domains as soon as these domains become known.

One option could be to automatically gather and analyze threat intelligence information, such as blacklists or malware analysis reports, and add suitable malicious domains to the RPZ file. This allows a timely sinkholing of new threats. Furthermore, it is possible to define different thresholds for the reputation of a domain or the trustworthiness of a source to ensure that only appropriate malicious domains are sinkholed.

3.4   Sinkhole System

Sinkhole systems, which receive connections of potentially infected systems, can be used to gather relevant details about the executed malware and the compromised system. Generally, the objective is to gather as much information as possible to may initiate further investigation steps or to inform the owner of the system.

For the identification of potentially infected systems, a sinkhole needs to determine the source IP address of the connection. Therefore, a sinkhole system can listen on all network ports that are relevant for malware communication and accept connection requests from arbitrary systems. If a potentially infected system tries to connect to a sinkholed domain, the sinkhole accepts the connection request and extracts the IP address of the system. To ensure that only the IP addresses of compromised systems are gathered, the sinkhole system should only be used for this dedicated purpose, otherwise IP addresses of uninfected systems are added to the list of compromised hosts.

Although the IP address is relevant to identify the system and initiate further steps, it is also necessary to gather additional information to identify the executed malware and to support further investigations. Therefore, sinkhole systems usually not only extract the IP address of the potentially infected systems, but also use additional approaches to gather more comprehensive details, such as transmitted data and header information, raw network packets and NetFlow or IPFIX (IP Flow Information Export) information. These additional details mainly focus on the collection of network related information, which can reduce the usefulness of the gathered details significantly. The reason for this is that malware usually uses custom protocols for their communication, which are not implemented in the sinkhole system. Therefore, the malware can recognize relatively fast that the communication party (sinkhole) is not able to use the intended protocol and this often leads to the termination of the connections. This has directly an impact on how many packets are send by the infected system to the sinkhole and therefore also how much details can be gathered by the sinkhole system. Furthermore, if malware uses standardized encryption protocols or custom encryption methods, even basic information, such as HTTP header information or initial requests or packets, can no longer be used to easily extract relevant information and identify the corresponding malware.

4   Enhanced Sinkhole System

Sinkhole systems should gather additional information to support investigations in a more comprehensive way and further improve detection as well as prevention capabilities. For the collection of detailed information our new approach for an enhanced sinkhole system leverages the fact that most systems within a company network are centrally managed and therefore also remotely accessible. In the following, we describe the general approach of the enhanced sinkhole system and relevant characteristics.

4.1   Approach

Compared to other sinkhole systems [9,11], which focus on the gathering of network related details, the proposed enhanced sinkhole system tries to collect further relevant information directly from the potentially infected system to provide more insights. The approach of the sinkhole also relies on DNS sinkholing, but allows to extract almost arbitrary information form the potentially infected system, such as DNS cache, running processes and open network connections.

Figure 1 shows the general approach of the enhanced sinkhole system. In a first step, a potentially infected system establishes a connection to a listening socket of the sinkhole. This socket has a high timeout value to ensure that the malicious process, which initiated the connection, will not be promptly terminated. Furthermore, due to high socket timeout the sinkhole does not need to send any responses to the connected system, which might have unwanted side effects on the behavior of the malware. After the connection is established, the sinkhole system initiates a connection to the potentially infected system with the help of corresponding credentials that also allow to execute functions and commands to gather relevant details. For example, it would be possible to dump the memory of the potentially malicious process that initiated the connection to the sinkhole. To identify this process and to dump the memory, the sinkhole first needs to extract all open network connections and afterwards identify the process that has an open connection to the sinkhole system. After the collection of all relevant details, the sinkhole closes all connections to the potentially infected system.

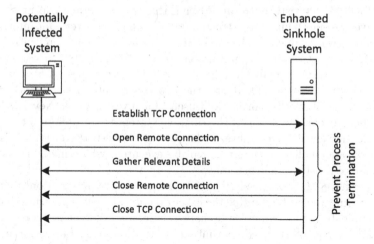

Fig. 1. Approach of enhanced sinkhole system

This approach requires that the enhanced sinkhole system is able to establish a direct connection to the potentially infected system to gather the system details. Therefore, within more complex and distributed networks, it might be necessary to use multiple systems within the different network segments to perform the collection of the relevant information from the potentially infected systems. Due to the fact that for such scenarios the general approach will not change, we will focus on environments with one enhanced sinkhole system to improve the understandability.

The enhanced sinkhole system approach uses built-in functions and commands of the operating system to gather the needed details of the potentially infected system. Therefore, it is possible to run everything directly in-memory without storing any kind of script or program on disk. Due to this, it is more difficult for a malware to detect the information gathering of the enhanced sinkhole system and change the behavior. Furthermore, this method ensures that less artifacts are changed on the potentially infected system and therefore the probability of unwanted side effects can be reduced. In general, it would also be possible to use already installed tools, such as forensic agents or toolkits, to perform the gathering of the details, but this could lead to falsified information.

4.2   Characteristics

The approach of the enhanced sinkhole system is not limited to certain protocols, because it is not necessary to have predefined knowledge about the protocols that are used by the different malwares. Due to the fact that the enhanced sinkhole system does not send any responses to the potentially infected system, the approach also works if the malware uses obfuscated, encrypted or custom protocols to communicate. Therefore, the sinkhole system can collect detailed information for a higher number of malwares to support investigations.

Another characteristic of the approach is that the malware is executed on real productive systems. Thus, the extracted details can provide relevant information about the malware, which can be used to improve detection and prevention capabilities. In contrast to this, if malware is executed on specific analysis systems, such as sandboxes, the malware might be able to detect these specific systems and change the behavior. Therefore, the analysis results of such sandbox systems might not always be correct and useful for investigations. Nevertheless, it should also be considered that if the sinkhole system is not able to interrupt all communication paths of a malware, the productive system can be misused by an attacker and malicious functions can be executed, which might lead to the exfiltration of sensitive information.

Furthermore, the enhanced sinkhole system collects information about the potentially infected system during the execution of a malicious program that tries to communicate with a sinkholed domain. Therefore, different methods that try to hinder analysis efforts, such as runtime decryption or deobfuscation of code, are no longer effective, because the malware already decrypted or deobfuscated the code by itself. This allows our approach to easily gather relevant details, such as other malicious domains or indicators, without any static analysis of the malware.

5   Evaluation

For the evaluation of the proposed approach, we implemented a prototypical enhanced sinkhole system that is able to gather comprehensive details from infected systems. Furthermore, we deployed and configured an environment to simulate a company network with all relevant services and systems. Within this environment we executed real-world malware and used DNS sinkholing as well as the enhanced sinkhole system to collect relevant information from the infected system.

5.1 Lab Environment

For the evaluation of the proposed enhanced sinkhole system we deployed and configured a Windows-based environment. The reason for this is that most company networks use Windows as operating system for central server systems and client systems. Due to this, also complex and sophisticated attacks usually target Windows-based infrastructures.

The deployed lab environment consisted of one domain controller with Windows Server 2016, one client system with Windows 7 and one client system with Windows 10. The domain controller as well as the two client systems were joined to an Active Directory. Furthermore, a BIND 9.10 DNS server and the enhanced sinkhole system, which runs on Windows 10, were part of the environment.

By default, the domain controller of an Active Directory serves as a DNS server for the domain joined clients. Therefore, we configured the Windows DNS server in such a way that all DNS requests, which could not be resolved locally, will be forwarded to the BIND DNS server. This BIND server was then used to implement DNS sinkholing. If a malware wants to establish a connection to a malicious domain, the DNS request is first send to the domain controller and then the domain controller forwards the request to the BIND DNS server. Due to the configured DNS sinkholing, the BIND server then answers with the IP address of the enhanced sinkhole system.

Additionally, it was necessary to create a group policy object (GPO) that enables the WinRM (Windows Remote Management) service on all client systems and to configure a corresponding firewall rule to allow access to this service. The WinRM service can be used for various central management tasks, such as remote configuration of systems and software deployment. This service is also used by the enhanced sinkhole system to connect to a potentially infected system and to gather relevant details.

5.2 Proof of Concept System

The proof of concept implementation of the enhanced sinkhole system consists of two main components. The first component is written in Python and used for handling the incoming connections of potentially infected systems. Furthermore, this connection handler component keeps the connections open to allow the information gathering. The second component uses PowerShell cmdlets and system commands to collect details about the potentially infected system and the executed malware. Figure 2 shows the different steps that are performed by the enhanced sinkhole system when a connection of a potentially infected system is redirected to the sinkhole.

The connection handler component listens on different ports for incoming connections from potentially infected systems. For the evaluation of the enhanced sinkhole approach, we configured the sinkhole system in such a way that it listens on the ports 80, 443 and 8443 for connections. If the system should listen on other or additional ports, the configuration of the proof of concept system can be changed accordingly. Furthermore, the handling of the incoming

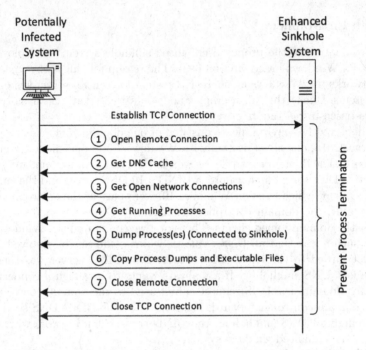

Fig. 2. Information gathering steps of the enhanced sinkhole system

connections is fully multi-threaded to support multiple concurrent connections from different systems. In the first step, the enhanced sinkhole system accepts incoming connections and sets the timeout of the corresponding socket to 60 s. This should ensure that all information gathering steps can be completed before the connection is terminated. After the establishment of the connection, the connection handler component triggers the collection of the system details by calling a PowerShell script. This script requires the IP address of the connecting system as input parameter.

The information collection component uses a PowerShell script to perform the subsequent steps to gather the relevant details of the potentially infected system. Due to the fact that different Windows systems and PowerShell versions support different PowerShell cmdlets, it was necessary to implement different collection methods. Therefore, different system commands and PowerShell cmdlets were used to enable the collection of system details from Windows 7 and Windows 10 systems. Before the corresponding information gathering commands can be executed, the enhanced sinkhole system needs to establish a connection to the potentially infected system with the *New-PSSession* cmdlet. Afterwards, the sinkhole determines the operating system version of the remote system to executed the correct collection methods. Table 1 lists the different system commands or PowerShell cmdlets that are used for the gathering. Further supporting functions are used to create and delete firewall rules and directories.

Table 1. Used PowerShell cmdlets[¶] and system commands[‡] for information gathering

Step: Purpose	Windows 7	Windows 10
Step 1: Open Remote Connection	New-PSSession[¶]	
Step 2: Get DNS Cache	ipconfig[‡]/displaydns	Get-DnsClientCache[¶]
Step 3: Get Open Network Connections	netstat[‡]-o -a -n	Get-NetTCPConnection[¶]
Step 4: Get Running Processes	tasklist[‡]-v Get-WmiObject[¶]win32_process	Get-Process[¶]-IncludeUserName Get-WmiObject[¶]win32_process
Step 5: Dump Process	Dedicated PowerShell Script [7]	
Step 6: Copy Dumps and Files	New-PSDrive[¶] + Copy-Item[¶]	
Step 7: Close Remote Connection	Remove-PSSession[¶]	

The most relevant part of the information collection is to identify the process that tried to resolve a sinkholed domain and established a connection to the sinkhole. All processes that have an open connection to the enhanced sinkhole system can be determined based on the collected information. This allows the sinkhole to dump the corresponding process memory and identify the image path of the process to also download the corresponding file. Sometimes also the parent process of a malicious process can be relevant for an investigation and therefore the sinkhole system also dumps the memory and image path file of the parent process.

All the gathered details about a potentially infected system, including the process memory and files, are stored on the sinkhole system for later analysis. For each potentially infected system a folder is created and within this folder the different details are stored in CSV files. This should allow a later analysis and extraction of relevant information. Furthermore, the sinkhole system also directly displays some relevant details, such as date, time, IP address, send network packets, dumped process IDs and image paths, on the screen.

5.3 Malware Execution

For the evaluation of the enhanced sinkhole system we used a real-world malware to show that our approach is feasible and provides useful information. We selected a malware (MD5 hash *8de1ebacb72f3b23a8235cc66a6b6f68*) that is difficult to detect with traditional signature-based detection approaches [18]. This malware uses an VBA macro within an Excel document to execute a malicious PowerShell script. This script is then used to load additional shellcode from a server. To establish a connection to the remote server, the malware resolves the domain *spl[.]noip[.]me* to get the corresponding IP address of the system. To sinkhole the connections of this malware, we added this domain to our DNS sinkhole so that all connection will be redirected to our enhanced sinkhole system.

After the execution of the malware in our lab environment, the corresponding process of the malware established a connection to our sinkhole system. Afterwards, the sinkhole started to gather details about the infected system. Figure 3 shows the output of the enhanced sinkhole system, which provide an overview of the identified and dumped processes. In this case, the sinkhole identified that the process with the ID 3200 established the connection to the sinkhole and the image path of this process leads to executable file of PowerShell. The parent process ID is 3988 and the image path points to the executable file of Excel. Based on these few details it is already possible to get a rough understanding of the malware behavior and used methods.

```
++++++++++++++++++++++++++++++++++++++++++++++++++++
>> 192.168.0.101
>> 2017-01-08 12:34:20.979000
----------------------------------------------------
             spl.noip.me
----------------------------------------------------
>> Dumping Process: 3200
   >> Image Path: C:\Windows\SysWOW64\WindowsPowerShell\v1.0\powershell.exe
>> Dumping Parent Process: 3988
   >> Image Path: C:\Program Files (x86)\Microsoft Office\Office15\EXCEL.EXE
++++++++++++++++++++++++++++++++++++++++++++++++++++
```

Fig. 3. Output of enhanced sinkhole system

Furthermore, it is possible to analyze the additional information that was gathered by the enhanced sinkhole system and extract more relevant details. For example, the command line argument of the PowerShell process (ID 3200), which is part of the collected process information, directly reveals the malicious script. Figure 4 shows a truncated version of this script. These few lines already reveal that the script is encoded and compressed to hinder detection. For further investigations it is necessary to decode and decompress the code to understand the functionality of the script. To perform this step, the script needs to be slightly modified to get readable code. Figure 5 shows some lines of the decoded and decompressed code. Through the usage of the enhanced sinkhole system it was possible to extract these details without manually analyzing the Excel document and the VBA macro code.

```
Write-Output $(New-Object IO.StreamReader
   ($(New-Object IO.Compression.DeflateStream
   ($(New-Object IO.MemoryStream
   (,$([Convert]::FromBase64String(" nZdJj9tGEIXv8yuIgQ [...]" )))),
   [IO.Compression.CompressionMode]::Decompress)),
   [Text.Encoding]::ASCII)).ReadToEnd();
```

Fig. 4. Encoded and compressed PowerShell script (Truncated)

```
$c = @"
[DllImport("kernel32.dll")] public static extern IntPtr VirtualAlloc([...]);
[DllImport("kernel32.dll")] public static extern IntPtr CreateThread([...]);
[DllImport("msvcrt.dll")] public static extern IntPtr memset([...]);
"@
$o = Add-Type -memberDefinition $c -Name "Win32" -namespace Win32Functions [...]
```

Fig. 5. Decoded and decompressed PowerShell script (Truncated)

It is possible to perform further analyses of the dumped process memory to get additional insights. For example, the memory dump of the Excel process allows to recover the location of the malicious Excel document. With the help of memory analysis tools, it is also feasible to extract parts of the macro and the document from the dumped memory. Although, the collected process dumps enable this type of analyses, they can be very time consuming and require additional efforts.

The results of this evaluation show that the enhanced sinkhole system is able to provide relevant details about the malware behavior and the used methods. With the collected details it is possible to support investigations and to improve security systems, for example with new or more detailed signatures.

6   Conclusion and Future Work

In this paper, we presented a new approach for an enhanced sinkhole system that enables the collection of detailed information form potentially infected systems to support investigations and to improve prevention and detection capabilities. For our approach it is necessary that DNS sinkholing is used to redirect connections from malicious processes to an enhanced sinkhole system. The proposed system listens for incoming connections and uses a socket with a high timeout value to prevent the termination of the malicious process. Afterwards, built-in remote management functionalities and additional methods of the operating system are used to gather detailed information about the potentially infected system and the corresponding malicious process. Due to the usage of standard operating system commands and functions no additional tools are needed, which reduces the footprint of the collection approach and makes it more difficult for malware to detect the information gathering.

For the evaluation of our approach we implemented a prototypical enhanced sinkhole system and executed real-world malware in a lab environment to collected detailed information. Although the executed malware uses encoded and compressed code, it was possible to collect relevant details without manually analyzing the malware. For example the identified parent process revealed that the malicious code is embedded into an Excel document and with the help of the collected process parameters it was possible to extract the used PowerShell script. The results of the evaluation show that the proposed approach is able to provide relevant insights into the behavior and the used methods of malware. With these details it is possible to support investigations and improve security systems.

For future work it might be interesting to identify further details that can be extracted with the approach of the enhanced sinkhole system. For example the extraction of all process handles could provide further insights, such as loaded libraries or opened files. Nevertheless, it is always necessary to consider needed configuration changes and possible side effects, because otherwise these details might be difficult to collect in real-world environments. Another task for future work could be to implement and evaluate automatic analysis approaches that use the collected details to extract the most relevant facts.

References

1. Avalanche   (2016).   http://blog.shadowserver.org/2016/12/01/avalanche/. Accessed 18 Dec 2016
2. DNS Response Policy Zones (2016). https://dnsrpz.info/. Accessed 02 Dec 2016
3. Balzarotti, D., Cova, M., Karlberger, C., Kruegel, C., Kirda, E., Vigna, G.: Efficient detection of split personalities in malware. In: Proceedings of the Symposium on Network and Distributed System Security (NDSS) (2010)
4. Bayer, U., Moser, A., Kruegel, C., Kirda, E.: Dynamic analysis of malicious code. J. Comput. Virol. **2**(1), 67–77 (2006). doi:10.1007/s11416-006-0012-2
5. Brengel, M., Backes, M., Rossow, C.: Detecting hardware-assisted virtualization. In: Caballero, J., Zurutuza, U., Rodríguez, R.J. (eds.) DIMVA 2016. LNCS, vol. 9721, pp. 207–227. Springer, Cham (2016). doi:10.1007/978-3-319-40667-1_11
6. Dell Incorporated: Dell Security Annual Threat Report 2016. Technical report (2016)
7. Graeber, M.: PowerShell Script: Out-Minidump.ps1 (2013). https://raw. githubusercontent.com/PowerShellMafia/PowerSploit/master/Exfiltration/ Out-Minidump.ps1. Accessed 05 Aug 2016
8. Hsu, C.-H., Huang, C.-Y., Chen, K.-T.: Fast-flux bot detection in real time. In: Jha, S., Sommer, R., Kreibich, C. (eds.) RAID 2010. LNCS, vol. 6307, pp. 464–483. Springer, Heidelberg (2010). doi:10.1007/978-3-642-15512-3_24
9. Jung, H.M., Lee, H.G., Choi, J.W.: Efficient malicious packet capture through advanced dns sinkhole. Wirel. Personal Commun. **93**, 21–34 (2016). doi:10.1007/ s11277-016-3443-1
10. Juwono, J.T., Lim, C., Erwin, A.: A comparative study of behavior analysis sand-boxes in malware detection. In: Proceedings of the International Conference on New Media (CONMEDIA) (2015)
11. Lee, H.-G., Choi, S.-S., Lee, Y.-S., Park, H.-S.: Enhanced sinkhole system by improving post-processing mechanism. In: Kim, T., Lee, Y., Kang, B.-H., Ślęzak, D. (eds.) FGIT 2010. LNCS, vol. 6485, pp. 469–480. Springer, Heidelberg (2010). doi:10.1007/978-3-642-17569-5_46
12. Kirat, D., Vigna, G., Kruegel, C.: BareCloud: bare-metal analysis-based evasive malware detection. In: Proceedings of the 23rd USENIX Security Symposium (USENIX Security), August 2014
13. Krebs, B.: Security firm Bit9 hacked, used to spread malware. https://krebson security.com/2013/02/security-firm-bit9-hacked-used-to-spread-malware/. Accessed 03 Feb 2017
14. Markoff, J.: SecurID company suffers a breach of data security. http://www. nytimes.com/2011/03/18/technology/18secure.html. Accessed 03 Feb 2017

15. Mathews, L.: ThyssenKrupp attackers stole trade secrets in massive hack (2016). http://www.forbes.com/sites/leemathews/2016/12/08/thyssenkrupp-attackers-stole-trade-secrets-in-massive-hack/LeeMathews,Lee. Accessed 10 Dec 2016

16. Raiu, C.: Microsoft seizes 22 NO-IP domains, disrupts cybercriminal and nation state APT malware operations (2014). https://securelist.com/blog/events/64143/microsoft-seizes-22-no-ip-domains-disrupts-cybercriminal-and-nation-state-apt-malware-operations/. Accessed 14 Dec 2016

17. Raiu, C., Baumgartner, K.: Sinkholing volatile cedar DGA infrastructure (2015). https://securelist.com/blog/research/69421/sinkholing-volatile-cedar-dga-infrastructure/. Accessed 18 Dec 2016

18. Regalado, D., Karim, T., Jain, V., Hernandez, E.: Ghosts in the endpoint (2016). https://www.fireeye.com/blog/threat-research/2016/04/ghosts_in_the_endpoi.html. Accessed 18 Nov 2016

19. Rossow, C., Dietrich, C., Bos, H.: Large-scale analysis of malware downloaders. In: Flegel, U., Markatos, E., Robertson, W. (eds.) DIMVA 2012. LNCS, vol. 7591, pp. 42–61. Springer, Heidelberg (2013). doi:10.1007/978-3-642-37300-8_3

20. Rossow, C., Dietrich, C.J.: ProVeX: detecting botnets with encrypted command and control channels. In: Rieck, K., Stewin, P., Seifert, J.-P. (eds.) DIMVA 2013. LNCS, vol. 7967, pp. 21–40. Springer, Heidelberg (2013). doi:10.1007/978-3-642-39235-1_2

21. Schwartz, M.J.: Lockheed martin suffers massive cyberattack. http://www.darkreading.com/risk-management/lockheed-martin-suffers-massive-cyberattack/d/d-id/1098013. Accessed 03 Feb 2017

22. Symantec Corporation: Internet Security Threat Report. Technical report 21 (2016)

23. Willems, C., Holz, T., Freiling, F.: Toward automated dynamic malware analysis using CWSandbox. IEEE Secur. Priv. 5(2), 32–39 (2007). doi:10.1109/MSP.2007.45

24. Willems, C., Hund, R., Fobian, A., Felsch, D., Holz, T., Vasudevan, A.: Down to the bare metal: using processor features for binary analysis. In: Proceedings of the 28th Annual Computer Security Applications Conference (ACSAC). ACM (2012). doi:10.1145/2420950.2420980

An Autonomous System Based Security Mechanism for Network Coding Applications in Content-Centric Networking

Li Xu$^{(\boxtimes)}$, Hui Li, Jiawei Hu, Yunmin Wang, and Huayu Zhang

Shenzhen Key Lab of Information Theory and Future Internet Architecture Future
Network PKU Lab of National Major Research Infrastructure,
Huawei and PKU Jointly Eng. Lab of Future Network Based on SDN,
Shenzhen Graduate School, Shenzhen Engineering Lab
of Converged Networking Technology, Peking University, Shenzhen, China
xuli0925@pku.edu.cn, lih64@pkusz.edu.cn

Abstract. Content-Centric Networking *(CCN)*, is built on the notion
of content-based security. With the integration of Network Coding *(NC)*
into CCN to contribute to the best performance, security, one of the key
features of CCN has been left behind. Though the permission for encod-
ing/recoding content packets at producers and intermediate routers provides performance benefits, it also introduces additional security issues
and disables existing security practices. In this paper, we fill the gap
by analyzing new security challenges brought accordingly and proposing an Autonomous Systems (AS-s) based security mechanism for NC
applications in CCN. It can not only guarantee the optimal performance
of NC, but also offer the assurance for *Integrity, Origin Authentication*
and *Correctness* of content packets, together with proving trustworthiness among border routers. More importantly, we also shed light on the
performance issues and implementation problems of the mechanism.

Keywords: Content-Centric Networking · Security · Network coding

1 Introduction

In the last few years, with the Internet struggling to accommodate the needs
of modern systems and applications, new network architectures are being proposed, among which Content-Centric Networking *(CCN)*, proposed by Jacobson
et al. [1] has emerged as a promising next-generation Internet architecture. It
comes with a potential for a wide range of benefits, including reduced congestion,
improved delivery speed, simpler configuration of network devices and security at
the data level, etc. In particular, departing from traditional connection-focused
approach to security, CCN is built on the notion of content-based security: protection and trust travel with the content itself, rather than being a property of
the connections over which it travels. In CCN, all content is authenticated with

© Springer International Publishing AG 2017
S. Bouzefrane et al. (Eds.): MSPN 2017, LNCS 10566, pp. 34–48, 2017.
DOI: 10.1007/978-3-319-67807-8_3

digital signatures, and private content is protected with encryption [1]. Specifically, CCN requires that content packets be cryptographically signed by its producer. This way, globally addressable and routable content can be authenticated by anyone within the network. Meanwhile, consumers who request content are expected to verify content signature in order to assert [2]:

- *Integrity* - a valid signature (computed over a content hash) guarantees that signed content is intact;
- *Origin Authentication* - a signature is bound to the public key of the signer, so anyone can verify whether the received content originates with its claimed producer;
- *Correctness* - since a signature binds content name to its payload, a consumer can securely determine whether delivered content corresponds to what was requested;

With the flourishing of CCN, more and more research forces have been trying to exploit existing technologies to bring the best performance out of it. The application of the technique of NC in CCN has been first explored in [3] to better cope with the information dissemination problems in CCN. Since then, the potential of NC in CCN has been explored from various angles of CCN architecture and application scenarios, which all prove that NC can become an indispensable part for the desirable performance of CCN. However, among all the researches exploring the contributions NC can make, there is no research having taken into consideration new security challenges raised accordingly. For example, the universal operation NC brings to CCN is that content packets are encoded at producers and recoded at intermediate routers, but how to justify the recoding process from the security prospective? How to achieve the validity of intermediate routers? CCN requires that content packets be cryptographically signed by its producer, but with the presence of encoding and recoding operation, how to coordinate signing implementation and encoding/recoding process? Most importantly, how to enable consumers to ascertain the *Integrity, Origin Authentication* and *Correctness* of encoded packets as usual?

These are the questions that have been left untouched in existing researches. Therefore, as the first effort to address security issues in NC employed CCN settings, we would like to focus on these questions. We hold that security consideration should be explicitly built into any NC employed CCN applications while not undermining the performance advantages gained through NC. Specifically, in this work, we analyze the new security issues raised accordingly and propose an autonomous systems based security mechanism that guarantees content security in terms of AS and confine particular security operations to border routers to insure security of content communication among AS-s. The proposed mechanism can not only ensure the optimal performance of NC, but also offer the assurance for *Integrity, Origin Authentication* and *Correctness* of content packets, together with proving trustworthiness among border routers. More importantly, we also shed light on the performance issues and implementation problems of the mechanism.

To the best of our knowledge, it is the first time that security issues are addressed in NC employed CCN environment. The rest of this paper is organized as follows. Section 2 introduces the fundamentals of CCN and security related existing work. Section 3 presents NC principles and the applications of NC in CCN. We give the detailed description of the proposed mechanism in Sect. 4. Performance analysis and implementation issues are introduced in Sect. 5. Finally in Sect. 6, we give the concluding remarks and further work.

2   CCN Fundamentals

2.1   Content Retrieval in CCN

Different from IP centering on end-points communication, CCN communication adheres to the *pull* model and emphasizes content by making it named, address-able and routable in the network. To enable the communication, there are two types of packets in CCN: *interest* and *content*. Both of these packets carry a hierarchically structured name which uniquely identifies a content package. Similar to the work in [5], we focus on content communication over wired networks represented by directed acyclic graphs $G = (V, L)$, where V and L denote the set of network nodes and the set of links connecting them, respectively. Each network consists of a set of source nodes, namely Producers S that generate and/or store content objects, a set of consumers U that demand content objects and a set of intermediate nodes R through which the content objects are requested and transmitted. Hence, we have $V = S \cup U \cup R$, where every node $v \in V$ is connected with its neighboring nodes through a set of faces F_v.

In CCN, content objects are split into smaller segments that fit into Data messages. Each segment is uniquely identified by a name. The detailed composition of a content packet will be given in the following section. We denote a content object as $C_p = \{c_{p,1}, \ldots, c_{p,N}\}$ where N is the number of segments in C_p and p is the name of the content object, which serves as a name prefix for the segments. The name of each segment $c_{p,n} \in C_p$ is generated by appending the segment id n to the content objects name p. For instance, the name of the segment $c_{p,1}$ is /producer/videos/smilevideo.h328/1, where /producer/videos/smilevideo.h328 is the name prefix p and 1 is the segment id.

Each source $s \in S$ stores content objects that can be requested by the clients. A client $u \in U$ that is interested in a content object $C_p = \{c_{p,1}, \ldots, c_{p,N}\}$ should send a set of Interest messages $I_P = \{i_{p,1}, \ldots, i_{p,N}\}$, one for each segment. These interests are sent over a set of faces F_u^p that are configured to forward Interests for content with name prefix p. The information about which faces a node can use to send Interests for specific name prefixes is stored in the *Forwarding Information Base (FIB)* table.

In CCN, each node $v \in V$ has a cache, or *Content Store (CS)* in CCN terminology, where segments that pass through the node can be stored. These segments can be used later to reply to Interests for segments with a matching name. Therefore, a node $v \in R \cup S$ holding a copy of the segment $c_{p,n}$ in its CS replies to any Interest $i_{p,n}$. If the CS of node v does not contain a segment matching the name of the Interest $i_{p,n}$, the node v first checks its *Pending Interest Table (PIT)*, that keeps track of the Interests forwarded by the node and all the faces over which those Interests have arrived. If the node v finds in its PIT an entry that matches the name in the Interest, it knows that it has already forwarded $i_{p,n}$ and hence the segment $c_{p,n}$ is expected. In this case, v does not forward $i_{p,n}$ again, but only adds the face f over which the Interest has arrived to the respective PIT entry. When the PIT does not have any entry that matches the Interest $i_{p,n}$, the node v forwards the Interest to its neighboring nodes over the set of faces F_u^p configured in its FIB and adds a corresponding entry to the PIT table.

Once the requested segment is found in the CS of an intermediate node or in a source node, it is transmitted to the client in a Data message over the reverse path of that followed by the Interest. When a node $v \in R \cup U$ receives a Data message with the segment $c_{p,n}$ over a face f, it first checks its CS. If a segment with the same name exists, the arrived segment $c_{p,n}$ is considered duplicated and it is not transmitted further. If there is no matching segment in the CS, the node checks its PIT for an entry that matches the name of the segment $c_{p,n}$. If there is no matching PIT entry, the segment $c_{p,n}$ is considered unsolicited and it is discarded. If a matching PIT entry exists, the segment is forwarded over all the faces specified in the corresponding PIT entry. Additionally, the segment $c_{p,n}$ may be added to the CS, according to the caching policy.

2.2 Security Practice in Original CCN

One key tenet of CCN is that each content packet should be digitally signed by its producer, while a consumer is required to conduct signature verification. Intermediate routers may choose to verify all, some or none of the data they handle, as their resources allow. They may also dynamically adapt, verifying more data in response to detected attack [1]. To verify the authenticity of a content packet $c_{p,n}$, we focus on the following fields of $c_{p,n}$, in addition to the data and other supporting information:

- *Signature* - a private key signature, generated by the content producer, covering the entire content, including all explicit components of the name and a reference to the public key needed to verify it.
- *Name* - the name used to route the content. It is adaptable concerning different mechanisms.
- *Content-digest* - the cryptographic digest of the content packet $c_{p,n}$.
- *KeyLocator* - The public key or certificate required to verify the signature. In our work, we require that it be the public key.

It is universally acknowledged that the primary means of security enforcement in CCN is encryption, which is commonly believed to be contingent upon a trust management architecture. The signature and verification processes in original CCN architecture go like this: For a fresh piece of source data segment, a producer first takes use of a Hash function to get its digest. Then it signs the digest and other components like name, nonce fields with its private key. Finally, it sends out the packet $c_{p,n}$ composed of signature, payload and other supporting information. When a consumer or an intermediate router receives $c_{p,n}$, it verifies the packet before making further decision. Specifically, it first uses the public key of the signer to decrypt the packet $c_{p,n}$. If it can be decoded, that means that it is from the expected producer *(Origin Authentication)*. Otherwise, the source of the packet $c_{p,n}$ is uncertain and it will be discarded. If the *Origin Authentication* is success, it hashes the payload of the packet and compares the result with the one in the decrypted signature *(Integrity)*. If they are equal, the payload is not changed and there is no transmission error. Otherwise, the packet will be discarded. If the name field is equal to the one in decrypted signature, it means that the packet is what had been requested *(Correctness)*. Otherwise, it is discarded.

2.3 Security Related Work

CCN is built on the notion of content-based security. Before NC meets CCN, previous research efforts have addressed security issues from different aspects, such as naming in content-oriented networks and its relationship to security [17–20], denial of Service (DoS) attacks [2, 21–24], trust and trust management systems [26–33] and privacy issues [34], etc.

CCN emphasizes that authenticity and trust are the keys to effective content-based security [25]. Based on previous techniques in [17–20, 25], Ghali *et al.* [2] has proposed IKB rule which stands for Interest-Key Binding rule, and sets that an interest must reflect the public key of the producer. However, it can not be applied to the NC employed CCN architecture, because intermediate routers are allowed to recode coded content packets, which, though, has no effect on the verification of a producer, the recoding process makes it hard to ensure the security of received packets and prevent content poisoning due to the absence of measures to verify routers who have recoded content packets.

In the same work [2], to further reduce communication and computation overhead, Self-Certifying Naming schemes *(SCN)* that have received a lot of attention [17–20] is optimized to specify the hash of requested content as the last component of the content name in the interest. It enables consumers and routers no longer need to verify signatures. Instead, they only need to recompute a content hash and check that it matches the one in the corresponding PIT entry, thus reducing overhead of publishing and network overhead. Unfortunately, this technique fails as well to address the new security challenges. In light of NC principles, the content of a packet is not static since it may experience recoding process several times before reaching a consumer, which makes the hash of content not stable and not reliable.

3 Network Coding in CCN

Contrary to the Internet perception that bits are meaningless, Network Coding *(NC)* considers data traffic as algebraic information [7]. The output of a network coder is a linear combination of a number of input packets. NC has been shown in an information theoretic manner to reduce the required number of transmissions to complete a file or stream operation over noisy or unreliable networks.

The application of the technique of NC in CCN has been first explored in [3] to better cope with the information dissemination problems in CCN. Since then, the potential of NC in CCN has been explored from various angles of CCN architecture and application scenarios, including cache performance [12–14], privacy issues [16], etc. The latest works are focusing on the contributions that NC can make to improve multi-path transmission [5] and video streaming [6] in CCN, which demonstrate further that NC can add robustness to losses and permits to exploit more efficiently the available network resources [5], and in the case of video streaming, NC can deliver significant performance gain, including better QoE, higher throughput [6].

The key idea behind introducing network coding in CCN is that consumers no longer need to request specific segments, but rather encoded segments as they all have the same amount of information. This removes the need to coordinate the forwarding of Interests and leads to a more efficient use of the available network bandwidth. It is true that NC does add complexity to network entities since it involves performing linear operations, yet these are quite simple for the current generation of network elements and end devices [3].

Among all the works for the integration of NC into CCN, Random Linear Network Coding *(RLNC)* has been popularly adopted. Though there are discrepancies in naming system, packet composition or packet processing in terms of the implementation, the consensus is that content packets delivered to consumers are coded at sources and intermediate nodes [6].

3.1   General NC Mechanism Without Security Measures

Network coding permits that intermediate routers can recode coded packets, which renders the fact that the original content packets are changed after the algebraic operation. The operation of NC is infused into CCN architecture.

As in the CCN protocol, the content object C_p is split into source data segments $\{c_{p,1}, \ldots, c_{p,N}\}$, that fit into content packets. Network coded packets $\hat{c_{p,g}}$ are random linear combinations of original segments with name prefix p. Similar to [5], g denotes the encoding vector associated with the coded packet $\hat{c_{p,g}}$. At the producers, coded packets are generated by randomly combining the set of non-coded segments with name prefix p that are stored in their CS. Thus, $\hat{c_{p,g}} = A \cdot CS_p = \sum_{l=1}^{L} a_l \cdot c_{p,l}$ where $A = a_1, \ldots, a_L$ is a vector of coding coefficients randomly selected from a finite field, $CS_p = \{c_{p,1}, \ldots, c_{p,L}\}$ is the set of segments with name prefix p stored in the CS of the router, and $L = |CS_p|$ is the size of the vector CS_p, with $L \leq N$. At the intermediate routers, network coded packets are generated by randomly combining the set of coded packets with name prefix p that are stored in their CS. Thus, $\hat{c_{p,k}} = \sum_{l=1}^{L} a_l \cdot \hat{c_{p,g_l}}$. The encoding vector k is generated as $k = \sum_{l=1}^{L} a_l \cdot g_l$, where g_l is the coding vector associated with the lth packet

The consumers and intermediate routers keep track of the received innovative encoding vectors for prefix p in an encoding matrix $G_p = [g_1, \ldots, g_L]$, with

$L = |CS_p|$. This allows the original set of segments to be retrieved at consumers by performing Gaussian elimination when the matrix G_p is full rank. Since the matrix G_p only contains linearly independent encoding vectors, its rank can be computed as $\text{Rank}(G_p) = L$. Thus, it is full rank when $L = N$.

4   Security Mechanism Based on Autonomous Systems

Based on the exiting security practice and the notion of Autonomous Systems (AS-s), we attempt to scale down security issues and address them in terms of AS-s. As Fig. 1 illustrates, the network is divided into several AS-s as *OSPF* does. There are content producers, routers within an AS, border routers and content consumers in the network. We start by dividing the communication between a producer and consumers into two categories-the one within an AS and the one outside an AS.

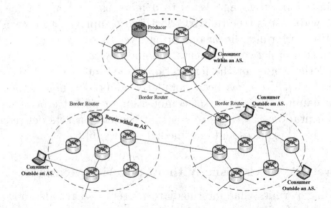

Fig. 1. Communication based on Autonomous Systems (AS-s)

For communication happening within an AS, we observe that only routers in the AS will get involved, which implies that if we can ensure routers in one AS are trustable, we can minimize the negative impact NC has on the original CCN security model by slightly adapting the signature generation, thus skillfully handling the relationship of NC and security measures. Given the current machine authentication technologies available, achieving the trustworthiness of routers in an AS is not difficult. Specifically, we set it a rule that a producer in the proposed security mechanism signs a source data segment over name, content digest and other supporting fields with its private key before conducting encoding procedure. Routers within an AS forward packets or recode them when they could, while being oblivious of the signatures from a producer. Consumers within an AS perform decoding procedure first and then conduct signature verification to ascertain the *Integrity*, *Origin Authentication* and *Correctness* of content packets. In this way, the security of content packets within an AS is well achieved.

For communication happening outside an AS, we have border routers who are speakers for communications both within and outside an AS. We adopt a second signature at them to offer the trustworthiness of routers from one AS for routers in other AS-s. Specifically, when a coded packet circulates within an AS, it only carries one signature. When it reaches a border router and is about to leave the AS, the border router will sign it over its name, content digest and other supporting fields while the inner signature from the producer remains transparent, regardless of performing recoding or not. Consumers in other AS-s perform at most two signature verification processes, the first one (might be spared by border routers) for the trustworthiness of routers, the *correctness* and the *integrity* of the packet while the second signature for the *origin* and the *integrity* of the packet. By delegating the security information of content packets passing one AS to border routers via adding a second signature and keeping the original practice of inner signature, the security of content packets among AS-s is finely achieved as well.

In the following parts, we will examine the implications of the proposed mechanism on producers, routers within an AS, border routers and consumers, respectively.

4.1   Implications for Producers

No prior work has explored the coordination issue of signature generation and encoding procedure. In the proposed mechanism, we set it a rule that producers sign the content chunks before performing encoding procedure.

Specifically, a producer first segments a requested content object C_P into source data segments $\{c_{p,1}, \ldots, c_{p,N}\}$. When the segmentation finishes, the producer signs them individually with its private key and we will get the first-stage content chunks denoted as $\{t_{p,1}, \ldots, t_{p,N}\}$. It is worth attention that these signatures are only for consumers to verify and of which intermediate routers are oblivious. Note that, before packets are ready to be sent out, we only call them chunks. Afterwards, they need to go through the encoding process that is similar to the one without considering security measures in [5]. After the encoding procedure, we get the coded packets denoted as $\hat{t_{p,g}}, \ldots, \hat{t_{p,k}}$, where g and k denote different encoding vectors associated respectively. Subsequently, we get the final content packets $\hat{c_{p,g}}, \ldots, \hat{c_{p,k}}$. This procedure is outlined in Algorithm 1.

Algorithm 1. The Processing Logic for Producers

---

1 **Require:** C_p
2 **Output:** $\hat{c_{p,g}}$, g denotes the encoding vector associated.
3 Segment C_p into $\{ c_{p,1}, \ldots, c_{p,N} \}$
4 Sign $\{ c_{p,1}, \ldots, c_{p,N} \}$ one by one
5 Get the first-stage content chunks $\{ t_{p,1}, \ldots, t_{p,N} \}$ that are composed of $c_{p,n}$, signature, name, keyLocator, etc.
6 Encode $\{ t_{p,1}, \ldots, t_{p,N} \}$ and get coded packets $\hat{t_{p,g}}, \ldots, \hat{t_{p,k}}$
7 Get the final content packets $\hat{c_{p,g}}, \ldots, \hat{c_{p,k}}$

4.2   Implications for Routers Within an AS

When a packet is circulating within an AS, routers within an AS will check the novelty of the coding vector resided in the packet first. If the packet increases the Rank of G_P, the routers will accept it and perform recoding procedure without being aware of the signature it carries. Otherwise, the packet is duplicated and will be discarded accordingly.

Specifically, upon receiving a coded content packet $\hat{c_{p,g}}$, the router verifies the uniqueness of the packet given the presence of network coding. If $\hat{c_{p,g}}$ is innovative for the fact that the encoding vector g is linearly independent of the encoding vectors in G_p, the packet will be processed further. otherwise, it is a duplicate packet and discarded accordingly. When it is innovative, $\hat{t_{p,g}}$ from $\hat{c_{p,g}}$ will be inserted into CS_p for further recoding operation. However, if $\hat{t_{p,g}}$ is the only one in the CS_p, namely, the Rank of G_p is 1, the router is unable to perform the recoding process. So it stops the recoding logic and undertakes forwarding and caching procedure. While, if there are more than one chunks from coded packets in the CS_p, the recoding process will begin. When the recoding operation finishes, we get recoded packets $\hat{t_{p,k}}$, where the encoding vector k is generated as $k = \sum_{l=1}^{L} a_l \cdot g$, and g is the coding vector associated with $\hat{t_{p,g}}$. Subsequently, we get the final content packet $\hat{c_{p,g}}$, which is then forwarded. The whole procedure is outlined in Algorithm 2.

Algorithm 2. The Processing Logic for Routers within an AS.

---

1   **Require:** $\hat{c_{p,g}}$
2   **Output:** $\hat{c_{p,k}}$, $k = \sum_{l=1}^{L} a_l \cdot g$
3   if g increases the Rank of G_p then
4   $\qquad$ if $|G_p| = 1$ then
5   $\qquad\qquad$ process forwarding and caching.

6   $\qquad$ else
7   $\qquad\qquad$ get $\hat{t_{p,g}}$ and encode it with those in the CS_p
8   $\qquad\qquad$ get $\hat{t_{p,k}}$
9   $\qquad\qquad$ get the final packet $\hat{c_{p,k}}$

10   else
11
12   $\qquad$ discard it.

4.3   Implications for Border Routers

Border routers are the routers who will communicate with routers both within and outside an AS. Specifically, for the communications within an AS, border routers assume the role of routers within an AS, as described in the former section. While for the communications outside an AS, border routers are expected to sign coded packets they have received with their private keys, in order to prove trustworthiness for border routers in other AS-s. Without a doubt, given the position and NC principles, borders routers are most likely to conduct the recoding process. However, no matter whether they conduct recoding or not, they need to perform the outer signature generation process for coded packets that are leaving the AS. While, for packets that are entering this AS, border router need not generate a signature.

Algorithm 3. The Processing Logic for Border Routers

---

1 **Require:** $\hat{c_{p,g}}$
2 **Output:** $\hat{c_{p,k}}$, $k = \sum_{l=1}^{L} a_l \cdot g$
3 **if** *g increases the Rank of* G_p **then**
4   **if** *outer signature exists* **then**
5   get public key from the keyLocator in $\hat{c_{p,g}}$
6   verify the signature
7   **if** *the verification successful* **then**
8   get $\hat{t_{p,g}}$
9   insert $\hat{t_{p,g}}$ into the CS_p
10   **else**
11
12   discard it and break.
13   **if** $|G_p| = 1$ **then**
14   process forwarding.
15   **else**
16   encode $\hat{t_{p,g}}$ with those in the CS_p and get $\hat{t_{p,k}}$
17   **if** $\hat{c_{p,g}}$ *leaving the AS* **then**
18   sign $\hat{t_{p,k}}$
19   get the final packet $\hat{c_{p,k}}$
20   **else**
21   get the final packet $\hat{c_{p,k}}$

22 **else**
23
24   discard it.

In particular, upon receiving a coded content packet $\hat{c_{p,g}}$ that is heading out of the AS, a border router will verify its novelty and when it is novel to the ones in its CS_P, it will check that whether it carries a signature. If there is a signature available, the router will verify the signature to achieve the trustworthiness and *correctness* as well as *integration* of the packet. If no discrepancy occurs, the router will undertake the recoding procedure. After the recoding, it will sign the recoded content chunk with its private key while the signature from the producer remains transparent. While preparing the final content packet, it directly puts its public key in the field of *KeyLocator* and subsequently sends the final content packet out. While, for a coded content packet that is entering the AS, a border router performs similar operation, yet the difference is that before forwarding it, the border router needs not to sign it. So the packet only carries one signature within the AS. The whole procedure is outlined in Algorithm 3.

4.4 Implications for Consumers

In the proposed mechanism, consumers are distinguished by the components of received packets they handle. For example, when there is an outer signature available before performing decoding process, a consumer will go through two signature verification processes. Otherwise, only one signature verification necessitates.

Algorithm 4. The Processing Logic for Consumers

---

1 **Require:** $c_{\hat{p},g}$
2 **if** *g increases the Rank of G_p* **then**
3   **if** *outer signature exists* **then**
4   get the public key from the keyLocator field in $c_{\hat{p},g}$
5   verify the signature
6   **if** *the verification successful* **then**
7   get $t_{\hat{p},g}$
8   insert $t_{\hat{p},g}$ in the CS_p.
9   **else**
10
11   discard it and terminate.
12   **if** $|G_p| = N$ **then**
13   decode $t_{\hat{p},g}, \ldots, t_{\hat{p},k}$ in the CS_p
14   get $\{ c_{q,1}, \ldots, c_{q,N} \}$
15   verify the signature of $\{ c_{q,1}, \ldots, c_{q,N} \}$
16   **if** *the verification successful* **then**
17   get the original segments $\{ c_{p,1}, \ldots, c_{p,N} \}$
18   **else**
19   discard it.
20   **else**
21   break.
22 **else**
23
24 discard it.

As Algorithm 4 outlines, upon receiving a content packet $c_{\hat{p},k}$, a consumer needs to figure out whether it is novel. When it is novel, the consumer proceeds to check whether there is an outer signature it carries. If the outer signature presents and the signature verification is successful, the consumer gets the confidence that the last signer is trustable and gets the transitional content chunks $t_{\hat{p},k}$, a coded chunk after the outer signature verification. After inserting $t_{\hat{p},g}$ into the CS_p, the consumer needs to test whether the Rank(G_p) = N, namely, whether the matrix G_p is full rank. If the coded packets in CS_p are decodable, the consumer will decode them according to network coding principles and get $\{t_{p,1}, \ldots, t_{p,N}\}$, which are source data segments, each with the signature of the producer.

Suppose no error occurs during the decoding process. With the decoded chunks $\{t_{p,1}, \ldots, t_{p,N}\}$ the consumer needs to ascertain whether these packets are from the expected producer. Then the verification of the inner signature unfolds. If the result is success, the consumer gets source data segments. Otherwise, further actions should be adopted, which is beyond the scope of this article.

5 Performance and Implementation Issues

As mentioned before, the proposed security mechanism based on the notion of autonomous systems implies that consumers outside an AS should perform at most two verification processes using the public keys of intermediate routers' and the producer's. Routers within an AS should perform one verification for the uniqueness of a packet, while a portion of them will recode coded content packets. Similar to the practice that a producer signs once in original CCN architecture where network coding is absent, a producer in the proposed mechanism is expected to sign source data segments first before they are encoded. At first glance, this mechanism seems to be complicated and questionable, but given the security requirements and security practice in CCN, it seems to be deliberate and inevitable.

As is known to all, CCN is built on the notion of content-based security: protection and trust travel with the content itself. All content is authenticated with digital signatures, and private content is protected with encryption. Consumers are expected to verify content signatures in order to assert *Integrity*, *Origin Authentication* and *Correctness*. We argue that when NC is introduced into CCN architecture, security should not be compromised and the security principles should be equally followed.

Notably, the *Origin Authentication* asks for the verification of the source for a content packet. When NC is not integrated into CCN, the verification performed by consumers can offer corresponding information. But when NC joins the architecture, intermediate routers are obligate to recode coded packets, which brings about issues. For example, how to interpret the recoding process performed by intermediate routers from security perspective especially for routers and consumers outside an AS, and can they be regarded as producers and be verified as well? How to achieve the validity of intermediate routers? Most importantly, how to ascertain the Integrity, Origin Authentication and Correctness of recoded content packets as usual when they reach consumers? Learning from experience, obviously, one signature could not satisfy this task. But how many signatures will be sufficient and how to effectively and efficiently sign them are the questions that concern us. After an exhaustive survey on existing CCN security solutions and cryptology theory, we hold that the proposed security mechanism is the answer.

First, the proposed mechanism can work effectively. AS reaching a consumer outside an AS, if coded packets carry outer signatures, the verification of the outer signatures will offer information concerning the validity of routers who have recoded them, the correctness and integrity of the packets. If outer signatures are gone, the corresponding security information has been achieved by border routers, thus a consumer only conducts inner signature verification that will ascertain the origin and integrity of the content packet. The verification performed by border routers will ensure the trustworthiness of other border routers, the correctness and integrity of the packets in accordance to their PIT entries. Without a doubt, the promise of content security in original CCN architecture is equally delivered by the proposed mechanism.

Second, this mechanism can work efficiently. Based on the existing works, signature verification in the proposed security mechanism will not induce extra cost for fetching and managing public keys, as they are readily available in the packets and consumers can obtain the producer's key before issuing an interest. For border routers in communications outside an AS, the implementation of the security mechanism and the NC operation will add to the complexity of the processing logic and consume a little bit more space (the size of a signature, to be exact) in a content packet, however the future is quite promising. Given the studies in [8,9], the implementation of network coding can be quite efficient, and a network coding coder and decoder can operate at wire-speed with rates of up to 1000 MPs. In addition, the previous work [35] suggests that per-packet RSA signatures for real-time data are practical on commodity end-user platforms today. As to the extra space consuming, there is no consensus on the exact size of a content packet, but with the increasingly cheaper and more superior storage technique, the extra space cost will not pose much limitation to our scheme, combined with fine compression technique in [11].

Last, this mechanism can be easily implemented. Compared to the original security scheme, the proposed mechanism does not impose substantial changes to the original CCN architecture. In particular, it ensures content security within as AS first and delegates security practice to border routers for across AS-s communications by requiring them to verify outer signature and add one signature. Apparently, the mechanism can be easily carried out.

6   Conclusion and Future Work

In this paper, we have analysed the new security issues brought by the integration of NC into CCN and propose an Autonomous System based security mechanism in accordance to the security requirements and existing practice of CCN. Our proposed mechanism can not only deliver the optimal performance of network coding in CCN, but also ensure the security assurance of *Integrity*, *Origin Authentication* and *Correctness* for content packets, which will definitely benefit NC application innovations in CCN. Moreover, we also take into consideration the performance issues and implementation problems of the mechanism. In the future, we are going to implement this mechanism in NC employed CCN applications and hope that this work can awaken more awareness for the security issues in CCN.

Acknowledgments. This work was supported in part by National Keystone R&D Program of China (No. 2016YFB0800101), the Natural Science Foundation of China

(NSFC) (No. 61671001, No.61521003), together with the Guangdong Research Programs 2016B030305005 and Shenzhen Research Programs (ZDSYS201603311739428, JCYJ20150331100723974 & 20140509093817684).

References

1. Jacobson, V., Smetters, D.K., Thornton, J.D., Plass, M.F., Briggs, N.H., Braynard, R.L.: Networking named content. In: ACM CoNEXT 2009, December 2009
2. Ghali, C., Tsudik, G., Uzun, E.: Network-layer trust in named-data networking. ACM Sigcomm Comput. Commun. Rev. **44**(5), 12–19 (2014)
3. Montpetit, M.-J., Westphal, C., Trossen, D.: Networking, network coding meets information-centric: an architectural case for information dispersion through native network coding. In: 1st ACM NoM Workshop, June 2012
4. Sundararajan, J., Shah, D., Medard, M., Jakubczak, S., Mitzenmacher, M., Barros, J.: Network coding meets TCP: theory and implementation. Proc. IEEE **99**(3), 490–512 (2011)
5. Saltarin, J., Bourtsoulatze, E., Thomos, N., Braun, T.: Netcodccn: a network coding approach for content-centric networks, arXiv preprint (2015). arXiv:1512.00259
6. Ramakrishnan, A., Westphal, C., Saltarin, J.: Adaptive video streaming over CCN with network coding for seamless mobility. In: 2016 IEEE International Symposium on Multimedia (ISM), San Jose, CA, pp. 238–242 (2016). doi:10.1109/ISM
7. Koetter, R., Mdard, M.: An algebraic approach to network coding. IEEE/ACM Trans. Networking **11**(5), 782–795 (2003)
8. Pedersen, M., Heide, J., Vingelmann, P., Fitzek, F.: Network coding over the $2^{32}-5$ prime field. In: IEEE ICC 2013, June 2013
9. Zhang, M., Li, H., Chen, F., Hou, H., An, H., Wang, W., Huang, J.: A general co/decoder of network coding in HDL. In: 2011 International Symposium on Network Coding, July 2011
10. Thomos, N., Frossard, P.: Toward one symbol network coding vectors. IEEE Commun. Lett. **16**(11), 1860–1863 (2012)
11. Lucani, D.E., Pedersen, M.V., Heide, J., Fitzek, F.H.P., Codes, F.N.: A Code for Fluid Allocation of Complexity (2014). http://arxiv.org/abs/1404.6620
12. Wu, Q., Li, Z., Xie, G.: Codingcache: multipath-aware ccn cache with network coding. In: Proceedings of the 3rd ACM SIGCOMM Workshop on Information-Centric Networking, pp. 41–42. ACM (2013)
13. Miyake, S., Asaeda, H.: Network coding and its application to content centric networking, Witmse (2013)
14. Wang, J., Ren, J., Lu, K., Wang, J., Liu, S., Westphal, C.: An optimal cache management framework for information-centric networks with network coding. In: IFIP/IEEE Networking Conference, June 2014
15. Wang, J., Ren, J., Lu, K., Wang, J., Liu, S., Westphal, C.: A minimum cost cache management framework for information-centric networks with network coding. Comput. Netw. **110**, 1–17 (2016)
16. Wu, Q., Li, Z., Tyson, G., Uhlig, S., Kaafar, M.A., Xie, G.: Privacyaware multipath video caching for content-centric networks. IEEE J. Sel. Areas Commun. **34**, 2219–2230 (2016)
17. Fayazbakhsh, S.K., Lin, Y., Tootoonchian, A., Ghodsi, A., Koponen, T., Maggs, B., Ng, K., Sekar, V., Shenker, S.: Less pain, most of the gain: incrementally deployable ICN. In: Proceedings of the ACM SIGCOMM 2013 Conference on SIGCOMM, pp. 147–158. ACM (2013)

18. Ghodsi, A., Koponen, T., Rajahalme, J., Sarolahti, P., Shenker, S.: Naming in content-oriented architectures. In: Proceedings of the ACM SIGCOMM Workshop on Information-Centric Networking, pp. 1–6. ACM (2011)

19. Ghodsi, A., Shenker, S., Koponen, T., Singla, A., Raghavan, B., Wilcox, J.: Information-centric networking: seeing the forest for the trees. In: Proceedings of the 10th ACM Workshop on Hot Topics in Networks, p. 1. ACM (2011)

20. Koponen, T., Chawla, M., Chun, B.-G., Ermolinskiy, A., Kim, K.H., Shenker, S., Stoica, I.: A data-oriented (and beyond) network architecture. ACM SIGCOMM Comput. Commun. Rev. **37**(4), 181–192 (2007)

21. Gasti, P., Tsudik, G., Uzun, E., Zhang, L.: DoS DDoS in named-data networking. In: Proceedings of the International Conference on Computer Communications and Networks (ICCCN) (2013)

22. Afanasyev, A., Mahadevan, P., Moiseenko, I., Uzun, E., Zhang, L.: Interest flooding attack and countermeasures in named data networking. In: Proceedings of the IFIP Networking Conference (2013)

23. Compagno, A., Conti, M., Gasti, P., Tsudik, G.: Poseidon: mitigating interest flooding DDoS attacks in named data networking. In: Proceedings of the 38th IEEE Conference on Local Computer Networks (LCN) (2013)

24. Ghali, C., Tsudik, G., Uzun, E.: Needle in a haystack: mitigating content poisoning in named-data networking. In: The Workshop on Security of Emerging NETWORKING Technologies (2014)

25. Smetters, D., Jacobson, V.: Securing network content. Technical report, PARC (2009)

26. Blaze, M., Feigenbaum, J., Lacy, J.: Decentralized trust management. In: Proceedings of the IEEE Symposium on Security and Privacy, pp. 164–173 (1996)

27. Cho, J.-H., Swami, A., Chen, R.: A survey on trust management for mobile ad hoc networks. IEEE Commun. Surv. Tutorials **13**(4), 562–583 (2011)

28. Conner, W., Iyengar, A., Mikalsen, T., Rouvellou, I., Nahrstedt, K.: A trust management framework for service-oriented environments. In: Proceedings of the 18th International Conference on World Wide Web (WWW), pp. 891–900 (2009)

29. Li, W., Joshi, A., Finin, T.: Coping with node misbehaviors in ad hoc networks: a multi-dimensional trust management approach. In: Proceedings of the 11th International Conference on Mobile Data Management (MDM), pp. 85–94 (2010)

30. Lopez, J., Roman, R., Agudo, I., Fernandez-Gago, C.: Trust management systems for wireless sensor networks: best practices. Comput. Commun. **33**(9), 1086–1093 (2010)

31. Omar, M., Challal, Y., Bouabdallah, A.: Certification-based trust models in mobile ad hoc networks: a survey and taxonomy. J. Netw. Comput. Appl. **35**(1), 268–286 (2012)

32. Zahariadis, T., Leligou, H.C., Trakadas, P., Voliotis, S.: Trust management in wireless sensor networks. Eur. Trans. Telecommun. **21**(4), 386–395 (2010)

33. Mahadevan, P., Uzun, E., Sevilla, S., et al.: CCN-KRS: a key resolution service for CCN. In: Proceedings of the 1st International Conference on Information-Centric Networking. ACM (2014)

34. Chaabane, A., Cristofaro, E.D., Kaafar, M.A., et al.: Privacy in content-oriented networking: threats and countermeasures. ACM Sigcomm Comput. Commun. Rev. **43**(3), 25–33 (2013)

35. Jacobson, V., Smetters, D.K., et al.: VoCCN: voice over content-centric networks. In: ACM ReArch 2009, December 2009

An Ultra-Lightweight Authentication Scheme for Heterogeneous Wireless Sensor Networks in the Context of Internet of Things

Hamza Khemissa[1,2]([✉]), Djamel Tandjaoui[1], and Samia Bouzefrane[3]

[1] Computer Security Division, CERIST: Research Center on Scientific
and Technical Information, Algiers, Algeria
{hkhemissa,dtandjaoui}@cerist.dz
[2] LSI, USTHB: University of Sciences and Technology Houari Boumediene,
Algiers, Algeria
h.khemissa@usthb.dz
[3] CEDRIC Lab, CNAM: National Conservatory of Arts and Crafts, Paris, France
samia.bouzefrane@lecnam.net

Abstract. The Internet of Things (IoT) is in a continuous development, the basic notion of IoT is that each object within the global network is accessible and interconnected. In such an environment, Wireless Sensor Networks play a crucial role, since they support different applications domains. Nevertheless, security issues are the major obstacle for their deployment. Among these issues, authentication of the different inter-connected entities and exchanged data confidentiality. In this paper, we propose a new ultra-lightweight authentication scheme for heterogeneous wireless sensor networks in the context of IoT. This scheme allows both of the sensor and the user to authenticate each other in order to secure the communication. The proposed scheme uses only nonces, exclusive-or, concatenation operations to achieve mutual authentication. Moreover, it terminates with a session key agreement between the sensor node and the user. To assess our scheme, we carry out a performance and security analysis. The obtained results show that the proposed scheme provides authentication with low energy consumption, and ensures a resistance against different types of attacks.

Keywords: Internet of things · Wireless sensor networks · Identity · Authentication · Session key agreement

1 Introduction

The Internet of Things (IoT) is designed as a network of highly heterogeneous connected devices (things) that have locatable, addressable, and readable counterparts on the Internet [11]. It includes several kinds of objects, and different in terms of capability and functionality such as Radio-Frequency IDentification (RFID) tags, sensors, smartphones, wearable, etc. These heterogeneous objects interact to reach common goals [2,11,16].

© Springer International Publishing AG 2017
S. Bouzefrane et al. (Eds.): MSPN 2017, LNCS 10566, pp. 49–62, 2017.
DOI: 10.1007/978-3-319-67807-8_4

IoT deployment will open doors to a multitude of application domains, such as healthcare, military, logistics, environmental monitoring, and many others [2]. Wireless Sensor Networks (WSN) are considered as one of actual and most effective IoT applications network. Nowadays, we talk about heterogeneous WSNs since sensor networks can be built with different types of nodes, and some more computational and energy capabilities than others.

The most of communications are wireless in the IoT, which have the risk of eavesdropping. Thus, IoT is vulnerable to different types of attacks. Involved devices in the IoT have also low capabilities in terms of energy and computation. Hence, they cannot support the implementation of complex security schemes [2]. Security issues are the major obstacle for several IoT applications. Among these issues, authentication is an important concept that allows to verify the identity of each connected objects. Also, data integrity and confidentiality are required to secure communications [2,16].

In the literature, there are five basic authentication models for WSNs [21]. They need four messages to achieve authentication. In four of them, the user initiates the authentication scheme by firstly contacting the gateway node, then the sensor node. When developing our proposed ultra-lightweight authentication scheme for heterogeneous WSNs, we use the fifth authentication model, such as it is the only one that initiates the authentication scheme by firstly contacting the specific sensor. In our network architecture (see Fig. 1), a sensor node is the initiator of the authentication. Thus, it has to initiate the authentication scheme with the user directly through the Internet and does not need to first connect with the gateway node.

In this paper, we propose an ultra-lightweight authentication scheme for heterogeneous WSNs in the context of IoT. This scheme authenticates both of a sensor node and the user, and establishes a secure channel between the sensor node and the user. The proposed scheme uses only nonces, exclusive-or, concatenation operations to achieve mutual authentication. To assess our proposed scheme, both in terms of security properties and energy savings, we proceed with a security and a performance analysis. The obtained results show that is resistant against several attacks, and it provides authentication with low energy consumption.

The remainder of the paper is organized as follows. In Sect. 2, related work on authentication in the context of IoT are presented. Section 3 presents in details the network architecture, used notations, and the proposed authentication scheme. In Sects. 4 and 5, we continue with a security and performance analysis of the proposed scheme. Finally, Sect. 6 concludes the paper and provides future works.

2   Related Work

During the past few years, the research community focuses on proposing new security protocols adapted to the constrained environment of the IoT. In the related work discussion, we mainly discuss several proposed authentication schemes in the context of IoT. Among critical security issues in the IoT, Authentication is an important aspect used in different applications domains [2, 16].

Traditional authentication schemes usually interacts with centralized servers and identity providers [4]. These interactions generally require a high energy and computation capabilities. Nevertheless, most objects that constitute the IoT are limited in these resources. Many research works aim to propose lightweight and ultra-lightweight schemes adapted to IoT environment limits. Several research works on authentication in the context of IoT are cited in [2, 16]. Recent proposed authentication schemes in the context of IoT can be divided into two classes, namely: authentication with certification, and certificateless authentication.

In the first class, authentication is achieved by using digital certificates, such as each object has its digital certificate. Among these protocols, DTLS (Datagram Transport Layer Security) [14] authentication handshake has been proposed for the IoT [8]. This authentication scheme ensures a secure authentication between the two involved objects. However, its high consumption of energy caused by asymmetric encryption based RSA and the use of PKI certificates exchanges constitute its main drawbacks. For this reason, Elliptic Curve Cryptography (ECC) has raised as an interesting approach compared to RSA based algorithms. Indeed, for the same level of security, it consumes less energy and uses less key size for the same level of security [17].

In order to reduce the energy cost of the authentication process, authors in [12, 13] have proposed an authentication protocol for WSNs in distributed IoT applications. This scheme uses ECC based implicit certificate [1]. The analysis shows that it offers an authentication with less energy consumption and computation overhead.

In the second class, authentication schemes do not need certification. They are based on cryptographic operations such as exclusive-or operation (Xor), concatenation operation, hash functions, and other symmetric cryptography functions. Thus, this class of authentication schemes is known for its high energy saving.

In 2013, authors in [19] have proposed a user authentication and key agreement scheme based on the IoT notion for heterogeneous ad hoc WSNs. This scheme uses only symmetric cryptographic operations between a remote user, a gateway, and a sensor node. It terminates by a session key establishment that secures communication between the remote user and the sensor node.

In 2014, Farash et al. [5] reviewed this scheme, and they showed some security weaknesses. In order to overcome these weaknesses, they proposed a new and an efficient user authentication and key agreement scheme. The results of security analysis confirm the security properties of the proposed scheme.

In 2016, authors in [7] have proposed a new lightweight authentication for heterogeneous WSNs in the context of IoT. The scheme uses nonces and keyed-hash message authentication (HMAC) [9]. In addition, the HMAC computation is based on sensor node identity without sending the identity on the clear message. The analyses prove that the proposed scheme is classified as lightweight since it provides authentication with low energy cost.

Tewari et al. [18] have proposed an ultralightweight authentication scheme that uses only bitwise operation for IoT devices using RFID tags. The analysis of the scheme showed that is resistant against several attacks such as desynchronization, secret disclosure and traceability attacks. Nevertheless, authors in [15] have showed that is not resistant against the mentioned attacks. Furthermore, they presented a passive attack that retrieves all secret parameters of the tag by only eavesdropping a session between the legitimate reader and the target tag in a very short time.

Recently, authors in [6] have proposed a lightweight anonymous authentication protocol for securing real-time application data access in WSNs. The security analysis of this scheme showed that it provides several security features with a high security level. However, the sensor identity is not protected since it is sent on clear in the authentication phase. Based on the performance analysis of the scheme, it has low communication and computation costs. Consequently, it is suitable to be applied in resource constrained environments.

In this work, we propose a new utlra-lightweight authentication scheme with a high level of security and very low energy cost. This scheme is adaptable to each object that can be involved on heterogeneous WSNs in the context of IoT. It provides mutual authentication and key establishment to maintain a secure communication channel for confidential exchanges.

3 The Proposed Scheme

In this section, we present the proposed authentication scheme that aims to provide a mutual authentication between a sensor node and a user. This latter achieves authentication with low resources consumption. Firstly, we describe the network architecture and the used notations. Secondly, we define in details the functioning of the proposed authentication scheme.

3.1 Network Architecture

The network architecture is mainly composed of: the sensor nodes, the gateway node, and the user (see Fig. 1). The used authentication model enables a direct transmission of collected data from a sensor node to the mobile user after a successful mutual authentication between a sensor node and the user.

According to the network architecture, we make some assumptions:

- Objects can be divided into two categories: Sensor nodes are constrained on computational and energy capabilities. The gateway node and the user are non-constrained since they have more computational and energy resources.
- Each sensor has an identity Id_i and a masked identity $MSId_i$, it has the capacity to perform symmetric encryption. The gateway node and the user are able to perform asymmetric encryption to secure data transmission outside the WSN.

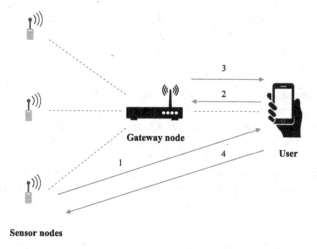

Fig. 1. Network architecture

3.2 Notations

The notations used in the proposed scheme are defined in Table 1.

3.3 Functioning

The proposed authentication scheme provides a mutual authentication and a session key agreement between a sensor node and a user that aims to collect data from the WSN. The scheme is divided into three phases:

- The registration phase, where the sensor nodes must first be registered in gateway node. Then, a registration part between the gateway and the user.

Table 1. Used Notations

Notation	Description
‖	Concatenation
⊕	Exclusive-or operation (Xor)
N	Nonce value of the sensor node
M	First nonce value of the user
L	Nonce value of the gateway node
P	Second nonce value of the user
H()	A one way hash function
$Enc(N, X_i)$	AES-128 encryption of the value N using the secret key X_i
F(N)	If (N != 16 bytes): The Function F applies an hash function h() that returns 16 bytes

- The authentication phase between the sensor nodes, the gateway, and the user in order to achieve mutual authentication.
- The key establishment, where a session key is established between each sensor node and the user.

In the following, we will present each phase in details.

(1) Registration phase

The registration phase between the sensor nodes, the gateway node, and the mobile user is the first phase of the proposed scheme. This phase is divided into two parts. The first registration part is between the sensor node and the gateway node, we assume that the communication channel has been previously secured. The second registration part is between the gateway node and the user (see Fig. 2).

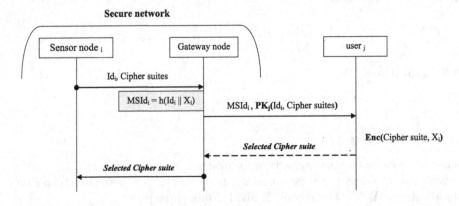

Fig. 2. Registration phase

First, the sensor node sends its identity Id_i and a list of supported cipher suites to the network gateway node through a secure channel. Once the gateway node receives the message, it selects the used cipher suite, and calculates the masked identity of the sensor node $MSId_i$ using the sensor identity Id_i and its secret key X_i. Second, it sends a message containing the masked identity of the sensor node, and the encryption of both the identity of the sensor node Id_i and the selected cipher suite by the public key of the user PK_j. (We assume that the gateway node knows the secret key of the sensor node and the public key of the user during the pre-deployment of the network).

As a response, the user sends an encrypted message *Selected Cipher suite* using the secret key of the sensor. This message contains the selected cipher suite. Finally, the gateway node transmits the *Selected Cipher suite* message to the sensor node. The sensor node receives, decrypts the message, and the registration phase terminates successfully.

Once the registration phase terminates, both of the gateway node and the user store the security related information in a binding table (see Table 2).

Table 2. Security related information

Node	Cipher suite	Masked Identity: $MSId_i = h(Id_i \| X_i)$
Id_1	Cipher1 & X_1	$MSId_1$
Id_2	Cipher2 & X_2	$MSId_2$
Id_3	Cipher3 & X_3	

(2) Authentication phase

The authentication phase aims to mutually authenticate both of the sensor nodes and the user. The authentication process must be executed to ensure a secure communication between each sensor node and the user. Our proposed authentication scheme is as follows (see Fig. 3):

(a) The sensor node generates a random nonce N on 8 bytes, calculates the value Z=(N $\|$ Id_i) $\oplus$ X_i, devises the value Z into two parts of 8 bytes: Z1 and Z2, applies a Xor between the two parts (Z1 $\oplus$ Z2), and puts the result on Z. Then, it sends a message composed of the masked identity of the sensor $MSId_i$, the generated nonce N, and the value Z to the user. The value Z will be used by the user to check the message.

(b) Upon receiving the message by the user, the message is verified by computing the value Z, and checking whether the received Z equal the computed value. If not equal, it is an authentication failure (F1), else the user generates a random nonce M on 8 bytes, calculates the value W=(M $\|$ Id_i) $\oplus$ X_i, devises the value W into two parts of 8 bytes: W1 and W2, applies a Xor between the two parts (W1 $\oplus$ W2), and puts the result on W. Then, it sends a message composed of the masked identity of the sensor $MSId_i$, the nonce N, the generated nonce M, and the value W to the user. The value W will be used by the gateway node to check the message.

(c) When the gateway node receives the message, it also verifies the message by calculating the value W, and checking whether the received W equal the computed value. If not equal, it is an authentication failure (F2), else the gateway node generates a random nonce L on 8 bytes, calculates the value S=N $\oplus$ M $\oplus$ L, calculates the T=(L $\|$ Id_i) $\oplus$ X_i, devises the value T into two parts of 8 bytes: T1 and T2, applies a Xor between the two parts (T1 $\oplus$ T2), and puts the result on T. Then, it sends a message composed of the nonce N, the nonce M, and the values S and T to the user. The value T will be used by the user to check the message.

(d) Upon receiving the message by the user, it computes the value L=N $\oplus$ M $\oplus$ S, and verifies the message by checking whether the received T equal the computed value. If not equal, it is an authentication failure (F3), else the user generates a random nonce P, calculates the value Q=P $\oplus$ L, computes the value R=(P $\|$ Id_i) $\oplus$ X_i, devises the value R into two parts of 8 bytes: R1 and R2, applies a Xor between the two parts (R1 $\oplus$ R2), and puts the result on R. Then, it sends a message composed of the nonce N, the nonce L, and the values Q and R to the sensor node. The value R will be used by the sensor node to check the message.

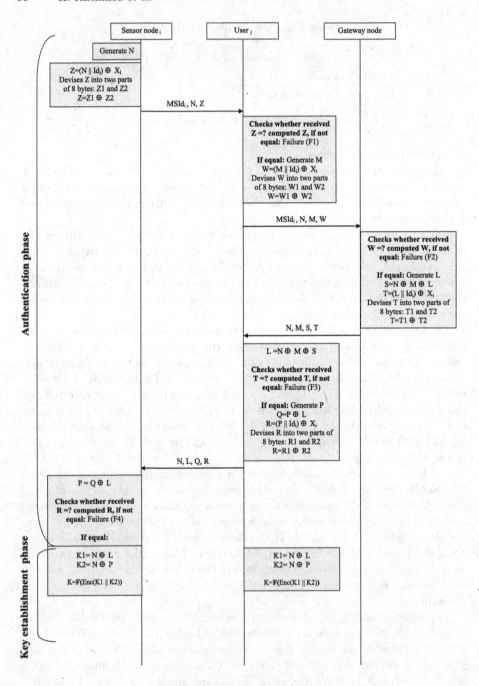

Fig. 3. Authentication scheme

(e) When the sensor node receives the message, it computes the value P=Q $\oplus$ L, and verifies the message by checking whether the received R equal the computed value. If not equal, it is an authentication failure (F4), else mutual authentication between objects terminates successfully.

(3) Key establishment phase

After a successful authentication phase, a shared symmetric key K is established to secure the communication between the sensor node and the user. This key is calculated by a personalized function as: K=F(Enc(K1 $\|$ K2,X_i)). First, the values K1 and K2 are calculated by applying respectively a Xor of the value N with the nonces L and P. Second, the concatenation of the two values K1 and K2, and apply an encryption with the associated secret key of the sensor node X_i. Thus, the key establishment phase terminates.

4   Security Analysis of the Proposed Scheme

In order to show the security efficiency of the proposed authentication scheme, we conduct a security analysis of the scheme. Our proposed scheme offers a resistance to several possible attacks. We are interested especially to:

- *Replay attack:*

If an attacker intercepts a previous exchanged message in the authentication phase, and tries to replay it in order to impersonate the sensor node, the user, or the gateway node, the message will be rejected and he cannot successfully impersonate the sensor node, the user, or the gateway node because new nonces are generated for each authentication to provide mutual authentication.

- *Impersonation attacks:*

First, an attacker cannot impersonate a sensor node since his identity is masked by the value $MSId_i$. Second, it cannot also impersonate the user or the gateway node without computing the value that checks the exchanged message using the sensor identity Id_i and the secret key X_i.

- *Denial-of-service attack:*

This attack is extremely dangerous in a resource constrained IoT environment. The Denial-of-service (DoS) attack has different types of attacks e.g. Jamming, Flooding, Tampering, etc. [20]. We threat the case of Flooding attack, since it can affect the proposed authentication scheme. The Flooding attack is not possible since each exchange in the authentication phase requests a response message that indicates the rejection or the acceptance of the received message, and ensures that is not a DoS attack. Furthermore, the proposed scheme uses random nonces, which are accepted only once in the authentication phase. Thus, it provides resistance against DoS attacks.

The proposed authentication scheme provides also advanced features that enhance security such as:

- *Mutual authentication:*

As a result of the authentication phase, both of the authenticity of the sensor node and the user is proven. This process is called mutual authentication.

Therefore, both of the sensor node and the user are sure of the identity of each other.

- *Session key establishment:*

After a successful authentication, a shared secret key is established between the sensor node and the user. This key is used as a session key to ensure a secure communication channel.

- *Data integrity:*

In the authentication phase of the proposed scheme, the integrity of a message is verified by the check of the computed value sent with the message. Thus, we are sure that transmitted data are not altered, and the integrity of exchanged messages is ensured.

- *Sensor identity protection:*

In order to disallow the revelation of the sensor identity Id_i, a masked identity $MSId_i$ is calculated for each sensor node. This value will be also known by the gateway node and the user.

- *Synchronization independence:*

In the proposed authentication scheme, we use random nonces to guarantee the freshness of messages. Thus, the proposed scheme does not require the use of timestamps to synchronize between involved objects. Therefore, the synchronization independence enhances the security of the proposed scheme.

- *Extensibility and scalability:*

The proposed authentication scheme allows new sensor nodes to be integrated into the network system through the registration phase. Thus, a new sensor node is registered into the gateway node and the user, and the security related information table is updated with its identity, masked identity, and used cipher suite.

As a result of security analysis, the proposed scheme is suitable for insecure IoT environments in which an attacker can eavesdrop communications between involved objects.

5   Performance Analysis of the Proposed Scheme

In this section, we provide a performance analysis of the proposed authentication scheme. We focus on the energy evaluation of the sensor node as a constrained object. We use a TelosB sensor node equipped with a CC2420 radio. This latter typically runs on two AA batteries, which combine about 18500 J. To estimate the energy consumption of the proposed scheme, we compute the energy required for the execution of the cryptographic primitives along with the energy required for communication (transmission and reception of data, with 12 bytes of protocol headers).

Authors in [3], have presented an energy evaluation of wireless sensor nodes regarding the communication cost. In addition, the cost of the different used symmetric cryptography functions has been evaluated in [10]. Table 3 summarizes the deduced values, which are used as an energy model.

Table 3. Estimated energy costs on the sensor node [3, 10]

Operation	Cost
Transmission of 1 byte	5.76 μJ
Reception of 1 byte	6.48 μJ
AES-128 encryption of 16 bytes	42.88 μJ

Based on the estimated values, we evaluate the energy consumption of the proposed authentication scheme in the authentication phase and the key establishment phase. Furthermore, we study the different cases of an authentication failure, and we evaluate the energy consumption in the authentication failure' cases: F1, F2, F3 and F4 as shown in Table 4.

As described in the proposed scheme, a sensor node has to send its masked identity (20 bytes), the generated nonce value (8 bytes), and the computed value (8 bytes). Thus, the length of the transmitted message is 48 bytes (20 bytes + 8 bytes + 8 bytes + 12 bytes of protocol headers) which requires 276.48 μJ to be transmitted. As a response from the user, the sensor receives a message of 44 bytes (8bytes + 8 bytes + 8 bytes + 8 bytes + 12 bytes of protocol headers) which requires 285.12 μJ to be received. Hence, the total energy cost of the authentication phase is equal to 561.6 μJ.

In the key establishment phase, an encryption of the concatenation of the two values K1 and K2 requires about 42.88 μJ (result of encryption on 16 bytes), and applying the function F if necessary (In our case, the result of the computation of the shared key K is on 16 bytes, we do not apply the function F). Therefore, the total energy cost of the key establishment phase is 42.88 μJ.

The total cost of the scheme is the cost of the authentication phase plus the cost of the establishment phase: 604.48 μJ. A very low energy cost proving that the proposed scheme is ultra-lightweight and suitable to be applied in a resource constrained IoT environment.

Table 4. Analysis of the authentication scheme

Case of authentication	Energy consumption	Number of sent messages	Number of received messages
F1	276.48 μJ	1	0
F2	276.48 μJ	1	0
F3	276.48 μJ	1	0
F4	561.6 μJ	1	1
Successful authentication	604.48 μJ	1	1

As a result from the evaluation of different scenarios of the authentication scheme (see Fig. 4), we deduce that the proposed scheme also saves energy in the different cases of an authentication failure. The energy consumption in the

Energy cost (μJ)

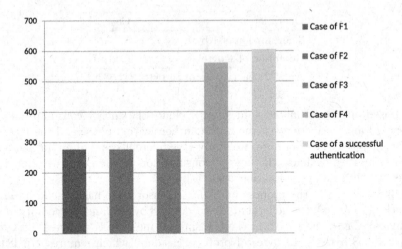

Fig. 4. Energy cost analysis of the proposed authentication scheme

authentication failures F1, F2, and F3 is just $276.48\,\mu$J, and $561.6\,\mu$J in the authentication failure F4. Consequently, the obtained results enhance the scheme performance.

The energy cost of the proposed scheme is very interesting compared to our previously proposed lightweight authentication scheme in [7] that consumes $883.98\,\mu$J (see Fig. 5).

Energy cost (μJ)

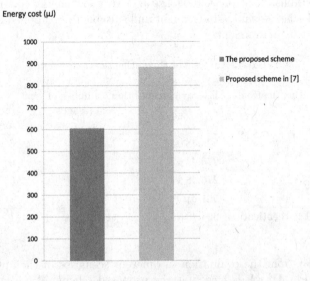

Fig. 5. Energy cost comparison of the proposed authentication scheme

6   Conclusion

In this paper, we have proposed a new ultra-lightweight authentication scheme for WSN applications in the context of IoT. This scheme uses only nonces, exclusive-or, concatenation operations in the authentication phase. Besides, it uses the concept of masked identity to protect the sensor identity, and only one symmetric encryption in the key establishment phase. The proposed scheme has low costs of communication and computation with a high level of security, and saves energy in the different cases of an authentication failure. Thus, it is suitable to be deployed in a resource constrained environment.

In order to obtain more accurate analysis study especially on memory consumption and execution time, we aim to simulate the proposed authentication scheme using Cooja simulator of Contiki OS and to test it in a real deployment.

References

1. SEC4: Elliptic Curve Qu-Vanstone Implicit Certificate Scheme (ECQV), version 0.97, August 2013. www.secg.org
2. Atzori, L., Iera, A., Morabito, G.: The internet of things: a survey. Comput. Netw. **54**(15), 2787–2805 (2010)
3. De Meulenaer, G., Gosset, F., Standaert, O.X., Pereira, O.: On the energy cost of communication and cryptography in wireless sensor networks. In: IEEE International Conference on Wireless and Mobile Computing Networking and Communications. WIMOB 2008, pp. 580–585. IEEE (2008)
4. El Maliki, T., Seigneur, J.M.: A survey of user-centric identity management technologies. In: The International Conference on Emerging Security Information, Systems, and Technologies. SecureWare 2007, pp. 12–17. IEEE (2007)
5. Farash, M.S., Turkanović, M., Kumari, S., Hölbl, M.: An efficient user authentication and key agreement scheme for heterogeneous wireless sensor network tailored for the internet of things environment. Ad Hoc Netw. **36**, 152–176 (2016)
6. Gope, P., Hwang, T.: A realistic lightweight anonymous authentication protocol for securing real-time application data access in wireless sensor networks. IEEE Trans. Indust. Electron. **63**, 7124–7132 (2016)
7. Khemissa, H., Tandjaoui, D.: A novel lightweight authentication scheme for heterogeneous wireless sensor networks in the context of internet of things. In: Wireless Telecommunications Symposium (WTS), pp. 1–6. IEEE (2016)
8. Kothmayr, T., Schmitt, C., Hu, W., Brünig, M., Carle, G.: DTLS based security and two-way authentication for the internet of things. Ad Hoc Netw. **11**(8), 2710–2723 (2013)
9. Krawczyk, H., Canetti, R., Bellare, M.: HMAC: keyed-hashing for message authentication (1997)
10. Lee, J., Kapitanova, K., Son, S.H.: The price of security in wireless sensor networks. Comput. Netw. **54**(17), 2967–2978 (2010)
11. Nguyen, K.T., Laurent, M., Oualha, N.: Survey on secure communication protocols for the internet of things. Ad Hoc Netw. **32**, 17–31 (2015)
12. Porambage, P., Schmitt, C., Kumar, P., Gurtov, A., Ylianttila, M.: Pauthkey: a pervasive authentication protocol and key establishment scheme for wireless sensor networks in distributed IoT applications. Int. J. Distrib. Sensor Netw. **10**, 357–430 (2014)

13. Porambage, P., Schmitt, C., Kumar, P., Gurtov, A., Ylianttila, M.: Two-phase authentication protocol for wireless sensor networks in distributed IoT applications. In: 2014 IEEE Wireless Communications and Networking Conference (WCNC), pp. 2728–2733. IEEE (2014)

14. Rescorla, E., Modadugu, N.: Datagram transport layer security version 1.2 (2012)

15. Safkhani, M., Bagheri, N.: Passive secret disclosure attack on an ultralightweight authentication protocol for internet of things. Technical report, Cryptology ePrint Archive, Report 2016/838 (2016). http://eprint.iacr.org/2016/838

16. Sicari, S., Rizzardi, A., Grieco, L., Coen-Porisini, A.: Security, privacy and trust in internet of things: the road ahead. Comput. Netw. **76**, 146–164 (2015)

17. Szczechowiak, P., Oliveira, L.B., Scott, M., Collier, M., Dahab, R.: NanoECC: testing the limits of elliptic curve cryptography in sensor networks. In: Verdone, R. (ed.) EWSN 2008. LNCS, vol. 4913, pp. 305–320. Springer, Heidelberg (2008). doi:10.1007/978-3-540-77690-1_19

18. Tewari, A., Gupta, B.: Cryptanalysis of a novel ultra-lightweight mutual authentication protocol for IoT devices using RFID tags. J. Supercomput. **73**, 1–18 (2016)

19. Turkanović, M., Brumen, B., Hölbl, M.: A novel user authentication and key agreement scheme for heterogeneous ad hoc wireless sensor networks, based on the internet of things notion. Ad Hoc Netw. **20**, 96–112 (2014)

20. Wood, A.D., Stankovic, J., et al.: Denial of service in sensor networks. Computer **35**(10), 54–62 (2002)

21. Xue, K., Ma, C., Hong, P., Ding, R.: A temporal-credential-based mutual authentication and key agreement scheme for wireless sensor networks. J. Netw. Comput. Appl. **36**(1), 316–323 (2013)

Authentication Based Elliptic Curves Digital Signature for ZigBee Networks

Ouassila Hoceini[1(✉)], Hossam Afifi[2], and Rachida Aoudjit[1]

[1] Computer Science Department,
Mouloud Mammeri University, Tizi Ouzou, Algeria
ouassila.hoceini@gmail.com, rachida_aoudjit@yahoo.fr
[2] RST Department, Institut des Mines, Télécom Sud Paris, Évry, France
hossam.afifi@telecom-sudparis.eu

Abstract. Elliptic Curve Cryptography (ECC) is emerging as an attractive public-key cryptosystem, in particular for internet of things. Compared to the well known cryptosystems such as RSA, ECC offers equivalent security with smaller key sizes. In this paper, we propose an authentication mechanism based on ECDSA (Elliptic curve digital signature algorithm) signature for ZigBee networks. Our system guarantees an end to end authentication between communicating entities. Security analysis and performance evaluations show that our new mechanism is resource efficient and it can resist several kinds of attacks.

Keywords: Authentication · Security · ECC · ECDSA · Cryptography · ZigBee · Internet of things

1 Introduction

The rapid deployment of connected devices and the increase in wireless communication are becoming a major concern, especially regarding security issues. In the near future, billions of IoT devices (Internet of Things) will be connected in a wireless way.

The lack of secured links exposes data to attacks, alteration and theft. Moreover, fraudsters show an increasing interest in this area. End-to-end authentication mechanisms are essential to meet security requirements in an IoT network. This can be achieved by signing by the sender and verifying the signature by the receiver, using signature methods such as MAC (Message Authentication Code). The principle of MAC signature is if a message is modified on its way to the recipient, the signature verification fails.

Traditionally, Message Authentication Codes (MAC) relied on symmetric algorithms such as secure hash algorithms that require secret keys. Symmetric encryption is when taking plaintext and converting it to ciphertext using the same key to encrypt and decrypt. And it is comparatively fast compared to other types of encryption. However, asymmetric algorithms use two interdependent keys, one to encrypt the data, and the other to decrypt it. The robustness of both relies on the level of protecting keys. The management and generation of the secret keys, then, can be challenging.

© Springer International Publishing AG 2017
S. Bouzefrane et al. (Eds.): MSPN 2017, LNCS 10566, pp. 63–73, 2017.
DOI: 10.1007/978-3-319-67807-8_5

And in critical applications we need a high level of security, and sometimes we opt to increase the length of keys; longer keys give more security but require more memory storage, more computation and more energy consumption.

To ensure a high level of security and conserve resources, memory and energy, a new alternative to this issue is the use of elliptic curves cryptography (ECC) that meets energy and memory resources requirements. The Digital Signature Standard, issued by the National Institute of Standards and Technology (NIST), specifies suitable elliptic curves, the computation of key pairs and digital signatures [1].

ZigBee is the one of the most standard used in Internet of things and it faces many security issues while many attacks threat the authentication of links in a ZigBee network. Moreover, this standard focus only on the security provided by physical and MAC IEEE 802.15.4 layers, and it does not define any mechanism to ensure an end to end authentication. Nowadays, data transported by ZigBee networks, is easily recovered, altered or deleted by fraudsters. Some works address this issue, but not in an efficient way. Moreover, methods that will be employed for such problems must use advanced cryptographic techniques, to cope with the several attacks that attempt to expose secret keys, like eavesdropping [2, 3] and Man-In-The-Middle [4, 5].

For this purpose, we propose a new authentication scheme that is based on ECDSA algorithm.

The rest of this paper is organized as follows. Section 2 provides an overview of ZigBee standard. In Sect. 3 we highlight ECDSA algorithm. Section 4 presents some related works to ZigBee security. In Sect. 5 we present our contribution; Authentication based elliptic curves digital signature for ZigBee Networks.

Then, in Sect. 6 we discuss the security analysis and in Sect. 7, we detail the performance analysis of the proposed work. And finally, in Sect. 8, we conclude the paper.

2   ZigBee Standards

ZigBee is defined by ZigBee Alliance and outlines a suite of high level, low-rate and low-power network protocols. It is classified among the most used standards in internet of things with a range of 100 m [6]. Some of prominent ZigBee applications incorporate building or home automation, monitoring systems, industrial automation, heating, cooling control and health.

ZigBee is built upon the physical and medium-access control layers defined in the IEEE 802.15.4 standard. Basically, ZigBee stack is composed of the application (APL) layer that provides data services to the applications, and the network layer that handles the routing [7]. According to the definition of the ZigBee protocol, there are three types of logical devices: the coordinator, routers and terminal equipment. According to the different performance, they can be divided into two types: FFD (Full Function Device) as the main equipment, which undertakes the network coordinator function. If the network enabled security mechanisms, network coordinator can become Trust Center (TC). Another device RFD (Reduced Function Device), it just has simple functions, it cannot be used as the network coordinator, and can just communicate with the network coordinator.

ZigBee security is based on AES-128 (Advanced Encryption Standard) block encryption method. The process of encryption is carried out by rounds.

2.1 ZigBee Key Management

ZigBee Trust Center (ZTC) maintains a list of cryptographic keys; master keys, network key, and link keys. Master keys are encrypted during the transfer from the devices to ZTC. Network key is transferred in cipher text. Link keys that are generated by ZTC and transferred Over the Air, are unencrypted. Moreover, IEEE 802.15.4 standard provides basic security services and interoperability between devices. Among them: maintaining an access control list (Control List Access, ACL) and the use of symmetric encryption algorithm to protect the transmission of data [8].

At present, most ZigBee applications have Network and Link keys, if the use of Network Key, although it can save the node's storage resources, but when a node is captured, the entire network will be threatened. When Link Key is used, only a small part of the node is affected when a node is captured in the network, but the system overhead is increased.

The strength of security systems depends on the authenticated links in a network. One of the ZigBee limits is the weak links: no an end to end authentication method defined [9]. As a result, ZigBee standard became not suitable for massive IoT networks that need high security protocols for small devices.

Yet, there has been a lack of studies about end to end authentication in ZigBee network, especially in massive networks which can be subject of a lot of interactions and uncountable kinds of attacks. However, there needed further studies to include new algorithms verifying devices authentication. The purpose of this paper is to block unauthorized nodes to interact with the legitimate ones, authenticate devices entering in communication and ensure messages integrity. So, we allow a more secure, reliable, and scalable network as well as performances will be more robust and improved.

3 ECDSA Algorithm

Neal Koblitz and Victor Miller proposed elliptic curve cryptography (ECC). This is an efficient technique, which provides security for wireless communication networks [10–12]. Studies have proven the effectiveness of ECC system compared to RSA; ECC offers smaller key sizes, faster computation, as well as memory, energy and bandwidth savings and is thus better suited for small devices with resource constraints [13]. Elliptic curve cryptography gives a greater strength-per-key-bit. It uses arithmetic with much shorter numbers 256 bits instead of 2048 bits of RSA and provides the same level of security.

ECDSA (Elliptic curve digital signature algorithm) is one of the most advanced and promising techniques in the field of signature based on elliptic curve discrete logarithmic problem and is the most secure digital signatures scheme [14]. It offers many advantages over other systems of signing. ECDSA Algorithm was first proposed in

1992 by Scott Vanstone in response to NIST's proposal of DSS (Digital Signature Standard) [16, 20].

ECDSA is analogue to the digital signature algorithm (DSA) and has been standardized by many standards organizations around the world including NIST, IEEE, ANSI and ISO [17].

4   Related Works

In the literature, there is not enough works addressing authentication in ZigBee network. We present in this section some of them.

In [18], authors have proposed a scheme that combines AES algorithm with ECC for ZigBee networks. They implement a multiple key protocol that ensures the protection of cryptographic keys. The number of generated keys is different with a tradeoff to security levels. Each message is divided into n 128-bit-blocks, and each block (sub message) is encrypted with 128-bit key Ki. The maximum number of secret keys is equal to the number of blocks. This scheme protects keys from disclosure but there are too many keys and exchanged packets generating an important overhead in the network. Moreover, it does not ensure an end to end authentication. Moreover devices authenticity and messages integrity are not verified.

Shamir [19] proposed an Identity-Based Encryption (IBE) by using unique ID (Identity) to generate a public key for ZigBee networks. A fully functional IBE was developed by applying pairing in the algorithm.

This scheme removes the need for certificate issuance by a third party CA (Certificate Authority) to obtain recipient's public key by only using the recipient's unique ID to generate them and encrypt messages for given entities. Only the legitimate entities can decode the message.

In [15], Kulkarni et al. propose a secure routing protocol that makes use of aggregated MAC for authentication code for ZigBee networks. It provides end-to-end, hop-to-hop and whole route authentications in a path. Although, it permits an end to end authentication but it uses only two keys, which does not ensure the secrecy of communication. In addition, these keys are not well protected against disclosure. There is any key management strategy defined in the work.

Each node has a shared secret key with each other in a network, and to calculate secret keys, no authentication mechanism between devices is allowed. Hence, launching several kinds of attacks is easily feasible like Man-In-The-Middle. Moreover, no key freshness technique is employed to protect against device tampering attacks. In fact, the only assumption to authenticate a node is that it owns the keys. However, there are several ways to expose these keys. If an adversary takes physical control of nodes, he can manipulate network communications as he wants. Additionally, the fact that the secret key is shared with each node in the network, consumes large memory space; a great number of keys are stored unnecessarily.

5 Authentication Based Elliptic Curves Digital Signature for ZigBee Networks

To secure information in ZigBee networks from disclosure and authenticate both the sender and the receiver in a whole path, we propose a new scheme, which define two MACs (message authentication codes) and enables keys protection. Our scheme adapts the ECDSA algorithm to meet authentication requirements for an IoT network.

We assume a ZigBee network using AODV (Ad Hoc On Demand Distance Vector Routing) as routing protocol. Moreover, we assume the presence of several Trust Centers (TCs) for a large scale network. Knowing that TCs are not constraint in memory and computation, each TC manages a few hundreds of ZigBee devices.

Our architecture defines three kinds of keys:

- Master key: K_M is used to authenticate nodes that want to join a network. The access control is carried out by the Trust Center.
- Group key: K_G is used to encrypt packets between devices and between devices and TC.

Our scheme is divided into different steps. We detail them in the following paragraphs.

5.1 Access Control

We assume that the network is composed of ordinary nodes and trust centers (TCs). All devices are pre-loaded with the master key in off-line, to get access to the network. To join the network, nodes must request TC, and then TC proves their authenticity by verifying MAC addresses. At this time, TC responds by sending the group key encrypted with the master key. When a device recovers the group key, it can enter in communication with the other legitimate nodes in the network.

5.2 Group Key Calculation

Each TC chooses an elliptic curve [21] and calculates the secret key K_G of its group of nodes based on the chosen curve [22, 23].

Each period of time, a trust center computes a new group key (K_G), by choosing other parameters at the same curve. It then sends the new group key K_G to the group after encrypting it with the previous group key. When devices recover the new group key, they delete the older one. The purpose of freshness technique is to secure network from node tampering attacks that attempt to expose secret keys by getting physical access to devices. Furthermore, frequent key revocation minimizes damages that can be observed if secret keys are exposed by attackers.

5.3 End to End Authentication

In this phase we employ a method that allows an end to end authentication by calculating the signature based on ECDSA algorithm and MAC_{GK} with the group key.

NodeA (the sender) creates the ECDSA and the MAC_{GK} signatures, and attaches them to the data. MAC_{GK} is calculated using SHA-256 [24] with the group key K_G.

At the reception *nodeB* (the receiver) verifies the two signatures. If they match, then the massage is accepted and the source is authenticated. Otherwise, the message is omitted. Figure 1 demonstrates the process of authentication.

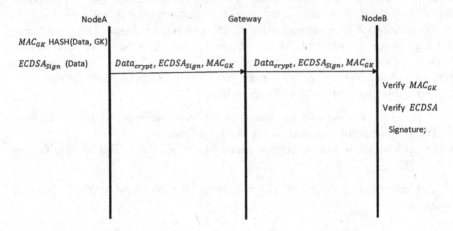

Fig. 1. End to end authentication process

In the following paragraphs, we explain the different steps of ECDSA algorithm.

- **ECDSA key pairs**

An entity nodeA's key pairs associated with a particular set of EC (Elliptic curve) domain parameters D. This association can be assured cryptographically (e.g., with certificates) or by context (e.g., all entities use the same domain parameters). The entity nodeA must have the insurance that the domain parameters are valid prior to key generation.

Given $P \in E(Fp)$ and $Q = aP$, find a $(1 <= a <= n)$.

An elliptic curve E defined over Fp with large group E(Fp) of order n and a point P of larger order are chosen by nodeA and made public to all users.

- NodeA follows these steps:

1. First, it chooses a random integer $d \in [2; n -2]$.
2. Then, it calculates $Q = d.P$.
3. In the end, it publishes its public parameters (E; P; n; Q) and it keeps safe its private key d.

- **ECDSA Signature Generation**

- NodeA signs a message m following these steps:

1. It selects a random integer $k \in [2; n - 2]$.
2. It calculates $k.P = (x1; y1)$ and $r = x1 \bmod n$. If $r = 0$ then it return to select a new k.
3. It computes $k -1 \bmod n$.

4. It computes s = k −1. (H(m) + d.r) mod n. H is the secure hash algorithm (SHA).

   If s = 0, nodeA needs to start from the beginning.

5. The pair of integers (r; s) is the signature for the message m.

– **ECDSA Signature Verification**

– NodeB verifies NodeA's signature (r; s) on the message m by performing the following steps:

1. It calculates c = s −1 mod n and H(m).
2. It computes u1 = H(m).c mod n and u2 = r.c mod n.
3. It computes u1.P + u2.Q = (x0; y0) and v = x0 mod n.
4. NodeB approves the signature if v = r.

   When:
   $Data_{crypt}$: is the DATA encrypted.
   $ECDSA_{Sign}$: ECDSA signature.
   MAC_{GK}: The Message authentication code with the group key.

5.4 Adding New Nodes to the Network

Our scheme allows increasing scalability, according to the network requirements in scale. Hence, additional nodes can join the network. To avoid that an adversary uses the older master key to launch an attack, we assume that a new master key will be pre-loaded in the new nodes and will be sent to the TC to perform network access control. And access control policy stays the same of the Sect. 5.1.

6 Security Analysis

In this section, we analyze and demonstrate the robustness of our proposed work and discuss its resistance to some attacks.

6.1 Access Control

One way to enable security and privacy is to implement access control, which covers both authentication and authorization. Because the ease access to a network is the breach to all attacks, it is mandatory to maintain the control and access restriction methods. In our solution, the trust centers authenticate nodes that request to join the network. During initialization, a TC gives access to a node that owns the Master key that is pre-loaded before connection to the network, and after this the authentication is done using the group-key based ECC system. Moreover, the computation of group keys with ECC has a lot of advantages in terms of security and robustness. In fact, it is difficult to break an ECC key in a short time. In addition, employing freshness techniques to ECC keys protects widely the network access in our scheme.

6.2   Protection Against Man-in-the-Middle Attack

One of the most successful methods for gaining control of sensitive user information is through Man-in-the-Middle (MiTM) attacks. In a man-in-the-middle attack, a third party pretends to be the *nodeA* with which a *nodeB* is trying to connect.

Our proposed scheme guarantees the resistance to such kinds of attack by defining two signatures, to protect from illegitimate nodes. Then both inside and outside attackers of the network can neither alter exchanged messages, nor pretend to be legitimate devices.

6.3   Resistance to Eavesdropping

The simple and the most frequent attack in wireless networks is eavesdropping, it is simple to achieve and difficult to detect, because this kind of attack can be launched without disrupting the functionalities of the network and without altering data. For these reasons, this presents a dangerous attack because the adversary can hear information using simple devices and use it in the future to launch more dangerous attacks. However, there are limited damages if the cryptographic keys are often changed. Our proposed work allows resistance to such kind of attacks, and protects keying information by employing on one side robust elliptic curves keys and in another side key freshness technique. The most cryptographic attacks became more difficult if only a limited amount of cipher text was generated under one key. If an adversary wants to recover long pieces of cipher text, he has to recover several keys, which makes attacks harder.

7   Performances Analysis

Tests and evaluations are developed under OMNET++ [25], using the micro-ecc Library to implement the different elliptic curve cryptography algorithms [26]. We compare our protocol performance to another protocol from the state of the art, with respect to the important parameters:

• Energy, Authentication delay and memory.

7.1   Energy Consumption

Energy is crucial in these small devices, with resources constraints. Our scheme consumes a minimum energy amount, because the use of elliptic curves is less greedy and better optimized. We compare our work to the one presented in [15] by Kulkarni and al. Having a shared key with each node in the network is unfeasible. That is the case of the authentication scheme proposed in [15]. Then a large memory space is used to store a great number of keys. Moreover, the great number of packets circulating in the network to establish shared keys with each node generates overhead and consumes a lot of energy, which leads to a rapid mortality of nodes.

As illustrated in Fig. 2, we compared the energy consumed in our scheme with the work proposed in [15].

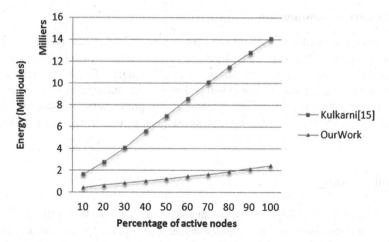

Fig. 2. Energy consumption according to the percentage of active nodes

7.2   Delay of Authentication Between Two Devices

Authentication delay must be as short as possible; otherwise attackers can exploit long delays to get control of communications. In the Fig. 3 we compare our scheme to the one proposed in [15] and we have shown an important difference between the two delays. This can be explained, by the inefficient method employed in [15] that is the verification of MACs (Message Authentication Codes) in each hop of the path. This generates further computations and verifications uselessly. And increase the time of authentication. Then, it creates slow services, slow responses and it opens new security breaches. However, in our work, verification of MACs is just carried out at the receiver device and it is enough. This ensure authentication in short time without overloading the network with computations, so giving a faster response time.

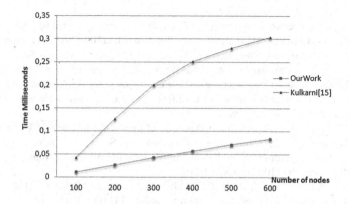

Fig. 3. Authentication delay according to the number of active nodes

7.3   Resources Consumption

As known ECC is hardware friendly. It is fast and requires a relatively few resources; with lower computing power and battery resources usage. Additionally, ECC uses small keys as strong as long key for RSA, i.e., less data that are transmitted, and requires less processing power, bandwidth and memory, resulting significantly in faster response times. Besides, our system generates new group keys, without exhausting nodes of the network, TCs that are not constraints in resources, are in charge of generation and updating of new keys.

8   Conclusion

ZigBee focus on the basic security mechanisms provided by IEEE 802.15.4. As a result, this standard became more vulnerable and more exposed to several attacks that attempt to recover secret information.

In this paper we proposed a new scheme that employs an end to end authentication method in large scale Zigbee networks, using advanced cryptographic techniques such as elliptic curves cryptography. Analysis shows that our scheme performs better security in ZigBee network in terms of protecting information and ensuring mutual authentication between the sender and the receiver. In addition, tests under Omnet++ demonstrate that energy consumption as well as memory are well conserved. For our future work, we aim to test our contribution under realistic scenarios.

References

1. Digital Signature Standard (DSS), National Institute of Standards and Technology (NIST) (2013)
2. Wang, K., et al.: Strategic anti-eavesdropping game for physical layer security in wireless cooperative networks. IEEE Trans. Veh. Technol. **PP**(99), doi:10.1109/TVT.2017.2703305. IEEE Vehicular Technology Society
3. Xu, J., et al.: Proactive eavesdropping via cognitive jamming in fading channels. IEEE Trans. Wireless Commun. **16**(5), 2790–2806 (2017). doi:10.1109/TWC.2017.2666138, Print ISSN 1536-1276, IEEE Communications Society IEEE Signal Processing Society
4. Saqib, N., et al.: Key exchange protocol for WSN resilient against man in the middle attack. In: IEEE International Conference on Advances in Computer Applications (ICACA), 24 October 2016, Coimbatore, India. IEEE (2016). INSPEC Accession Number: 16776896, doi:10.1109/ICACA.2016.7887963
5. Eigner, O., Kreimel, P., Tavolato, P.: Detection of man-in-the-middle attacks on industrial control networks. In: 2016 International Conference on Software Security and Assurance (ICSSA), 24–25 August 2016, St. Polten, Austria, NSPEC Accession Number: 16693204. IEEE (2016). doi: 10.1109/ICSSA.2016.19
6. Baalbaki, B.A.I., Pacheco, J., Tunc, C., Al-Nashif, Y.: Anomaly Behavior Analysis System for ZigBee in Smart Buildings, 978-1-5090-0478-2/15/$31.00 ©2015 IEEE
7. http://www.zigbee.org
8. Xu, X., Gao, Y., Zhang, W., Li, J.: Research on the Wireless Network Transmission Security Based on IEEE 802.15.4. Research (2009)

9. Hyncica, O., Kacz, P., Fiedler, P., Bradac, Z., Kucera, P., Vrba, R.: On security of PAN wireless systems. In: Vassiliadis, S., Wong, S., Hämäläinen, T.D. (eds.) SAMOS 2006. LNCS, vol. 4017, pp. 178–185. Springer, Heidelberg (2006). doi:10.1007/11796435_19
10. Koblitz, A.H., Koblitz, N., Menezes, A.: Elliptic curve cryptography: the serpentine course of a paradigm shift. J. Numb. Theory **131**, 781–814 (2011)
11. Koblitz, N.: Elliptic curve cryptosystems. Math. Comput. **48**, 203 (1987). 209MATH MathSciNetCrossRef
12. Miller, V.S.: Use of elliptic curves in cryptography. In: Williams, H.C. (ed.) CRYPTO 1985. LNCS, vol. 218, pp. 417–426. Springer, Heidelberg (1986). doi:10.1007/3-540-39799-X_31
13. Gura, N., Patel, A., Wander, A., Eberle, H., Shantz, S.C.: Comparing elliptic curve cryptography and RSA on 8-bit CPUs. In: Joye, M., Quisquater, J.-J. (eds.) CHES 2004. LNCS, vol. 3156, pp. 119–132. Springer, Heidelberg (2004). doi:10.1007/978-3-540-28632-5_9
14. Akhter, F.: Faster scalar multiplication algorithm to implement a secured elliptic curve cryptography system. (IJACSA) Int. J. Adv. Comput. Sci. Appl. **7**(1) (2016). doi:10.14569/IJACSA.2016.070187, License: CC BY-NC-ND 4.0
15. Kulkarni, S., Ghosh, U., Pasupuleti, H.: Considering security for ZigBee protocol using message authentication code. In: IEEE INDICON 2015, pp. 1–6 (2015). doi:10.1109/INDICON.2015.7443625
16. Elgamal, T.: A public key Cryptosystem and a signature scheme based on discrete logarithms. IEEE Trans. Inform. Theory **31**(4) (1985), 469–472 (1985)
17. Federal Information Processing Standards Publication, "Digital Signature Standard (DSS)," Gaithersburg, MD, Technical report, July 2013
18. Al-alak, S., Ahmed, Z., Abdullah, A., Subramiam, S.: AES and ECC mixed for ZigBee wireless sensor security. World Acad. Sci. Eng. Technol. Int. J. Electr. Comput. Energ. Electron. Commun. Eng. **5**(9) (2011)
19. Shamir, A.: Identity-based cryptosystems and signature schemes. In: Blakley, G.R., Chaum, D. (eds.) CRYPTO 1984. LNCS, vol. 196, pp. 47–53. Springer, Heidelberg (1985). doi:10.1007/3-540-39568-7_5
20. Hankerson, D., Menezes, A., Vanstone, S.: Guide to Elliptic Curve Cryptography. Springer, New York (2004)
21. Koblitz, N.: Elliptic curve cryptosystems. Math. Comput. **48**(177), 203–209 (1987)
22. https://tools.ietf.org/search/rfc4492#section-6
23. http://csrc.nist.gov/groups/ST/toolkit/documents/dss/NISTReCur.pdf
24. https://tools.ietf.org/html/rfc6234
25. https://omnetpp.org
26. https://github.com/kmackay/micro-ecc

Formal Modeling and Performance Evaluation of Network's Server Under SYN/TCP Attack

Naouel Ouroua$^{(\boxtimes)}$ ⑩, Wassila Bouzegza, and Malika Ioualalen

Department of Computer Science, University of Sciences and Technology,
USTHB, Algiers 16111, Algeria
ourna@yahoo.fr, bwassila_mail@yahoo.fr,
mioualalen@usthb.dz

Abstract. This paper describes the modeling of a network's server under SYN/TCP attack, using Deterministic and Stochastic Petri Nets, which is a formalism allowing qualitative and quantitative analysis for the modeled system. This high level formalism allows also to cope with the complexity of such systems and to express the stationary performance indices as a function of Petri Net elements. The objective is thus to evaluate the unavailability of server during this attack, by computing probability of connection loss, and the impact of system parameters on this metric. Some other performance metrics, such as buffer occupancy of half-open connections for attack traffic and legitimate traffic and the mean number of legitimate SYN packet received, are also evaluated. By these results we show how the attack load severely degrade the performance of the network under attack, and the change of some system crucial parameters such as the buffer size and the holding time for half-open connections in order to guarantee the service availability, is effective only if the attack load is limited.

Keywords: DoS/DDoS attacks · SYN/TCP attack · Formal modeling · performance evaluation · Stochastic and deterministic petri nets

1 Introduction

Millions of people frequently use internet services, which have become a necessity of daily life. Unfortunately, Denial of Service (DoS) flood attacks and Distributed Denial-of-Service (DDoS) flood attacks can easily deny regular internet services to be accessed by legitimate users. DoS flood attacks consist in sending the victim (the network's server) a higher volume of traffic than it can handle. This can be achieved either by saturating the server's network connection or by using weaknesses in the communication protocols that typically allow to generate high server resource usage for a limited attacker effort. Distributed denial-of-service (DDoS) flood attacks are simply DoS flood attacks performed by multiple agents, most frequently simultaneously.

SYN/TCP attack called also "SYN Flooding" is one of DoS/DDoS flood attack, perpetrated against network's servers, which use TCP protocol, to block access to their various services such as Ftp, Http, and Mail [1].

The SYN flooding attacks exploit the limitation of TCP's three-ways handshake mechanism, in maintaining half-open connections. This mechanism is the way used to

© Springer International Publishing AG 2017
S. Bouzefrane et al. (Eds.): MSPN 2017, LNCS 10566, pp. 74–87, 2017.
DOI: 10.1007/978-3-319-67807-8_6

initiate any "reliable" internet connection, which uses the protocol TCP [2]. When a server receives a SYN request, it returns a SYN-ACK packet to the client. The connection remains in half-open state for a period up to the TCP connection timeout, until the client acknowledged SYN-ACK packet. The server has built in its system memory a backlog queue to maintain all half-open connections. Once the limit of the backlog queue is reached, all connection requests will be dropped. If a SYN request is spoofed, the victim server will never receive the final ACK packet to complete the three-way handshake. Flooding spoofed SYN requests can easily exhaust the victim server's backlog queue, causing the drop of the incoming SYN requests and so the unavailability of the server. Furthermore, many other system resources, such as CPU and network bandwidth used to retransmit the SYN/ACK packets, are occupied.

Many defense mechanisms have been proposed in the literature to defend against DoS flood attacks [3, 4]. Most of those methods are experimental studies; few works have employed rigorous mathematical models to analytically study SYN/TCP attack. They used queueing model or Markov chains, to evaluate the system performances of a computer network under DoS attacks [5–7].

In this paper, we proposed PetriDos, a formal model of network's server under SYN/TCP attack using Deterministic and Stochastic Petri Nets (DSPNs). The objective is to evaluate the probability of connection loss P_{loss}, the impact of system parameters on this metric and on some other performance parameters. The DSPNs are an important graphical and mathematical high level formalism, adapted to describe and analyze the performances of the systems characterized by competition and synchronization, which allow us to incorporate features that may be difficult to model directly by Markov chains. They are also appropriated for describing and analyzing stochastic systems. They allow to check the qualitative properties and to obtain performance parameters either with analytic means or by numerical algorithms.

The paper is organized as follows: Sect. 2 provides an overview of related work. Section 3 introduces DSPN, the formalism used for modeling. In Sect. 4, we describe PetriDos, the proposed model of the system under SYN/TCP attack. In Sect. 5, we present the qualitative analysis of this model, several numerical examples for evaluation of loss connection probability, the impact of system parameters on this metric with some comments and the evaluation of some other performance parameters. Finally, Sect. 6 concludes the paper.

2 Related Works

SYN/TCP Attack has interested the researchers [3, 4]. Most of the works are experimental and directed towards the detection of this type of attacks, by proposing mechanisms of detection to be used in firewalls or inside the victim server [8–10], in routers [11–16] or in intrusions detection systems (IDS) [17–19]. Few works have employed rigorous mathematical models to study SYN/TCP attack, most of them used queueing model or embedded Markov chain, and were directed towards the determination of parameters used for attack detection [5], or performance evaluation of the computing system under attack [6, 7].

In [5] authors use a simple model M/M/1/K with round robin discipline to analyze the impact of DoS flood and complexity attacks on some parameters as response time or queue-growth-rate. In [6], the authors use a two dimensional embedded Markov chain model to study the network under DoS attacks, in which the input queue and service times are stochastic processes. With this model, they developed a memory-efficient algorithm for finding the stationary probability distribution which can be used to find performance metrics such as the connection loss probability and buffer occupancy percentages of half-open connections for regular traffic and attack traffic. In [7] the author considers the model studied in [6], the difference is that the distribution of service times is arbitrarily distributed and he takes into consideration the possibility of connection failures. With his model he obtains explicit formulas for the steady-state probabilities of the underlying stochastic process. The goal is to quantify the damage that a successful attacker can have on the performance of the network such as the loss probability and buffer occupancy of half-open connections.

The queueing theory is used for a quantitative evaluation of the systems; however it is not adapted to qualitative study of the modeled system, or to express certain mechanisms of the parallel systems such as synchronization and concurrency. In Markov chain the process of modeling is a very tiresome task which implies the enumeration of all the possible states and all the possibilities of transitions between states. For that, we choose to use Deterministic and Stochastic Petri Net, a tool of modeling which offers power of expression, allows qualitative and quantitative analysis for the modeled system, and permits automated edition and analysis thanks to availability of software package, which facilitates the process of modeling and performance evaluation.

3 Petri Nets

Petri nets [20] are graphical and mathematical tools which provide a uniform environment for modeling, formal analysis, and design of discrete event systems. One of the major advantages of using Petri net models is that the same model is used for the analysis of behavioral properties and performance evaluation. Petri nets can be used to model properties such as process synchronization, asynchronous events, concurrent operations, and conflicts or resource sharing.

These properties characterize discrete-event systems such as industrial automated systems, communication systems, and computer-based systems. Petri nets, allow the performance evaluation of the systems. Both deterministic and stochastic performance measures can be evaluated by using a class of Petri Net models incorporating in their definitions deterministic and/or probabilistic time functions. The performance evaluation can be conducted using either analytical techniques, based on solving the underlying (semi)-Markov processes, or discrete event simulation.

3.1 Description of Petri Net

A Petri net may be identified as a particular kind of bipartite directed graph populated by three types of objects, places, transitions, and directed arcs connecting places to transitions and transitions to places. Places are depicted by circles and transitions as bars or boxes. In its simplest form, a Petri net may be represented by a transition together with its input and output places. This elementary net may be used to represent various aspects of the modeled systems. For instance, input (output) places may represent preconditions (post conditions), the transition an event. Input places may represent the availability of resources, the transition their utilization, output places the release of the resources.

We can study dynamic behavior of the modeled system, by changing distribution of tokens on places, which may reflect the occurrence of events or execution of operations, for instance. Frequently, in the graphical representation, parallel arcs connecting a place (transition) to a transition (place) are represented by a single directed arc labeled with its weight. The following rules are used to govern the flow of tokens.

3.2 Enabling Rule

A transition t is said to be enabled, if each input place p of t contains at least the number of tokens equal to the weight of the directed arc connecting p to t.

- An enabled transition t may or may not be fired depending on the additional interpretation, and
- A firing of an enabled transition t removes from each input place p the number of tokens equal to the weight of the directed arc connecting p to t. It also deposits in each output place p, the number of tokens equal to the weight of the directed arc connecting t to p.

The modeling power of Petri nets can be increased by adding the zero testing ability, i.e., the ability to test whether a place has no token, used to model the unavailability of shared resource for example. This is achieved by introducing an inhibitor arc. The inhibitor arc connects an input place to a transition, and is pictorially represented by an arc terminated with a small circle.

Responding to the need for the temporal performance analysis of discrete-event systems, time has been introduced into Petri nets in a variety of ways [21].

3.3 Deterministic and Stochastic Petri Nets (DSPN).

DSPN [22] is an extension of a Petri Net, defined by taking of account the concept of time. It is characterized by, timed transitions having exponentially distributed firing delays to describe the operations requiring a random time to be carried, timed transitions with constant firing delay and immediate transitions (without firing delay), under the restriction that at most one of deterministic transition is enabled in each marking.

Formally, a Deterministic and Stochastic Petri net can be defined as follows:
DSPN = a tuple <P, T, Arc, Π, W, M0>,

P: set not empty of places.
T: set not empty of transitions partitioned into three disjoints sets T^I, T^E and T^D immediate, exponential and deterministic transitions respectively, with $P \cap T = \varnothing$.

Arc: finite set of arcs = {→,⊸}, two types of arcs, simple arc, and inhibitor arc

Π: T → IN is the priority function.

W: T → IR$^+$, the function which associates a period of firing to each timed transition.

M_0:   P → IN is the initial marking which describes the initial state of the system

4   Description of SYN/TCP Attack Model

We consider the same assumptions as in [6], the arrivals and service time are stochastic processes. In general, the arrival of SYN packets contains the regular (legitimate) request packets and the attack (illegitimate) packets. The victim has a connection buffer of the backlog queue, at most N half-open connections are allowed simultaneously and so N maximum number of connection requests can be served at the same time. The arrivals of both regular and attack packets are Poisson processes with rate λ1 and λ2 respectively. We suppose that each half-open connection in the buffer is maintained at latest a given period B (a timeout), which is the time interval since half-open connection began (the arrival of SYN packet) until it is abandoned (not arrival of ACK). We suppose that half-open connections for the legitimate packets are maintained for random duration, which is distributed exponentially with a parameter μ (the arrival of the ACK). The two arrival processes are independent of each other and of the holding times for half-open connections. All connection requests that arrive when the server is saturated are rejected.

We model the attack, with DSPN, to evaluate the performances of the system during the attack. We evaluate the probability of connection loss P_{loss}, which is the probability of server unavailability during the attack, and it can help us to conclude if there is an attack or not. So if P_{loss} is large, the network should be under SYN/TCP attack. We may use a threshold value h > 0, small enough to indicate the network security status, if P_{loss} < h; we can conclude that the network is not under attack. If there is an attack, the attackers consume network resources such that $P_{loss} \geq$ h, which leads to network performance degradation. Other performance metrics are also evaluated.

4.1   DSPN Model of SYN/TCP Attack

Figure 1 shows PetriDos, the DSPN model of above described system. The place represents the state of the system; the transition represents the event, causing the change of system's state. There are two types of transitions, those with an exponential distribution firing delay, represented by full white rectangles, those with constant firing delay, represented by full black rectangles.

Table 1 gives the meaning of each place, transition and the different firing rate of timed transitions. The service in our model is the half-open state of the packet which arrived and found a space in buffer. Attack packet is a request packet which does not complete the third step of the three-ways handshake and does not send an ACK, so it is

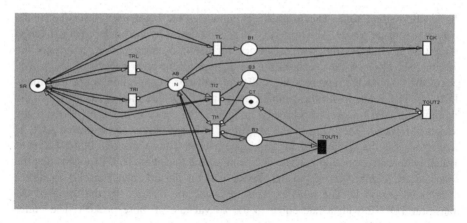

Fig. 1. PetriDos model.

kept in buffer until the expiration of the timeout B. The initial marking of the net is: $M0 = \{M(SR), M(AB), M(B1), M(B2), M(B3), M(CT)\}$; $M0 = \{1, N, 0, 0, 0, 1\}$. This represents that all the N spaces on buffer are initially free. No legitimate or attack parquets are on service.

If the place AB contains at least one free space in buffer, one of the exponential transitions TL, TI2 or TI1is fired. If there is conflict, the priority is to the transition with

Table 1. Meaning of places and transitions in PetriDos model.

Place	Meaning
SR	Source of legitimate and attack packets
AB	Available buffer space of the backlog queue
B1	Contains legitimate packets in service
B2	First attack packets in service
B3	Others attack packets in service
CT	Controls illegitimate packets timeout's
Transition	Meaning
TL	The legitimate packets arrival with a rate $\lambda 1$
TI1	The arrival of the first attack packet with a rate $\lambda 2$
TI2	The arrival of the other attack packets with a rate $\lambda 2$
TCK	The service end for legitimate packets with a rate μ
TOUT1	The service end for the first attack packet after a deterministic period B (not arrival of ACK)
TOUT2	The service end for other attack packets with a rate $\lambda 2$, triggered after the end of service of the first attack packet represented by the deterministic transition TOUT1
TRL	Reject legitimate packets when all servers are unavailable. with a rate $\lambda 1$
TRI	Reject attack packets when all servers are unavailable. with a rate $\lambda 2$

the smallest firing time. The firing of TL indicates the beginning of service of the arrived legitimate packet. The firing of TI1 is conditioned by the presence of a token in place CT; it indicates the start of service for the first attack packet, to trigger the timeout. The firing of TI2 synchronizes the timeout for the other packets of attack. The places B1, B2and B3 represent the buffer of half-open connections. The transitions TRL and TRI, related with the inhibitor arc to place AB, are fired at the arrival of the legitimate or attack packet respectively, finding no free space in buffer M(AB) = 0, the packet is rejected. The firing of the transition TCK means that the expected ACK is arrived, so it is the service end for legitimate packet. Thus a space in buffer becomes available to receive another packet. The firing of the transition TOUT1 means that the expected ACK didn't arrive, so the service end for the first attack packet is after a determined period B. The other packets of attack are released by the firing of the transition TOUT2 with a rate equal to the arrival rate of those packets. The buffer becomes free and ready to receive other packets.

The attack succeeds when the resources used by the victim to store the pending requests, are exhausted. This is expressed by the marking of AB, when it's equal to zero, then the packets are dropped and the server is unavailable.

5 Evaluation of Connection Loss Probability P_{loss}

5.1 Qualitative Analysis

To model and evaluate our system, we used the TimeNet package [23]. Firstly, the proposed model is specified using the graphical interface of the TimeNet. Then, to guarantee the stationary of the model, we verified the qualitative properties (boundedness and liveness). Finally we evaluated the performance metrics.

5.2 Numerical Examples for Evaluation of Loss Connection Probability

Our model is bounded and all transitions are live, so it admits a stationary state, we note $\pi = (\pi_1, \pi_2, ..., \pi)$ the distribution of the probabilities of marking to the stationary state. Then we can launch the stationary analysis to calculate the steady-state probability distribution vector π. Having the steady-state probability distribution, several performance measures can be derived.

We evaluate the connection loss probability P_{loss}, which is the probability of server unavailability during the attack, using the stationary probability distribution. The connection loss probability can be described as:

$$P_{loss} = \sum_{i:M_i(AB=0)} \pi_i \qquad (1)$$

M_i (AB) denotes the number of tokens in the place AB in the marking M_i. We consider now some numerical examples showing the impact of, SYN/TCP attack and some system parameters, on this metric.

We test the accuracy of our model (C2) with the model (C1) in [6], for the metric P_{loss}. In the work [6], the basic numerical data are as follows:

Let $\lambda 1 = 10$ packets/s be the parameter of the Poisson arrival process of regular request packets; $\lambda 2 = K * \lambda 1$ is the parameter of the Poisson arrival process of attack request packets. The attack parameter K is the ratio of arrival rates between the attack packets and the regular request packets. The exponential distribution is used with the parameter $\mu = 100$ packets/s, as the service time of regular request packets.

The values of the loss probabilities for both C1 and C2 are given in Tables 2 and 3 for different values of the attack parameter K, N and B. As in [6], we observe that the loss probability increases with the increase of the attack traffic load.

Table 2. Comparison of loss probabilities for two models, B = 5.

P_{loss}	N = 10		N = 20		N = 40	
K	C1	C2	C1	C2	C1	C2
0	0.01	0.001	–	0.0	–	0
0.2	0.5	0.132	–	0.0004	–	0
0.4	0.9	0.462	0.45	0.095	0.001	4.34e-6
0.7	0.9	0.672	0.9	0.408	0.2	0.024
1	0.9	0.762	0.9	0.568	0.82	0.202
1.25	0.9	0.807	0.9	0.649	0.9	0.347
1.6	0.9	0.853	0.9	0.732	0.9	0.500
1.9	0.9	0.876	0.9	0.775	0.9	0.579
2.3	0.9	0.893	0.9	0.805	0.9	0.636

Table 3. Comparison of loss probabilities for two models, N = 20.

P_{loss}	B = 1 s		B = 10 s		B = 50 s	
K	C1	C2	C1	C2	C1	C2
0	0.01	0	0.01	0.036	0.9	0.732
0.2	0.01	0	0.1	0.095	0.9	0.774
0.4	0.01	0	0.9	0.471	0.9	0.884
0.7	0.01	7.77e-6	0.9	0.685	0.9	0.933
1	0.02	4.81e-4	0.9	0.774	0.9	0.953
1.25	0.04	0.0041	0.9	0.818	0.9	0.962
1.6	0.16	0.0359	0.9	0.862	0.9	0.971
1.9	0.4	0.0947	0.9	0.884	0.9	0.976
2.3	0.64	0.1670	0.9	0.900	0.9	0.979

"Figure 2a", shows the P_{loss} of the system with respect to the attack traffic load for different values of N = 10, 20, 40 and B = 5s.

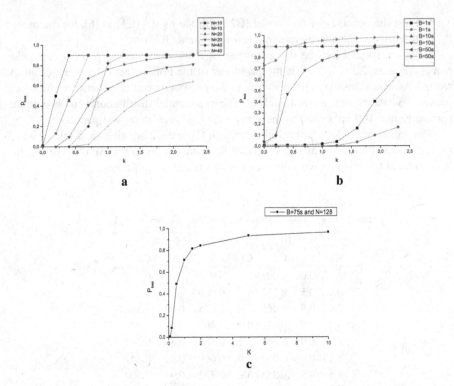

Fig. 2. The connection loss probability vs. the attack load for different parameters.

"Figure 2b", shows the P_{loss} of the system with respect to the attack traffic load for different values of B = 1s, 10s, 50s and N = 20. The dashed line corresponds to C1.

Either decreasing the holding time B (Fig. 2b), or increasing the maximum allowable number of half-open connections N (Fig. 2a), can reduce P_{loss} if the attack traffic load is limited.

We also try to evaluate P_{loss} with real values of B = 75s and N = 128, used in some operating systems. "Figure 2c" shows that P_{loss} increases rapidly with the increase of the attack traffic load. We conclude that the attack load K is a crucial factor, and it will severely degrade the performance of the network under attack.

In [6], to find the stationary probability distribution and the analytical results for a security performance metrics, a two-dimensional embedded Markov chain is used. However, constructing the two-dimensional embedded Markov chain and the transition probability matrices corresponding is a tedious and error-prone procedure, especially when the studied system is complex. Our model based on Deterministic and stochastic Petri nets is interesting because it facilitates the modeling and the evaluation of performance parameters, thanks to the automation of the generation of Markov chains and the performance parameters evaluation, provided by the DSPN corresponding software packages.

5.3   Evaluation of Some Other Performance Parameters

We also, evaluate five other performance parameters, represented by the formulas below, and the effect of the attack and the system parameters N and B on some of these performance parameters. In these formulas, M_i (P) indicates the number of tokens in the place P in the marking M_i, AM is the set of all accessible markings and E(t) is the set of markings where the transition t is enabled:

1. Buffer occupancy percentages of half-open connections for regular traffic (Pr), which is characterized by the mean ratio of the number of regular half-open connections to the maximum allowable number of half-open connections. This corresponds to the ratio of mean number of tokens in the place B1 to buffer capacity N:

$$Pr = \frac{\sum_{i:M_i \in AM} M_i(B1).\pi_i}{N} \tag{2}$$

2. Buffer occupancy percentages of half-open connections for attack traffic (Pa), which is represented by the mean ratio of the number of attack packets to the maximum allowable number of half-open connection. This corresponds to the ratio of mean number of tokens in the places B2 and B3 to buffer capacity N:

$$Pa = \frac{\sum_{i:M_i \in AM}(M_i(B2) + M_i(B3)).\pi_i}{N} \tag{3}$$

Pr and *Pa* can be used as security metric.

3. The mean number of legitimate SYN packets lost per unit time (NLL): This represents the mean rate of legitimate SYN packets lost. It corresponds to the throughput frequency of the transition TRL:

$$NLL = \sum_{i:i \in E(TRL)} M_i(SR). \lambda_1. \pi_i \tag{4}$$

4. The mean number of legitimate SYN packets received per unit time (NLR): This represents the mean rate of legitimate SYN packets received. It corresponds to the throughput frequency of the transition TL:

$$NLR = \sum_{i:i \in E(TL)} M_i(SR). \lambda_1. \pi_i \tag{5}$$

5. The mean response time ($\overline{R}$) for legitimate SYN packets:

$$\overline{R} = \frac{n}{NLR} \tag{6}$$

With n is the mean number of legitimate SYN packets in the system (buffer). This represents the mean number of tokens in the places B1:

$$n = \sum_{i:i \in AM} M_i(B1). \pi_i \tag{7}$$

For all graphs below, we also assume $\lambda = 10$ packets/s and $\mu = 100$ packets/s as the general parameters, and B = 5 and N = 20 as the basic parameters.

Figures 3 and 4, respectively, depict how the buffer occupancy percentages of half-open connections for legitimate traffic and attack traffic depend on the attack traffic load with different system parameter B and N.

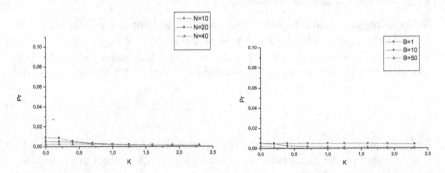

Fig. 3. Buffer occupancy percentages of half-open connections for regular traffic (Pr).

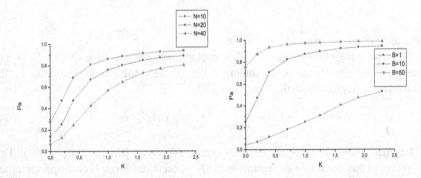

Fig. 4. Buffer occupancy percentages of half-open connections for attack traffic (Pa).

We observe that Pr remains at a similar level in the two figures of Fig. 3, which implies that it is not sensitive to B and N. On the other hand, in Fig. 4, we observe that Pa is much larger in the second figure, because the holding time B of attack packets is much longer, while in the first figure of Fig. 4 Pa increases in the same way for the various values of N. We can conclude that Pa is more sensitive to B than N and only Pa is sensitive to the attack load.

Figures 5 and 6, respectively, depict how the mean number of legitimate SYN packets received (NLR), and the mean number of legitimate SYN packets lost (NLL), depend on the attack traffic load with different system parameter B and N.

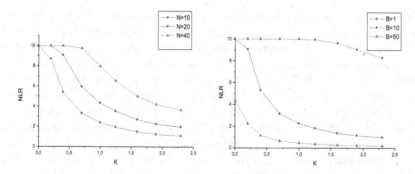

Fig. 5. The mean number of legitimate SYN packets received (NLR) vs. the attack load for different parameters.

In Fig. 5, we observe that NLR decreases, with the increase in the traffic of attack. The increase of N has not much effect, while NLR decreases rapidly, if B is increased. We observe in Fig. 6 that NLL increases with the increase of the attack traffic load, in the same manner if N is increased, and it increases rapidly if B is increased. That means that B has more impact than N, on these parameters of performance, and both NLR and NLL are sensitive to K, which means that K is an important factor of network degradation performance, under SYN/TCP attack.

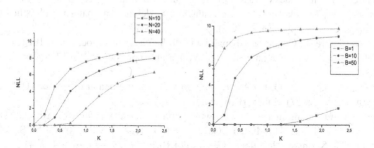

Fig. 6. The mean number of legitimate SYN packets lost (NLL) vs. the attack load for different parameters.

6 Conclusion

Several research works focused on the SYN flood attack, which can disrupt internet's important services, including Http, Ftp, and Mail server. Different experimental mechanisms and few formal models have been proposed to detect and combat SYN/TCP attack. In this paper, we proposed a formal model, to specify SYN/TCP attack with Deterministic and Stochastic Petri Net, which allowed us the conception of legible model, qualitative verification and quantitative evaluation of the model, facilitated by the use of TimeNet package. The objective consists of the calculation of connection loss probability, in order to evaluate the unavailability of server during the attack and other performance metrics, such as buffer occupancy of half-open connections for attack traffic and legitimate traffic, and number of legitimate SYN packet received and lost. By these results we show how the attack load severely degrade the performance of the network under attack, and the change of some system crucial parameters such as the buffer size and the holding time for half-open connections in order to guarantee the service availability, is effective only if the attack load is limited. The evaluation results of our model coincide with the results of the work [6], which used queueing theory. Constructing the two-dimensional embedded Markov chain and the transition probability matrices corresponding, used in [6] to find the stationary probability distribution and the analytical results for a security performance metrics, is a tedious and error-prone procedure. Our model is interesting because it facilitates the modeling and performance parameters evaluating. Indeed if the system is rightly modeled, the formulas of calculations of the performance parameters are correctly defined, and the automatic tools for verification and evaluation of the model are available, then the analytical study of systems becomes easier.

References

1. Eddy, W.: RFC 4987: Tcp Syn Flooding Attacks And Common Mitigations (2007)
2. http://www.wikipidia.com
3. Zargar, S.T., Joshi, J., Tipper, D.: A survey of defense mechanisms against distributed denial of service flooding attacks. IEEE Commun. Surv. Tutorials 15(4), 2046–2069 (2013)
4. Douligeris, C., Mitrokotsa, A.: DDoS attacks and defense mechanisms: classification and state-of-the-art. Comput. Netw. 44(5), 643–666 (2004)
5. Khan, S., Traore, I.: Queue-based analysis of DoS attacks. In: Proceedings IEEE Workshop on Information Assurance and Security West Point, pp. 266–273. IEEE Press, New York (2005)
6. Wang, Y., Lin, C., Li, Q.-L.: A queueing analysis for the denial of service (DoS) attacks. Comput. Netw. (2007). doi:10.1016/j.comnet.2007.02.011
7. Aissani, A.: Queueing analysis for networks under DoS attack. In: Gervasi, O., Murgante, B., Laganà, A., Taniar, D., Mun, Y., Gavrilova, M.L. (eds.) ICCSA 2008. LNCS, vol. 5073, pp. 500–513. Springer, Heidelberg (2008). doi:10.1007/978-3-540-69848-7_41
8. Lemon, J.: Resisting SYN flooding DoS attack with a SYN cache. In: Proceeding of USENIX BSDCon, pp. 89–98 (2002)
9. Mananet Reverse Firewall. http://www.cs3inc.com/pubs/ReverseFirewall.pdf
10. Ricciulli, L., Lincoln, P., Kakkar, P.: TCP SYN Flooding Defense. Computer Science Laboratory SRI International (2000)
11. Peng, T., Leckie, C., Ramamohanarao, K.: Protection from distributed denial of service attacks using history-based IP filtering. ICC 1, 482–486 (2003)
12. Wang, H., Jin, C., Shin, K.G.: Defense against spoofed IP traffic using Hop-Count filtering. IEEE/ACM Trans. Networking 15(1), 40–53 (2007)
13. Park, K., Lee, H.: On the effectiveness of route-based packet filtering for distributed DoS attack prevention in power-law internets. In: Proceedings of ACM SIGCOMM (2001)
14. Mizrak, A.T., Savage, S., Marzullo, K.: Detecting compromised routers via packet forwarding behavior. IEEE Network 22, 34–39 (2008)
15. Ferguson, P., Senie, D.: Network ingress filtering: defeating denial of service attacks that employ IP source address spoofing. In: Internet RFC 2827 (2000)

16. Wang, H., Zhang, D., Shin, K.-G.: Detecting SYN Flooding Attacks. EECS Department, the University of Michigan (2002)
17. Wang, H., Zhang, D., Shin, K.-G.: Change-point monitoring for the detection of DOS attack. IEEE Trans. Dependable Secure Comput. **1**(4), 193–208 (2004)
18. Gil, T.M., Poleto, M.: MULTOPS: a data-structure for bandwidth attack detection. In: Proceedings of 10th Usenix Security Symposium, Washington, DC, pp. 23–38 (2001)
19. Karthik Pai, B.H., Nagesh, H-R., Abhijit, B.: Detection and performance evaluation of DoS/DDoS attacks using SYN flooding attacks. In: International Journal of Computer Applications (0975 – 8887) International Conference on Information and Communication Technologies ICICT (2014)
20. Zurawski, R., Zhou, M.: Petri nets and industrial applications: a tutorial. IEEE Trans. Industr. Electron. **41**(6), 567–583 (1994)
21. Molloy, M.: performance analysis using stochastic petri nets. IEEE Trans. Comput. **31**(9), 913–917 (1982)
22. Marsan, M.A., Chiola, G.: On Petri nets with deterministic and exponentially distributed firing times. In: Rozenberg, G. (ed.) APN 1986. LNCS, vol. 266, pp. 132–145. Springer, Heidelberg (1987). doi:10.1007/3-540-18086-9_23
23. Zimmermann, A., Knoke, M.: TimeNET 4.0 software tool for the performability evaluation with stochastic and colored petri nets. Real-Time Systems and Robotics Group, Università Berlin Technical Report 2007-13, ISSN 1436-9915 (2007)

Empirical Evaluation of a Distributed Deployment Strategy for Virtual Networks

Carsten Hahn[✉], Stephan Holzner, Lenz Belzner, and Michael Till Beck

Ludwig-Maximilians-Universität München, Munich, Germany
{carsten.hahn,belzner,michael.beck}@ifi.lmu.de,
stephan.holzner@cip.ifi.lmu.de

Abstract. Network virtualization is a key technology for future network services, enabling the deployment of network services without changing dissimilar hardware devices. This leads to the problem of mapping virtual demands to physical resources, known as the $\mathcal{NP}$-hard Virtual Network Embedding problem. The DPVNE framework (*Distributed, Parallel, and Generic Virtual Network Embedding Framework*) has been presented as a distributed approach that is able to solve this optimization problem heuristically, spreading computational load to multiple distributed nodes. Previously, DPVNE has only been evaluated in simulation, but not in real, distributed test beds. In this paper, we present new empirical results on DPVNE's performance in large-scale setups.

Keywords: Deployment of virtual networks · Cloud computing

1 Introduction

The Internet and associated packet switched services have a major impact on our everyday lives. This results in an increased demand of those services. Nevertheless the inflexibility of traditional network architectures hinders the extensibility of those infrastructures and the integration of next-generation services. Network Virtualization aims to overcome these limitations by dynamically assigning network services to generic hardware resources. In virtualized environments, virtual network requests (VNRs) are embedded into a shared substrate network which offers processing and bandwidth resources. Each virtual resource has to be mapped to one or multiple substrate resources whereby also multiple virtual resources can be assigned to one substrate resource with regard to their processing and bandwidth constraints. The objective is to embed VNRs efficiently into the substrate network, e.g., in a cost-efficient way. The optimal mapping between VNRs and the substrate network is considered as the Virtual Network Embedding Problem (VNE) and is known to be $\mathcal{NP}$-hard [1]. As such, optimal solutions can only be computed for small problem instances in suitable time.

For this reason, several efficient, but non-optimal, heuristic approaches have been suggested. One of them is the *Distributed, Parallel, and Generic Virtual Network Embedding Framework* (DPVNE) [2]. DPVNE hierarchically partitions

© Springer International Publishing AG 2017
S. Bouzefrane et al. (Eds.): MSPN 2017, LNCS 10566, pp. 88–98, 2017.
DOI: 10.1007/978-3-319-67807-8_7

the substrate network and designates so called *embedder nodes* and *delegation nodes*. This allows embedder nodes to perform the embedding of multiple VNRs in parallel. Due to its distributed nature, DPVNE does not depend on a single, central instance that is responsible for computing the embedding of the VNRs. In scenarios where a large amount of VNRs need to be embedded, approaches relying on a central instance do not scale well with the number of requests. DPVNE's distributed embedder nodes refer to one of those non-distributed approaches for computing the actual embedding of the VNRs within its designated network part. Thus, DPVNE can be used in conjunction with those centralized solutions in order to improve their scalability. Compared to other distributed approaches, DPVNE comes with less communication overhead [3].

DPVNE has previously been evaluated in a simulation environment called *Alevin* [4]. *Alevin* is an extensive simulation tool that eases the evaluation of VNE algorithms. In the context of distributed scenarios, however, one drawback of *Alevin* is that it simulates the embedding process on just one CPU core.

As a consequence, despite of the distributed nature of DPVNE, the embedding process could previously not be simulated in parallel, as all simulations were performed on one CPU core. The contribution of this paper is the prototypical implementation and evaluation of DPVNE in a real distributed testbed. Multiple physically distributed nodes concurrently process arriving VNRs and embed them in substrate networks of various sizes. As shown in this paper, these new evaluation results are in line with the previously presented results and can thus be seen as a confirmation of those evaluation results.

2   The Virtual Network Embedding Problem

In cloud scenarios, typically, multiple virtual networks need to be deployed into a shared physical infrastructure [5]. Usually, structure and demands of each virtual network are specified by an external stakeholder, and the infrastructure provider is getting paid for hosting these virtual networks. The objective of the infrastructure provider is to ensure that all the virtual networks can successfully and efficiently be deployed within its network. Therefore, resource constraints of the virtual networks need to be considered: each virtual machine demands a certain amount of CPU or memory resources, and each virtual communication link requires bandwidth resources. Unfortunately, resources provided by the physical network are limited and thus, the assignment of these resources needs to be considered carefully.

This is depicted in Fig. 1: Here, two virtual networks need to be embedded into a shared substrate network. Virtual networks can be described as graphs with virtual nodes and virtual links. A virtual node demands a certain amount of resources, denoted as the weights of the nodes (e.g., CPU resources); likewise, virtual links demand substrate resources as well (e.g., bandwidth resources). The substrate network can be modeled as a weighted network graph as well: here, substrate nodes provide physical resources for hosting virtual nodes (e.g., CPU resources), and substrate links provide resources for hosting virtual links (e.g., bandwidth resources).

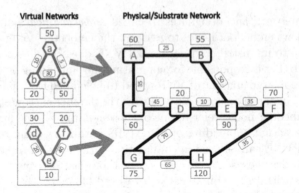

Fig. 1. Multiple virtual networks need to be deployed into a shared physical network infrastructure

The embedding of virtual networks into the infrastructure of the substrate network is shown in Fig. 2. Here, each virtual node is assigned to a suitable substrate node. To this end, it needs to be assured that all virtual nodes are assigned to substrate nodes offering sufficient resources for hosting those virtual nodes. E.g., substrate node A is capable of hosting both virtual nodes d and f, but not nodes a and c, as this would exceed available resources. Furthermore, virtual links need to be mapped to substrate paths. E.g., as virtual node a is hosted on substrate node C, and virtual node c to node B, a substrate path between nodes C and B needs to be assigned for hosting the respective virtual link.

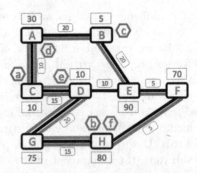

Fig. 2. A valid embedding of virtual networks within a physical network infrastructure

Assigning these virtual networks in an efficient and optimal way (e.g., such that embedding cost/resource usage is minimized) is known to be a $\mathcal{NP}$-hard optimization problem. This is known as the Virtual Network Embedding Problem [1].

3 Related Work

The proposed solutions for the VNE problem are mostly heuristic due to the $\mathcal{NP}$-hardness of the problem [1]. They can be divided into centralized and distributed approaches. In centralized scenarios, a centralized embedder node which benefits from full knowledge of the substrate network topology and available resources performs the embedding. Despite of their heuristic nature, many of those centralized solutions suffer from poor scalability in large network scenarios, as they rely on one single node performing the embeddings [3]. Distributed solutions like DPVNE were suggested which aim to overcome those limitations by solving the optimization problem not on one single node, but on several distributed nodes.

3.1 Centralized Approaches

Several centralized algorithms have been introduced in the past. Most of them are based on heuristics [6–13] or metaheuristics [14–17]. Centralized approaches typically suffer from the following shortcomings:

- Poor scalability: Many centralized approaches do not scale well in large-scale environments. Beck et al. analyzed runtime performance of several VNE algorithms [2], showing that runtime significantly increases for multiple strategies with increased network size.

  In contrast, DPVNE builds hierarchical partitions of the substrate network and assigns distributed embedding nodes to those network partitions. This way, computational workload is spread to multiple nodes. To this end, for each VNR, DPVNE aims to identify small network partitions offering suitable network resources for embedding the respective virtual network. One of the distributed nodes is then used to perform the actual embedding within the partition scope. This way, problem complexity can often be reduced in many scenarios.
- Serial processing of VNRs: Furthermore, centralized approaches can only process one VNR at a time. In scenarios where many VNRs arrive simultaneously, all VNRs need to be handled by one node, one-by-one. This leads to high utilization of the central node, introducing queueing delay. This might be unsuitable in highly dynamic cloud scenarios, where those non-distributed approaches suffer from poor scalability.

  In contrast to those centralized approaches, DPVNE is able to cope with multiple VNRs at once, effectively spreading VNRs among its distributed nodes.

One prominent centralized algorithm is ASID (*Advanced Subgraph Isomorphism Detection*) by Lischka and Karl [6]. It is a heuristic approach, aiming to detect suitable subgraphs of the substrate network which have the same or a similar structure as the virtual network. As DPVNE is more of a generic framework which is capable of running various centralized approaches in a distributed way, it can also be used to run the non-distributed ASID algorithm on several distributed nodes.

3.2   Distributed Approaches

A distributed approach besides DPVNE is ADVNE [18]. While performing the embedding of VNs it aims to guarantee a balanced load among all substrate nodes. For embedding, VNRs are divided into smaller subgraphs. Each subgraph is then forwarded and handled by a so called root node in the substrate network. This is done in order to parallelize the processing of VNRs. Recent studies, however, show that ADVNE comes with high message overhead, even in small- to mid-size scenarios [2]. This is due to the fact that ADVNE operates in a fully distributed way, involving all substrate nodes into the embedding process. In contrast, DPVNE chooses only a small set of nodes for computing the embeddings. Indeed, compared to ADVNE, DPVNE message overhead was shown to be much smaller in larger scenarios.

4   The DPVNE Algorithm

The DPVNE algorithm has extensively been discussed in [2,3]. The interested reader is directed to these publications for the full technical details behind the DPVNE framework. In the following, the key idea behind DPVNE is shortly sketched.

The substrate network is recursively split into smaller network parts. This is depicted in Fig. 3: The complete substrate network is shown in layer 0. The network is now recursively split into non-overlapping network parts: In layer 1, the network is divided in two smaller partitions. In layer 2, each of those smaller partitions was split into even smaller sub-partitions. Thus, a hierarchical partitioning of the substrate network is built.

Now, distributed embedding nodes are assigned to these network partitions. For each partition, an external embedding node is allocated that is in charge of embedding virtual networks within its partition scope. Embedding nodes work in a distributed manner: they coordinate the embedding process and collaboratively agree on where to embed the virtual networks. The actual embedding of a virtual network is then computed by one of the embedding nodes by referring to one of the well-known optimization strategies. Thus, DPVNE is a generic framework that is capable of running centralized VNE algorithms in a distributed way.

One effect of the hierarchical partitioning is that in many cases, the embedding of virtual networks can be performed in parallel. E.g., the nodes and links assigned to the left partition of layer 1 are not part of the layer's right partition. This means that an embedding node can perform the embedding process for a virtual network in the left partition, while at the same time, another embedding node assigns another virtual network within the right partition.

In scenarios where comparatively small, continuously arriving virtual networks need to be embedded into a large substrate network, this embedding strategy is advantageous. In other scenarios where only few virtual networks need to be embedded, a centralized approach is sufficient and is, in fact, beneficial, as system complexity can be kept at a minimum.

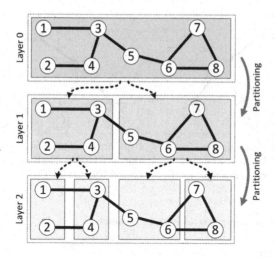

Fig. 3. The DPVNE algorithm

Previously, DPVNE's performance has not been analyzed in physically distributed environments. That's the focus of this paper.

5   Method

DPVNE has previously been evaluated on a single core machine, simulating partitioning of the substrate network and computation of embedding nodes [3]. Operations that are meant to be executed in parallel by DPVNE have therefore been executed sequentially on a single physical core, and parallelism only occured in simulation (i.e. virtually). While in principle the previous evaluation shows the scalability of the DPVNE approach due to its divide-and-conquer approach, the simulation results cannot be directly transferred to a real, physically distributed setting due to complex dependencies w.r.t. DPVNE's communication protocol and message delays arising in physical communication. Therefore, we implemented the DPVNE algorithm in a physically distributed way. I.e., we proceeded as follows.

1. We generated a VNE problem instance with the help of the Alevin simulation framework.
2. We determined the corresponding distribution tree and started a DPVNE agent for each embedding node, each one on a dedicated physical core.
3. We solved the generated VNE problem instance with DPVNE, where communication was physically performed via the network, in a truly distributed way.
4. We empirically observed the results.

By distributing DPVNE on multiple cores and measuring its performance this way, we were able to assess DPVNE's performance in a more realistic manner than in the previous, simulated experiments (cf. Fig. 4).

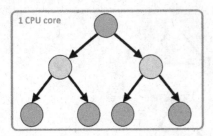
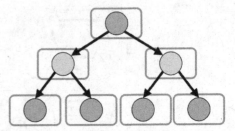

(a) Simulation on one physical host with a single CPU core and simulated communication between simulated hosts.

(b) Our physically distributed implementation of DPVNE. Each host application runs on a dedicated CPU core.

Fig. 4. Simulation on one physical host vs. simulation in a distributed environment.

6   Evaluation

DPVNE's performance was evaluated in multiple scenarios and compared to results obtained from the centralistic ASID algorithm.

6.1   Setup

Virtual networks were created by the Waxman network topology generator [19]. For the generation of the substrate network, the Barábsi Albert Model was used as it generates scale-free network topologies. Scale-free topologies are seen to be found in many real-world network structures [20]. Each substrate node and link was assigned a uniform distributed random value of free CPU respectively bandwidth capacity between 1% and 100%. Similarly, virtual nodes and links were assigned random CPU and bandwidth demands between 1% and 50%.

6.2   Results

In the following, we discuss the evaluation results obtained from our experiments.

Runtime. The first experiment evaluates the runtime of the prototypic DPVNE implementation w.r.t. the size of the substrate network and the number of available embedder nodes. For each configuration 20 VNRs had to be embedded. This was done with 3, 7, and 15 available embedder nodes (EN) as depicted in Fig. 5. In order to assure stability of the results, experiments were repeated 50 times. As can be seen in the Figure, runtime of the embedding with DPVNE generally decreases in scenarios with more embedder nodes present. In smaller substrate networks, however, the distributed approach does not lead to any performance improvements. This effect can be explained with the communication overhead between the distributed embedder nodes. Furthermore, it can be seen that ASID's runtime rapidly grows with larger number of nodes while the runtime of DPVNE almost stays constant for smaller substrate network sizes. For larger substrate networks with more than 5000 nodes the experiments show that runtime of DPVNE increases linearly on the given network sizes. The ASID algorithm was left out on purpose after a substrate network size of 10000 nodes as its runtime quickly becomes infeasible in this experiment.

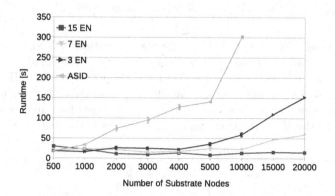

Fig. 5. Runtime in mid- to large-scale Scenarios

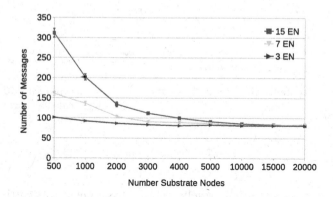

Fig. 6. Message overhead

Communication Overhead. Figure 6 depicts the amount of emerging messages between the embedder nodes for the embedding of 20 VNRs in various sized substrate networks. The large amount of messages for small substrate networks and respectively high number of embedder nodes can be explained by the fact that the partitions on the lowest level get too small to embed the VNRs. This means that the embedding of those requests fails on the lowest level and they have to be delegated to a higher level in the hierarchy for another embedding attempt.

It can be concluded that DPVNE performs faster than the centralized ASID in large networks with multiple VNRs due to the partitioning of the substrate network and the parallel embedding process. Nevertheless the number of embedder nodes has been carefully chosen w.r.t. the substrate network size and the expected VNRs because the number of embedder nodes determines the size of the resulting partitions and the associated message overhead.

Acceptance Ratio. Another metric for the evaluation of VNE algorithms is the acceptance ratio. It measures the amount of VNRs that could be embedded successfully. As can be seen in Fig. 7a, DPVNE outperforms ASID in terms of acceptance. One explanation for this effect is that DPVNE delegates VNRs between embedder nodes if an embedding in one partition failed while ASID simply rejects the VNR if the maximal search depth is reached.

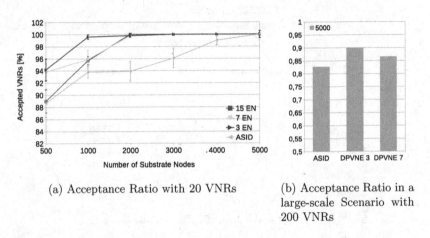

(a) Acceptance Ratio with 20 VNRs

(b) Acceptance Ratio in a large-scale Scenario with 200 VNRs

Fig. 7. Acceptance ratio

To further investigate these results another experiment was carried out. In this experiment substrate networks with the size 5000 nodes were created in which each nodes had 10 links. The structure of the VNs was unchanged to the previous experiments except for the fact that 200 instead of 20 VNRs had to be embedded. Figure 7b shows the results of the scenario. For 5000 nodes the acceptance ratio of DPVNE is better than the value of the ASID algorithm. It can be concluded that DPVNE comes with higher acceptance ratio and a faster embedding of VNRs compared to the centralized ASID algorithm.

7   Conclusion

This paper presents an empirical evaluation of the distributed DPVNE framework. Evaluation results show that DPVNE is able to efficiently spread compuational workload to distributed embedder nodes. The embedding of multiple virtual networks can efficiently be solved by DPVNE. In scenarios where virtual networks arrive continuously and need to be embedded into a large-scale substrate network, DPVNE is able to heuristically solve the $\mathcal{NP}$-hard problem efficiently.

Summarizing, results presented here are in line with those previously obtained with the help of the (non-distributed) Alevin simulation tool, emphasizing the integrity of those earlier experiments.

References

1. Fischer, A., Botero, J.F., Beck, M.T., De Meer, H., Hesselbach, X.: Virtual network embedding: a survey. IEEE Commun. Surv. Tutorials **15**(4), 1888–1906 (2013)
2. Beck, M.T., Fischer, A., Botero, J.-F., Linnhoff-Popien, C., de Meer, H.: Distributed and scalable embedding of virtual networks. J. Netw. Comput. Appl. **56**, 124–136 (2015)
3. Beck, M.T., Fischer, A., de Meer, H., Botero, J.F., Hesselbach, X.: A distributed, parallel, and generic virtual network embedding framework. In: 2013 IEEE International Conference on Communications (ICC), pp. 3471–3475. IEEE (2013)
4. Beck, M.T., Linnhoff-Popien, C., Fischer, A., Kokot, F., de Meer, H.: A simulation framework for virtual network embedding algorithms. In: 2014 16th International Telecommunications Network Strategy and Planning Symposium (Networks), pp. 1–6. IEEE (2014)
5. Mell, P., Grance, T.: The NIST definition of cloud computing. Nat. Inst. Stan. Technol. **53**(6), 50 (2009)
6. Lischka, J., Karl, H.: A virtual network mapping algorithm based on subgraph isomorphism detection. In: Proceedings of the 1st ACM Workshop on Virtualized Infrastructure Systems and Architectures, pp. 81–88. ACM (2009)
7. Zhu, Y., Ammar, M.H.: Algorithms for assigning substrate network resources to virtual network components. In: INFOCOM, vol. 1200, no. 2006, pp. 1–12 (2006)
8. Yu, M., Yi, Y., Rexford, J., Chiang, M.: Rethinking virtual network embedding: substrate support for path splitting and migration. ACM SIGCOMM Comput. Commun. Rev. **38**(2), 17–29 (2008)
9. Butt, N.F., Chowdhury, M., Boutaba, R.: Topology-awareness and reoptimization mechanism for virtual network embedding. In: Crovella, M., Feeney, L.M., Rubenstein, D., Raghavan, S.V. (eds.) NETWORKING 2010. LNCS, vol. 6091, pp. 27–39. Springer, Heidelberg (2010). doi:10.1007/978-3-642-12963-6_3
10. Fajjari, I., Aitsaadi, N., Pujolle, G., Zimmermann, H.: VNR algorithm: a greedy approach for virtual networks reconfigurations. In: 2011 IEEE Global Telecommunications Conference (GLOBECOM 2011), pp. 1–6. IEEE (2011)
11. Rahman, M.R., Aib, I., Boutaba, R.: Survivable virtual network embedding. In: Crovella, M., Feeney, L.M., Rubenstein, D., Raghavan, S.V. (eds.) NETWORKING 2010. LNCS, vol. 6091, pp. 40–52. Springer, Heidelberg (2010). doi:10.1007/978-3-642-12963-6_4
12. Cheng, X., Su, S., Zhang, Z., Wang, H., Yang, F., Luo, Y., Wang, J.: Virtual network embedding through topology-aware node ranking. ACM SIGCOMM Comput. Commun. Rev. **41**(2), 38–47 (2011)
13. Botero, J.F., Molina, M., Hesselbach-Serra, X., Amazonas, J.R.: A novel paths algebra-based strategy to flexibly solve the link mapping stage of VNE problems. J. Netw. Comput. Appl. **36**(6), 1735–1752 (2013)

14. Fajjari, I., Aitsaadi, N., Pujolle, G., Zimmermann, H.: VNE-AC: virtual network embedding algorithm based on ant colony metaheuristic. In: 2011 IEEE International Conference on Communications (ICC), pp. 1–6. IEEE (2011)
15. Zhang, Z., Cheng, X., Su, S., Wang, Y., Shuang, K., Luo, Y.: A unified enhanced particle swarm optimization-based virtual network embedding algorithm. Int. J. Commun. Syst. **26**(8), 1054–1073 (2013)
16. Cheng, X., Su, S., Zhang, Z., Shuang, K., Yang, F., Luo, Y., Wang, J.: Virtual network embedding through topology awareness and optimization. Comput. Netw. **56**(6), 1797–1813 (2012)
17. Zhang, S., Qian, Z., Guo, S., Lu, S.: FELL: a flexible virtual network embedding algorithm with guaranteed load balancing. In: 2011 IEEE International Conference on Communications (ICC), pp. 1–5, June 2011
18. Houïdi, I., Louati, W., Zeghlache, D.: A distributed virtual network mapping algorithm. In: IEEE International Conference on Communications. ICC 2008, pp. 5634–5640. IEEE (2008)
19. Waxman, B.M.: Routing of multipoint connections. IEEE J. Sel. Areas Commun. **6**(9), 1617–1622 (1988)
20. Barabási, A.-L., Albert, R.: Emergence of scaling in random networks. Science **286**(5439), 509–512 (1999)

Identifying Service Contexts for QoS Support in IoT Service Oriented Software Defined Networks

Hong Jin Kim, Moon Yong Jung, Won Sang Chin,
and Ju Wook Jang[(⊠)]

Department of Electronics Engineering, Sogang University, Seoul 04107, Korea
{chii92,myjung,mokey82,jjang}@sogang.ac.kr

Abstract. An important challenge for supporting variety of applications in the Internet of Things is the network traffic engineering and virtual network technologies such as SDN (Software Defined Network). To assign virtual network, it require service context (QoS) however, identifying service context is not easy. For that reason, the proliferation of new applications use port numbers already known (e.g. HTTP = 80). In addition, the encrypted packets (e.g. HTTPS) make it difficult to identify service contexts. This paper presents an identifying scheme for service contexts from real network traffic to support service-oriented IoT network. We use statistical properties of network traffic such as mean packet length, mean interpacket arrival time, and standard deviation interpacket arrival time to identify service contexts (e.g. Video Streaming, Video Conference, File Transfer Service). The contribution of our approach is in identifying services which have not been identified by previous methods. We devise a scheme which incrementally add dimensions to separate services until all services are identified. For example, Video Streaming and FTP shows identical statistical properties when we examine by two dimensions (MPL: Mean Packet Length, MIAT: Mean Inter-Arrival Time), hence not separable. However, if we add one more dimension (SDIAT: Standard Deviation of Inter-Arrival Time), the two services can be clearly separated. Our scheme can be used to find out which traffic needs what QoS in combined traffics, which can be used for traffic engineering in SDN.

Keywords: IoT · Network context · Service context · Statistical property · MPL · MIAT · SDIAT

1 Introduction

The number of sensors deployed around the world is growing at a swift speed. Naturally, large amount of data is being gathered from the devices, hence using data approach has been enlarged. In addition, the more data emerged, the more we need to define the data. For this, towards moving to the internet of things, context is considered to be extremely important. Perera et al. [1] claims, context-aware computing allows us to store context information linked to sensor data, therefore the interpretation can be done easily and more meaningfully. Furthermore, understanding context makes it easier to fulfill

© Springer International Publishing AG 2017
S. Bouzefrane et al. (Eds.): MSPN 2017, LNCS 10566, pp. 99–108, 2017.
DOI: 10.1007/978-3-319-67807-8_8

machine to machine (M2M) communication, as it is a core element in IoT vision. Accordingly, there have been several surveys conducted in relation to this field.

In identifying context, Figo et al. [2] claims that device can understand user's performance, such as walking or running, with analyzing accelerometer data. It is one example of identifying user context from device context. Eisenman et al. [3] presents BikeNet, a mobile sensing system for mapping the cyclists' experience. They claim that users could gain empirical knowledge of important factors, such as exposure to air and noise pollution, and danger due to car density with BikeNet. This can be explained by identification of service context from user and device contexts. To identify service context either way, we can use network context.

Our study initiated from building service oriented platforms, similar to Paganelli [4]. In this paper, as a first step, we identified service contexts from network contexts to lay the ground work for Software defined network (Fig. 1).

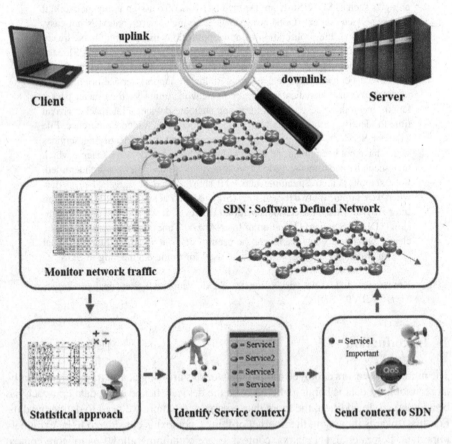

Fig. 1. Overall architecture

The remainder of this paper is arranged as followed. The different traffic classification methods are reviewed in Sect. 2. Section 3 presents our methodology and outline experimental results, respectively. Section 4 presents our conclusions.

2 Related Works

Due to its fundamental nature and its basis in other techniques, the field of traffic classification (to identify service) has maintained everlasting interest. For instance, Port-based approach is the most common technique for identifying internet network applications. For now, however, it's not easy to classify the network as well as identify service contexts due to the proliferation of new applications. Several new applications have no IANA registered ports, but instead use ports that are already registered (e.g. HTTP = 80, HTTPS = 443). In addition, application developers and users use assigned ports to disguise their traffic and circumvent filtering or firewalls. Furthermore, pervasive deployment of network and port address translation make it hard to classify traffic (e.g. several physical servers may offer services through the same public IP address but on different ports) [5].

As applications and user behaviors appeared on port-based flow classification undependable, payload-based approaches emerged. Payload-based approach, sometimes called deep packet inspection (DPI), relies on specific application data. This method can further divide into two parts which are protocol decoding - where the application protocol data has been used, and signature-based identification - where a search will be carried out to identify application's specific byte sequence in packet payload [6].

Nonetheless, it is easily circumvented by encryption, protocol obfuscation or encapsulation (e.g. tunneling traffic in HTTP), and prohibitively computationally expensive for general use on high-bandwidth links. These concerns with payload based techniques have motivated researchers to seek new discriminating properties of traffic classes and other classification techniques.

In other way, Erman et al. [7] claims, using a clustering approach is called clustering for the network traffic identification problem. We pursue this clustering approach, and in particular by using network statistical properties.

Classification involves two stages; sets of features with known traffic classes (creating "rules"), and applying these rules to classify unknown traffic and identify service contexts.

3 Acquiring Service Context Through Traffic Classification

3.1 Target Services

In this paper, our target service contexts are Video streaming, Video conference and File transfer service. Since these three applications need QoS based routing, in extreme cases, Video streaming needs less than 1% loss, less than 30 ms jitter, and less than 150 ms latency for their services [8]. YouTube and Netflix are examples of these kinds of Video streaming. Skype and Google Hangouts are included in Video conference. For File transfer service, various web services that use HTTP (Port 80) or HTTPs (Port 443) are examples.

3.2 Data Acquisition and Pre-processing

Data acquisition was carried out using the Wireshark packet sniffer. This network packet analyzer is able to capture network packets and tries to display that packet data as detailed as possible. We collected data packets from the client's side on Window OS environment. Figure 2 shows collected packet dissection data as a CSV file from Wireshark. Then we read it through R program, which is a statistical analysis software for data pre-processing. Dataset consists of *Timestamp, Source IP, Destination IP, Protocol, Packet Length, Source Port Number*, and *Destination Port Number*.

Time	srcIP	dstIP	Protocol	Length	srcPort	dstPort
7.721860	64.4.23.156	163.239.195.111	QUIC	68	443	36920
7.744289	65.54.184.18	163.239.195.111	TLSv1	155	443	6625
7.769936	157.55.235.142	163.239.195.111	TCP	60	40012	6624
7.769936	157.55.235.142	163.239.195.111	TCP	60	40012	6624
7.769983	163.239.195.111	157.55.235.142	TCP	67	6624	40012
7.780195	151.31.228.118	163.239.195.111	UDP	68	46428	36920
7.859076	104.49.209.2	163.239.195.111	UDP	68	23263	36920
7.893605	163.239.195.111	184.85.223.58	TCP	54	6153	80
7.928133	163.239.195.111	198.72.147.242	TCP	66	6717	55571
7.943580	163.239.195.111	65.54.184.18	TCP	54	6625	443
7.960041	163.239.195.111	184.85.223.58	HTTP	340	6153	80
8.054872	157.55.235.142	163.239.195.111	TCP	141	40012	6624
8.055376	163.239.195.111	35.32.194.187	TCP	66	6718	11239
8.106939	198.72.147.242	163.239.195.111	TCP	66	55571	6717
8.106994	163.239.195.111	198.72.147.242	TCP	54	6717	55571
8.107389	163.239.195.111	198.72.147.242	TCP	117	6717	55571
8.117192	163.239.195.98	163.239.195.111	UDP	70	22654	36920
8.253861	35.32.194.187	163.239.195.111	TCP	66	11239	6718
8.253885	163.239.195.111	35.32.194.187	TCP	54	6718	11239
8.254480	163.239.195.111	35.32.194.187	TCP	107	6718	11239
8.254599	163.239.195.111	157.55.235.142	TCP	54	6624	40012

Fig. 2. A CSV dataset imported from Wireshark

To obtain meaningful dataset, we constructed a flow table based on *SRC* (srcIP + srcPort), *DST* (dstIP + dstPort) 2 tuple (Fig. 3a). We set the value of K (count threshold) as 25, since we want to focus on large flows as previously stated(hence excluded DNS, SNMP, NBNS, and other mice flows) Fig. 3(b), shows the result of preprocessing. It consists of *Time, SRC, DST, packet lengths* and *flow*. Flows are classified by SRC, DST pair and seven bidirectional flows are identified.

3.3 Identifying Flows Based on Legacy Method

Legacy port-based classification method could be applied on our dataset. In this case, we can only identify HTTP and HTTPs among the classes. In other words, the majority of flows use same port (e.g. class 2, 3, 4, 5) that makes it difficult to interpret its application (Table 1). Therefore, we can find out that port based classification is not an efficient way to identify dataset that were collected from web services. Also in payload based classification case, as mentioned above, HTTPs traffics are encrypted so that it is

SRC	DST	count	Flow
163.239.195.119:1478	208.89.14.135:80	90	1
208.89.14.135:80	163.239.195.119:1478	47	1
163.239.195.119:1587	203.233.18.45:443	43	2
203.233.18.45:443	163.239.195.119:1587	57	2
163.239.195.119:1594	203.248.180.204:443	15003	3
203.248.180.204:443	163.239.195.119:1594	33266	3
163.239.195.119:1595	203.248.180.204:443	4540	4
203.248.180.204:443	163.239.195.119:1595	10073	4
163.239.195.119:1583	216.58.221.142:443	39	5
216.58.221.142:443	163.239.195.119:1583	64	5
163.239.2.30:55004	163.239.195.119:1036	38	6
163.239.195.119:1036	163.239.2.30:55004	38	6
139.150.3.75:5223	163.239.195.119:1598	56	7
163.239.195.119:1598	139.150.3.75:5223	40	7

(a)

Time	SRC	DST	Length	Flow
1.805392	163.239.195.119:1583	216.58.221.142:443	54	5
1.806882	216.58.221.142:443	163.239.195.119:1583	1484	5
1.806884	216.58.221.142:443	163.239.195.119:1583	1484	5
1.806926	163.239.195.119:1583	216.58.221.142:443	54	5
1.807668	216.58.221.142:443	163.239.195.119:1583	1484	5
1.807669	216.58.221.142:443	163.239.195.119:1583	1484	5
1.807711	163.239.195.119:1583	216.58.221.142:443	54	5
1.808453	216.58.221.142:443	163.239.195.119:1583	891	5
1.836507	163.239.195.119:1594	203.248.180.204:443	66	3
1.836670	163.239.195.119:1595	203.248.180.204:443	66	4
1.840021	203.248.180.204:443	163.239.195.119:1595	66	4
1.840055	163.239.195.119:1595	203.248.180.204:443	54	4
1.840080	203.248.180.204:443	163.239.195.119:1594	66	3
1.840100	163.239.195.119:1594	203.248.180.204:443	54	3
1.840234	163.239.195.119:1595	203.248.180.204:443	299	4
1.840330	163.239.195.119:1594	203.248.180.204:443	299	3
1.843947	203.248.180.204:443	163.239.195.119:1595	60	4
1.844699	203.248.180.204:443	163.239.195.119:1594	60	3
1.845642	203.248.180.204:443	163.239.195.119:1594	1514	3
1.846411	203.248.180.204:443	163.239.195.119:1594	1514	3
1.846412	203.248.180.204:443	163.239.195.119:1594	746	3

(b)

Fig. 3. Flow table (a), Pre-processed packet dissection dataset (b)

also difficult to find applications. We applied this method on our dataset which we obtained by wireshark (Sect. 3.2). However, 57% of the traffic were encrypted, making identifying service contexts hard. To solve these problems, we use statistical properties approach to identify service contexts.

Table 1. Port-based classification

Port	Class	Protocol
80	1	HTTP
443	2,3,4,5	HTTP
55004	6	Unregistered
5223	7	XMPP

3.4 Identification Based on Statistical Properties Flows

To use statistical classification, selecting a feature is the most significant way. Accordingly, there have been a lot of works conducted in relation to this field [9]. Roughan et al. [10] claims that average packet length and flow duration are the most important features to classify network traffic data. However, Roughan et al. [10] do not separately identify uplink traffic and downlink traffic. We refine identification of service contexts by considering uplink traffic and downlink traffic separately. We improved their method by introducing directions of flows (Client to Server or Server to Client), since we want to divide unidirectional transmission and duplex transmission.

Firstly, mean packet length (MPL) and mean interpacket arrival time(MIAT) are used. Figure 4 shows the result of flows direction with downlink (server to client) and uplink (client to server) state by mean packet length and mean interpacket arrival time property. We represented it on two dimension spaces for easy understanding. As Fig. 5, we notice that each of the flows indicate different statistical properties.

```
        MPL          MIAT Flow FlowVector
   496.62222 2.117699404    1            0
   653.10638 4.085726826    1            1
    92.86047 4.364129643    2            0
   544.36842 3.272716446    2            1
    57.25502 0.011233167    3            0
  1509.97788 0.005065977    3            1
    56.93084 0.009490680    4            0
  1508.10225 0.004277052    4            1
   128.53846 4.888866395    5            0
   987.10938 2.948863079    5            1
    63.00000 4.865143027    6            1
    60.50000 4.865120946    6            0
    64.95000 0.019693590    7            1
  1388.25000 0.013400945    7            0
```

Fig. 4. Classification of dataset flows with direction

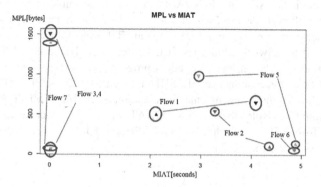

Fig. 5. Classification of dataset flows (2-dimension)

Subsequently, to identify our target services (Streaming, Video conference, File transfer service), we collect the representative traffics with packet sniffer. The clustering result was obtained through 10 experiments.

Figure 6 shows that result of services' mean of μ-packet length, mean of μ-interpacket arrival time. From this we can see the apparent differences of uplink and downlink statistical characteristics (especially the uplink MPL) between Video streaming flow and Video conference flow.

In contrast, Video streaming and File transfer service have similar features (MPL, MIAT). Still, using only two features does not seem to be enough to identify their services. (e.g. In Fig. 5 we try to identify flow 3 and 4, yet we do not know which is Steaming or File transfer). To solve this problem, the service is identified through protocol analysis and by adding features as followed.

3.5   MPL, MIAT and Standard Deviation Interpacket Arrival Time (SDIAT)

We now need a new dimension which separates MPEG-DASH [12] from FTP. We choose Standard Deviation Interpacket Arrival Time (SDIAT) as a new dimension based on the following observation: MPEG-DASH [12] is an adaptive bitrate streaming technique [Wikipedia]. MPEG-DASH works by breaking the content into a sequence of small HTTP-based file segments, each segment containing a short interval of playback time of content that is potentially many hours in duration, such as a movie or the live broadcast of a sports event. The content is made available at a variety of different bit rates, i.e., alternative segments encoded at different bit rates covering aligned short intervals of play back time are made available. While the content is being played back by an MPEG-DASH client, the client automatically selects from the alternatives the next segment to download and play back based on current network conditions. The client selects the segment with the highest bit rate possible that can be downloaded in time for play back without causing stalls or re-buffering events in the playback. Thus, an MPEG-DASH client can seamlessly adapt to changing network conditions.

Our reasoning is that since MPEG-DASH adjusts its transmission rate to available bandwidth and buffer space for each client, its traffic may exhibit higher standard deviation of inter-packet arrival time(SDIAT) than FTP. Both MPEG-DASH and FTP use TCP to adapt to network conditions in transport layer. However, MPEG-DASH adds adaptation in application layer, i.e. client program chooses segments of different bit-rate. Based on this reasoning we add SDIAT to differentiate MPEG-DASH from FTP. Figure 7 shows a three dimensional classification where MPL, MIAT and SDIAT serve as coordinates. Note that adding SDIAT as a new coordinate separates MPEG-DASH from FTP. Recall that MPEG-DASH and FTP are inseparable in a two dimensional classification as in Fig. 6.

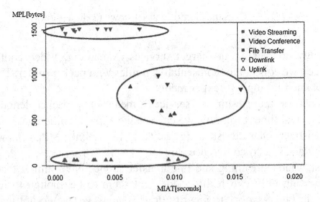

Fig. 6. Classification representative traffics (YouTube, Skype, File transfer service)

Figure 7 shows Video streaming and File transfer service in 3D graph, which have similar properties. FTP services and Video Streaming send almost the same packet length near 1500. However, in downlink SDIAT, video streaming service has long SDIAT than File transfer service as we conjectured in the above.

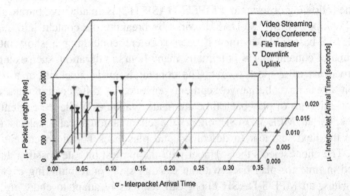

Fig. 7. Classification of File transfer service and DASH video stream

In this sense, we could identify both service contexts that have similar network properties. Thus, we can identify our target contexts (that were using same ports or not registered on IANA, which were so difficult to identify by legacy method) through MPL, MIAT and SDIAT.

Lastly, we applied the above method on our dataset (Fig. 8). Based on video streaming characteristics in the graph, video streaming flows are identified as flow 3 and 4.

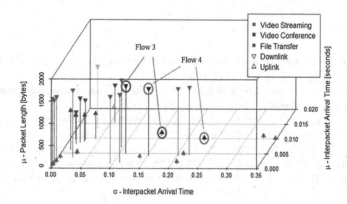

Fig. 8. Classification our dataset in 3D to identify video streaming

4   Conclusion

In this paper, we have introduced identification of service contexts from network contexts as Table 2. Port based classification scheme is used to infer the traffic service, but several ports are already used in same number (e.g. HTTP = 80, HTTPs = 443) so it is hard to classify. The other method, Payload based classification is also difficult to classify, since deep packet inspection method increases system complexity and processing load. In order to derive service contexts from network, we proposed network statistical properties approach. We assumed the traffic flows have statistical properties. To obtain meaningful flow classes, we utilized traffic packet lengths, interpacket arrival time and etc. Also, we introduced our traffic identification method in three stages. First, we demonstrated legacy port based classification. Second, we used traffic packet lengths and interpacket arrival time to identify services (e.g. YouTube and Skype). Finally, to classify analogous properties, we added standard deviation (e.g. DASH

Table 2. Identified services by statistical property method

Methods	Protocol
Legacy (Port based)	None
Statistical property (MPL, MIAT)	Video conference
Statistical property (MPL, MIAT, SDIAT)	Video streaming Video conference File transfer

Video stream and File transfer service). Future works will be carried out to verify new traffics with machine learning methodology and also place a priority on captured traffic to guarantee the network QoS.

Acknowledgement. This research was supported by the Institute for Information & Communications Technology Promotion(IITP) grant funded by the Korean government(MSIP) (No. 2017-0-00325, Block chain based IoT Reliability and Management System Development).

References

1. Perera, C., et al.: Context aware computing for the Internet of Things: a survey. Commun. Surv. Tutor. IEEE **16**(1), 414–454 (2014)
2. Figo, D., et al.: Preprocessing techniques for context recognition from accelerometer data. Pers. Ubiquitous Comput. **14**(7), 645–662 (2010)
3. Eiseman, S.B., et al.: BikeNet: a mobile sensing system for cyclist experience mapping. ACM Trans. Sens. Netw. (TOSN) **6**(1), 6 (2009)
4. Paganelli, F., Ulema, M., Martini, B.: Context-aware service composition and delivery in NGSONs over SDN. Commun. Mag. IEEE **52**(8), 97–105 (2014)
5. Dainotti, A., Pescape, A., Claffy, K.C.: Issues and future directions in traffic classification. Netw. IEEE **26**(1), 35–40 (2012)
6. Maldeniya, S.L., Atukorale, A.S., Vithanage, W.W.: Network data classification using graph partition. In: 2013 19th IEEE International Conference on Networks (ICON). IEEE (2013)
7. Erman, J., Arlitt, M., Mahanti, A.: Traffic classification using clustering algorithms. In: Proceedings of the 2006 SIGCOMM Workshop on Mining Network Data, pp. 281–286. ACM (2006)
8. Szigeti, T., et al.: End-to-End QoS Network Design: Quality of Service for Rich-Media & Cloud Networks, pp. 170–172. Cisco Press (2013)
9. Nguyen, T.T.T., Armitage, G.: A survey of techniques for internet traffic classification using machine learning. Commun. Surv. Tutor. IEEE **10**(4), 56–76 (2008)
10. Roughan, M., Sen, S., Spatscheck, O., Duffield, N.: Class-of-service mapping for QoS a statistical signature based approach to IP traffic classification. In: Proceedings of the 4th ACM/SIGCOMM Conference on Internet Measurement, Taormina, pp. 135–148. ACM (2004)
11. Seufert, M., et al.: A survey on quality of experience of HTTP adaptive streaming. Commun. Surv. Tutor. IEEE **17**(1), 469–492 (2014)
12. MPEG: Dynamic Adaptive Streaming over HTTP (DASH), ISO/IEC 23009 (2012)

A Fast Bit-Level MPLS-Based Source Routing Scheme in Software Defined Networks: SD-{W,L}AN

Ali El Kamel[(✉)], Manel Majdoub, and Habib Youssef

Prince Lab, University of Sousse, Sousse, Tunisia
ali.el.kamel@hotmail.com

Abstract. Today, more concerns are raised to Software Defined Networks (SDN) paradigm since it is a promising concept that offers programmability and scalability by decoupling control and data planes. However, many problems have arisen due to the huge amount of control messages exchanged periodically between the controller and Forwarding Elements (FE) and the limited space of Ternary Content-Addressable Memory TCAM into the switches. The standard Hop-by-Hop forwarding scheme requires that the controller installs at least one flow entry for each flow on each switch. This may lead to a significant bandwidth overhead and unbalanced flow tables. Unfortunately, this scheme seems to be no longer suitable for application neither in SD-LAN nor in SD-WAN.

Many solutions were proposed to avoid network performance degradation. The MPLS-based source routing is one of the most emergent schemes that have attracted attention due to its ability to overwhelm deficiency of the standard Hop-by-hop forwarding scheme. However, the MPLS-based forwarding scheme may induce a significant bandwidth overhead due to the fact that a per-hop routing information is carried using one MPLS label which may lead to a wasteful encoding space.

This paper aims to avoid wasting available encoding space by reserving exactly the required number of bits to encode each routing information. The proposed scheme is based on affecting a wildcard bit-pattern to each switch. A wildcard bit-pattern is a set of bits that is used to decode the routing path by means of the bitwise XOR operation. The routing path is initially appended to one MPLS label after being encoded. The MPLS label is embedded as a header to each packet. Our scheme is suitable for application in multicast scenarios using the same routing path as the unicast scenarios with no additional bandwidth overhead.

Simulation results show that the proposed scheme outperforms parallel solutions in terms of bandwidth overhead, Control traffic overhead and flow tables balancing.

Keywords: SDN · MPLS-based forwarding · Source routing

S. Bouzefrane et al. (Eds.): MSPN 2017, LNCS 10566, pp. 109–121, 2017.
DOI: 10.1007/978-3-319-67807-8_9

1   Introduction

Today, Software Defined Networks (SDN) [10] are considered a promising paradigm since they can help to enhance network performances by decoupling the control plane and the data plane. It consists of defining a central node, called the controller, which manages the overall network through a secure channel. Openflow [1,11] is the most raising protocol developed to ensure secure communication between the controller and programmable Forwarding Elements (FE) such as L3-switches.

The first forwarding scheme, the hop-by-hop forwarding scheme, consists of sending flow entries to flow tables of all switches in a path. Upon receiving a packet, the switch performs a lookup of one matching entry among its flow table and extracts the forwarding port number. Not only this induces a huge amount of control traffic, but it may also affect the overall performance of the network and can create multiple bottlenecks. Thereby, more concerns are given today to reduce control traffic overhead, especially, in large scale networks. Source routing is the most promising solution proposed in this way.

Source routing consists of embedding routing information in an extra header such as VLAN Id tags and MPLS labels and attaching it to the packet. Certainly, this may lead to a significant bandwidth overhead if the header space is not well managed. Compared to using the VLAN ID tag of 12 bits length, MPLS-based forwarding scheme is suitable for application both in SD-LAN and SD-WAN since the size of one label (32 bits) may be used to encode any port number.

This paper deals with MPLS-based source routing. It aims to achieve better exploitation of available bits of appended headers used to carry routing paths. Our scheme is able to reduce the control traffic overhead since the controller will only communicate with selective switches denoted the contact switches. Moreover, our scheme is suitable for multicast flows and may be used to transmit multicast packets with the same bandwidth overhead as achieved in unicast scenario.

This paper is structured as follows. Firstly, we discuss some related work. Especially, we focus on MPLS-based forwarding schemes. Secondly, we formulate an analytic model of our scheme and we describe it in detail. Then, we present the multicast scenario. Experimental results are given in Sect. 4. Finally, a conclusion resumes our contribution and points out future work.

2   Related Work

Many schemes were developed to deal with the problem of MPLS-based source routing in large scale networks. As an example, Google proposes the B4 [4] architecture which consists of deploying a private infrastructure to connect all their datacenters in the world. Due to the success of B4, many network-service providers focus on emerging the programmability concept to large scale networks. Therefore, it was proved that deploying SD-WAN is feasible, but it needs hard work.

Indeed, many limitations postpone the emergency of SD-WAN. The most important one is the limited space of Ternary Content-Addressable Memories (TCAM). Cohen et al. in [5] proclaim that flow entry placement schemes is an optimization problem that may be solved by linear programming. Moreover, they declare that the load of flow table is unbalanced among the switches in the network, and suggest to efficiently use the TCAM resources on each switch by decomposing a large flow table into small pieces and distributing these small flow tables across the network, while preserving the overall SDN policy semantics [6]. Although flow entries are reduced it was proved that these schemes may lead to an unwanted packet traveling inevitably, which may raise security problems. Moreover, decomposing the flow table is a hard problem [7]. To avoid hop-by-hop configuration, source routing was proposed. It consists of embedding the routing path once at the entry node into a header space, such as MPLS labels or VLAN ID tags, and appending the header to packets. However, more attention should be given to these headers since they may cause bandwidth overhead.

The problem of optimizing the bandwidth overhead becomes a very interesting challenge. In [8], a hierarchical Segment routing (H-SR) framework is proposed. It aims, by clustering a path routing for Carrier Ethernet networks into segment routing or routing sub-paths, to improve scalability of segment routed networks based on a hierarchical segment routing framework [9]. Indeed, the network is divided into clusters and specific contact switches are selected within every cluster. The contact node is an intermediate node which loads the complete routing path of a section into an MPLS label. However, selection of contact switches depends largely on the network topology and the resulting bandwidth overhead. Therefore, JumpFlow [2] is proposed as a forwarding scheme that uses the VLAN identifier (VID) field in the packet header to carry routing information. Although, JumpFlow has eliminated the bandwidth overhead, it has risen many drawbacks that make it unsuitable deployment in SD-WAN. Indeed, it assumes that the network consists of similar n-port switches (n = 8 or 16 ports) and all switches are treated similarly. However, switches in large scale networks may be heterogenous and the number of ports may reach 128, which requires over 7 bits to be encoded. Therefore, JumpFlow is no longer suitable for deployment in SD-WAN.

In [3], authors propose an efficient MPLS-based forwarding scheme called Arbitrary Jump Source Routing (AJSR) which aims to achieve a trade-off between the control traffic overhead and the bandwidth overhead by dividing the complete routing path of a particular flow into arbitrary length sections and distributing these sections at different switches along the flow's routing path. Since MPLS labels are used, AJSR can be deployed in SD-WAN. However, it seems to be not cost-effective since it can induce a significant bandwidth overhead due to carrying each per-hop forwarding information into one MPLS Label.

3   Proposed Mechanism

In this section, our scheme is described anxiously. Firstly, we formulate an analytic model of the problem and we criticise it by focusing on its limits. Secondly, we drive an analytic model of our scheme and we describe the contribution in detail. Finally, we provide an example on how to use our scheme in multicast scenarios.

3.1 Problem Formulation

Generally, a network is modeled as a directed graph G(S, L) where S and L represent the set of switches and the set of links, respectively. A routing path is a vector $P = (s_1, s_2, ..., s_N) \subseteq S^N$ between the source and the destination, where s_j ($1 \leq$ j $\leq$ N) is the jth switch of the routing path and N is the length of the path.

Let n_j ($1 \leq$ j $\leq$ N) be the number of ports on switch s_j. To encode any port, $\lceil \log_2(n_j) \rceil$ bits are required. As an example, 2 bits are enough to encode ports from a 4-port switch, 3 bits for a 8-port switch, k bits for a 2^k-port switch and so on.

Generally, given a path P, crossed switches may be heterogenous. Therefore, using the same number of bits to encode any port on any switch, like in jumpFlow, seems to be unsuitable for application especially in large scale networks. Routing path should be encoded basing on a per-hop required number of bits and not a common required number of bits.

Let $I_P = (i_1, \cdots, i_N)$ be the set of crossed ports along the path P. Let $n = \max\limits_{i_j}(\lceil \log_2(i_j) \rceil)$. If $n \leq 12$, JumpFlow scheme may be used. In this case, $\lceil \frac{Nn}{12} \rceil$ contact switches are required to keep packet forwarding. Especially, Jumpflow acts as the hop-by-hop forwarding scheme when $n = 12$. If the path P consists of 8-port (16-port, respectively) switches, no more than 4 hops (3 hops respectively) may be appended to the VID tag.

Using AJSR scheme, each i_j is carried using one MPLS label. Therefore, $N \times 32$ bits are required to forward one packet from the source to the destination. If a is the number of packets to be sent, the total communication overhead reaches $aN \times 32$ bits which may be extravagant as the path P goes more and more large.

Let $c_j = 1 - \frac{\lceil \log_2(i_j) \rceil}{n}$ be the encoding penalty of i_j. The encoding penalty expresses the unused number of bits resulting from encoding i_j using n bits. More the forwarding port number in a switch is close to 2^n, more the encoding penalty goes down and reciprocally. We formulate C_S as the penalty of encoding I_P according to a given scheme S as follows:

$$C_S = \sum_{i_j \in I_P} c_j = N - \frac{\sum\limits_{i_j \in I_P} \lceil \log_2(i_j) \rceil}{n} \tag{1}$$

Despite Jumpflow achieves reduced encoding penalty compared to AJSR, it is unsuitable for large scale networks due to the limited space of the VLAN ID tag. Moreover, using MPLS Label to encode routing information brings a lot of benefits. Firstly, an MPLS label is enough to encode any port in any switch. Secondly, the controller and the switch should perform pop, push and read actions on any MPLS label.

Unfortunately, significant bandwidth overhead may result in appending multiple MPLS labels to packets in order to carry routing information. Nevertheless, the bandwidth overhead can be significantly reduced by properly encoding forwarding ports with exactly the required number of bits. As an example, if the packet crosses the ports 2, 14 and 50 during forwarding, the routing information requires only $2 + 4 + 6 = 12$ bits to be forwarded, however, $3 * 32 = 96$ bits are used if we consider the MPLS-based forwarding scheme.

Obviously, the main shortcut of above schemes is the use of the same number of bits to encode any port from any switch. This leads to wasted bits during encoding process. To deal with this problem, the encoding number of bits should be chosen according to the number of ports n_j in a switch s_j. As an example, for a port number 6 in a 32-port switch, we use only 5 bits ($\log_2(32)$) for encoding. Therefore, the encoding penalty is formulated as follows:

$$C_S = \sum_{i_j \in I_P} c_j = N - \sum_{i_j \in I_P} \frac{\lceil \log_2(i_j) \rceil}{\lceil \log_2(n_j) \rceil} \tag{2}$$

3.2   Proposed Scheme

In this section, we describe our scheme. It is inspired both from Jumpflow and MPLS-based forwarding and aims to maximize the use of available bits on MPLS labels by reducing the encoding penalty as depicted in Eq. 2.

The proposed scheme consists of using one MPLS label to transmit routing path. Therefore, the routing path is divided into several sections where the number of bits used to transmit routing path in each section should not exceed the size of one MPLS label (32 bits). At the entry of each section, the first switch is a contact switch. A contact switch is a switch which loads the routing path for a flow in a section.

The controller affects a wildcard bit-pattern for each crossed switch in a section. The bit pattern is randomly created based on the number of ports belonging to the switch. Take Fig. 1 as an example, the first switch S_1 is a 4-port switch and the last switch is a 32-port switch. Accordingly, the controller affects the bit-pattern $w_1 = 10$ to S_1, since 2 bits are enough to express all ports, and $w_5 = 11001$ to S_5, since 5 bits are sufficient to represent all ports. Typically, the length of the w_i of the switch S_i is equal to $\lceil \log_2(k_i) \rceil$ where k_i represents the total number of ports in the switch S_i.

When a flow reaches an ingress switch, the controller establishes an end-to-end path that connects the source to the destination by using a routing protocol. The controller performs a logical bitwise exclusive OR operation between each port in the resulting path and the wildcard bit-pattern of associated switch. Resulting values are joined to form an encoded routing path. The controller communicates the encoded routing path toward the contact switch as well as the set of bit-patterns toward each involved switch.

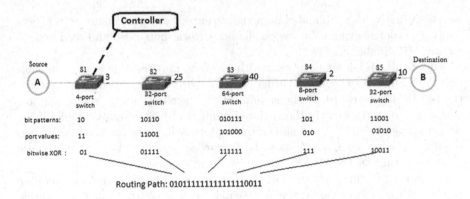

Fig. 1. Encoding routing path procedure

Extraction of separate routing information at each switch is straightforward (Fig. 2). Upon receiving a packet, each switch performs the logical bitwise exclusive OR operation between its wildcard bit-pattern and most significant n bits from the routing path, where n defines the length of the wildcard bit-pattern. The obtained value represents the local forwarding port to be used by the switch. Before sending the packet to the next hop, the switch performs a logical left-shifting by n bits.

3.3 Routing Path Clustering

To avoid the bandwidth overhead induced by using multiple MPLS labels to carry large routing path, we divide the routing path into sections so that one MPLS label space is enough to carry the routing path of one section. At the entry of a section, the first switch is elected as the contact switch. The controller will only perform append or update actions on routing path at the contact switch. Finally, we suggest the Algorithm 1 to be used by the controller to divide the routing path.

3.4 Encoding Routing Information Procedure

Given a path $P = (s_1, \cdots, s_L)$ between a source and a destination, where s_j is the jth switch and L is the length of the path. Let n_j be the number of ports in the switch s_j. Therefore, $\lceil \log_2(n_j) \rceil$ bits are required to encode all ports of the switch s_j. For each switch s_j, the controller creates a wildcard bit pattern w_j which is conveyed to s_j. Obviously, The controller can create over $2^{\lceil \log_2(n) \rceil}$ possible bit-patterns for a n-port switch.

Let $W_P = (w_1, \cdots, w_L)$ be the set of wildcard bit-patterns associated to switches belonging to path P. Let also $I_P = (i_1, \cdots, i_L)$ be the set of crossed ports along the path P. For each switch s_j, the controller computes the encoding routing information $r_j = w_j \oplus i_j$. Finally, all the encoding routing information

---

Algorithm 1. RoutingPathDiv

Require: $I_P = (i_1, \cdots, i_N)$
Ensure: $Sec = (S_1, \cdots, S_K)$

$\{\forall i, S_i$ are subsets from I_P. $\bigcup_{i=1}^{K} S_i = I_P$ and $\bigcap_{i=1}^{K} S_i = \emptyset\}$

$Sec \leftarrow \emptyset$
while $I_P \neq \emptyset$ **do**
$\quad S_k \leftarrow \emptyset$
$\quad$**for all** $i_j \in I_P$ **do**
$\quad\quad$**if** $|S_k| + |i_j| \leq 32$ **then**
$\quad\quad\quad S_k \leftarrow S_k \cup i_j$
$\quad\quad$**end if**
$\quad$**end for**
$\quad Sec \leftarrow Sec + \{S_k\}$
$\quad I_P \leftarrow I_P \backslash \{S_k\}$
$\quad$incr(k)
end while
return Sec

---

r_j are bring together to create the encoding routing path R_P. The controller conveys R_P to the contact switch which append it into an MPLS Label.

3.5 Decoding Routing Information Procedure

Upon receiving a packet, each switch s_j performs a logical bitwise exclusive OR operation between its wildcard bit-pattern w_j and n most significant bits of the routing path n-MSB, where n is the length of w_j. The switch can retrieve the port number i_j to be used to forward the packet as follows: $i_j = w_j \oplus n$-MSB. Before sending the packet to the next hop, the switch performs a left shifting by n bits on the routing path.

3.6 Multicast Scenario

In previous sections, we mainly consider unicast flows. In this section, we will prove that our scheme may be adopted for multicast flows. Generally, bandwidth overhead in multicast forwarding is greater than one's in unicast situation, since more routing information should be carried to allow multicast actions: (1) duplicating the multicast packet, and (2) forwarding packets via the corresponding ports.

In our scheme, no more routing information is appended to the routing path. Indeed, the controller should install a number of wildcard bit patterns as needed to keep packet forwarding.

Take Fig. 3 as an example. The multicast group consists of a sender S and 3 receivers A, B and C, respectively. S starts a multicast flow and sends multicast packets toward receivers through paths P_A, P_B and P_C of A, B and C, respectively. Assume that S sends a multicast packet through the route

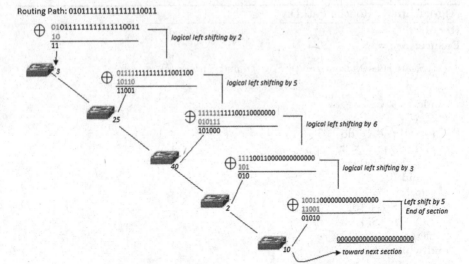

Fig. 2. Decoding routing path procedure

$R1(S_1 \rightarrow S_2 \rightarrow S_3)$ to switch S_3. At switch S_3, the packet is duplicated then copies are sent via R21 and R22 to S_4 and S_8, respectively. At switch S_{10}, the packet is duplicated another time and copies are sent via routes $R31(S_{10} \rightarrow S_{11} \rightarrow S_{11})$ and $R32(S_{10} \rightarrow S_{13} \rightarrow S_{14})$. Let f_3^1 and f_3^2 be port numbers used to forward multicast packet through $R21(S_3 \rightarrow S_4 \rightarrow S_5 \rightarrow S_6 \rightarrow S_7)$ and R22, respectively. To allow packet forwarding via multiple ports without appending more routing information, the controller selects a wildcard bit-pattern w_3^1 to be installed into S_3. Therefore, it encodes the port f_3^1 as follows: $r_3 = f_3^1 \oplus w_3^1$. The controller performs a bitwise XOR operation on r_3 and f_3^2 to obtain a new wildcard bit-pattern: $w_3^2 = r_3 \oplus f_3^2$. Finally, the controller conveys both bit-patterns w_3^1 and w_3^2 to switch S_3. The same procedure will be run at switch S_{10}.

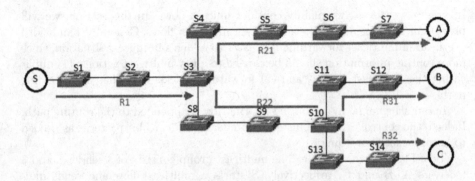

Fig. 3. Multicast scenario

The decoding procedure is straightforward. Let's denote w_{10}^1, w_{10}^2 and r_{10} the Master bit-pattern, the Slave bit-pattern and the encoded routing information at switch S_{10}, respectively. The port number used to forward multicast packet through R31 is computed as follows: $f_{10}^1 = w_{10}^1 \oplus r_{10}$. The port number used to forward multicast packet through R32 is computed as follows: $f_{10}^2 = w_{10}^2 \oplus r_{10}$.

4   Experiment and Results

In this section, we describe simulation results. We evaluate our scheme and the MPLS-based forwarding scheme. We used the Java Beacon Controller version 1.0.4, the Openflow1.0.3 protocol and the Mininet2.2.0 framework to define the controller, ensure control messages exchanges and installing experiment topology, respectively. The topology is described in Fig. 4. The path is defined by the greatest number of crossed hops to simulate large scale networks. We assume that all the nodes are 64-port switches. At each switch, the forwarding port is picked randomly from the interval [0, 63]. The simulation time is divided into 6 slots. At the source, we generate some 1 Mbps-CBR flows that should cross the path in red color. The rate of generating flows is incrementally picked from the set [10, 100, 200, 500, 700, 1000] in each slot. Since the number of transmitted packets has no impact, we limited a flow to 20 packets/flow. We run our simulation 30 times.

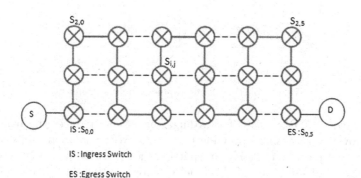

Fig. 4. Experimental topology (Color figure online)

4.1   Results Analysis

Figure 5 shows the total bandwidth overhead of MPLS-based forwarding scheme and our scheme as the flow arrival rate changes. The bandwidth overhead refers to the total number of bits used to forward a packet from the source to the destination. The bandwidth overhead of MPLS-based forwarding scheme increases exponentially as the flow arrival rate increases. However, it increases linearly for our scheme.

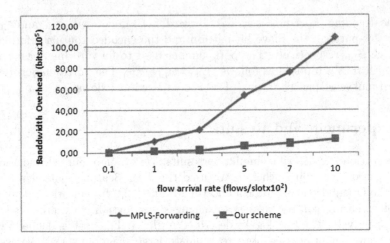

Fig. 5. Bandwidth overhead for different flow arrival rates

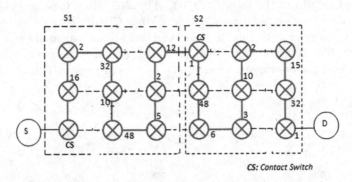

CS: Contact Switch

Fig. 6. Splitting of the topology into sections

Compared to MPLS-based forwarding, our scheme reduces the bandwidth overhead over 88,42% since available bits in the MPLS label are fully used to carry routing information. Moreover, splitting the network topology into two sections (Fig. 6) and using one MPLS label to carry routing path is cost-effective and helps to overwhelm the problem of encapsulating multiple MPLS labels. Indeed, MPLS-based forwarding scheme has used $17 \times 20 = 340$ MPLS labels for each flow (over 340×32 bits $= 10880$ bits) while less than $2 \times (20 \times 32) = 1280$ bits are used for each flow in our scheme. As shown in Fig. 7, the MPLS-based forwarding scheme used the minimum number of control messages. Indeed, only the ingress node communicates with the controller. The controller will install all required flow entries in the ingress switch. The most number of control messages is associated with the traditional hop-by-hop scheme since each switch should receive at least one flow entry to keep packet forwarding. Our scheme outperforms clearly the traditional scheme since control messages are sent only to contact switches. More the number of sections is reduced, more our scheme performance can be close to MPLS-based forwarding performance.

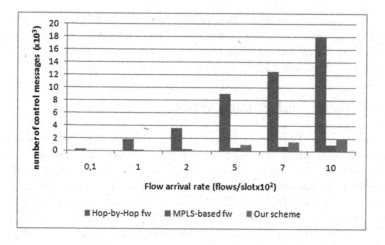

Fig. 7. Number of control messages

Figure 8 presents an evaluation of flow tables balancing performance. We used the Absolute Error function (AE) (Eq. 3) to compute the balancing of flow tables between the Hop-by-Hop forwarding scheme, the MPLS-based forwarding scheme, and our scheme. Unfortunately, MPLS-based forwarding scheme consumes a lot of flow entries which may lead to unbalanced usage of flow tables. Our scheme outperforms other schemes since the network is split into sections which may limits the number of flow entries per each contact switch.

$$AE(X) = \sum_{i \in [1..N]} |X_i - \bar{X}| \qquad (3)$$

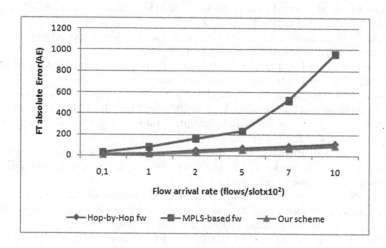

Fig. 8. Flow tables balancing

where N, X_i and $\bar{X}$ are the number of switches, the number of flow entries in switch s_i and the average of all X_i, respectively. In conclusion, our scheme is able to achieve a trade-off between bandwidth overhead and flow tables balancing, compared to MPLS-based forwarding and Hop-by-Hop forwarding.

5   Conclusion and Future Work

In this paper, an MPLS-based source routing scheme is proposed. It aims to minimize the bandwidth overhead by reducing the encoding penalty resulting from encoding the routing path. Our scheme encodes each routing information exactly with the required number of bits. Our scheme is suitable for application both on SD-LAN and SD-WAN. For scalability purposes, the network is divided into several sections. Only one MPLS label is required in each section.

To allow extraction of the per-hop forwarding port, a wildcard bit-pattern is defined on each switch. Performing a bitwise XOR operation between the bit-pattern and the encoded routing information helps to retrieve the port number to be used locally to send the packet.

As shown in results, our scheme outperforms parallel solutions such as MPLS-based forwarding in terms of flow rejection rate and bandwidth overhead. In future Work, more simulations need to be performed to prove efficiency of our scheme. More concern is to be addressed to multicast scenario and to fault tolerance.

References

1. Open Networking Foundation: The OpenFlow Switch Specification, Version 1.4.0, October 2013. https://www.opennetworking.org/images/stories/downloads/sdn-resources/onf-specifications/openflow/openflow-spec-v1.4.0.pdf
2. Zehua, G., et al.: JumpFlow: Reducing flow table usage in software defined networks. Comput. Netw. **92**, 300–315 (2015)
3. Dong, X., Guo, Z., et al.: AJSR: an efficient multiple jumps forwarding scheme in software-defined WAN. IEEE Access **5**, 3139–3148 (2017)
4. Jain, S., et al.: B4: experience with a globally-deployed software defined WAN. ACM SIGCOMM Comput. Commun. Rev. **43**(4), 3–14 (2013)
5. Cohen, R., Lewin-Eytan, L., Naor, J.S., et al.: On the effect of forwarding table size on SDN network utilization. In: INFOCOM IEEE, pp. 1734–1742 (2014)
6. Kanizo, Y., Hay, D., Palette, K.I.: Distributing tables in software- defined networks. In: Proceedings of IEEE INFOCOM, pp. 545–549 (2013)
7. Kang, N., Liu, Z., Rexford, J., et al.: Optimizing the one big switch abstraction in software-defined networks. In: ACM Conference on Emerging Networking Experiments and Technologies, pp. 3–24 (2013)
8. Bidkar, S., Gumaste, A., Somani, A.: A scalable framework for segment routing in service provider networks: the omnipresent ethernet approach. In: High Performance Switching and Routing (HPSR), pp. 76–83 (2014)
9. Bidkar, S., et al.: Field trial of a software defined network (SDN) using carrier ethernet and segment routing in a tier-1 provider. In: Global Communications Conference (GLOBECOM) (2014)

10. Kreutz, D., Ramos, F.M.V., Esteves Verissimo, P., et al.: Software-dened networking: a comprehensive survey. Proc. IEEE **03**, 10–13 (2014)
11. McKeown, N., et al.: OpenFlow: enabling innovation in campus networks. ACM SIGCOMM CCR **38**(2), 69–74 (2008)

Requirements and Complexity Analysis of Cross-Layer Design Optimization for Adaptive Inter-vehicle DSRC

Keyvan Ansari[1(✉)], Hannaneh Sadat Naghavi[2], Yu-Chu Tian[2], and Yanming Feng[2]

[1] The University of the Sunshine Coast, Sippy Downs, Australia
kansari@usc.edu.au
[2] Queensland University of Technology, Brisbane, Australia
{h.naghavi,y.tian,y.feng}@qut.edu.au

Abstract. Accurate implementation of communications protocol stacks is unavoidable, however the traditional protocol stack designed for Dedicated Short Range Communications (DSRC) does not efficiently support safety applications. DSRC protocol stack must satisfy some stringent performance requirements by safety applications in challenging scenarios such as heavy road traffic. Several communications solutions, and industry standards including the recently published SAE-J2945.1 standard, are proposed for vehicular safety systems, but by what means such systems can address the stringent requirements of safety applications and the scalability issue in their actual deployment is still an open question. With the current spectrum allocations for vehicular DSRC and the data traffic generated by cooperative applications, the radio channels could be easily saturated in the absence of effective control algorithms, resulting in unstable inter-vehicle communications and eventually failure of the system. The results of several simulation studies are presented in this paper to evaluate the DSRC channel and understand the parameters affecting its state.

This paper proposes a cross-layer designed controller for inter-vehicle safety messaging to address the channel congestion problem of vehicular networks. The proposed controller enjoys a design supporting direct and in-direct interfacing between layers with awareness control aiming at serving the stringent requirements of DSRC safety applications. The message dissemination controller receives feedback such as channel utilization, outdated packets and vehicle density information from cross-layer sources to control the load on the radio channels by adjusting the transmit power and message intervals. The necessity of instant adjustments requires the mechanism to be utilized with a decentralized yet cooperative coordination. The aim of this study is to validate the cross-layer design for DSRC and is fundamentally different to that of the message scheduling and congestion control algorithm presented as a part of the SAE-J2945.1 standard. The complexity verification and results of analysis show the proposed controller is an efficient and fair design.

Keywords: Cross-layer design · DSRC · Stack optimization · Vehicular networks

© Springer International Publishing AG 2017
S. Bouzefrane et al. (Eds.): MSPN 2017, LNCS 10566, pp. 122–137, 2017.
DOI: 10.1007/978-3-319-67807-8_10

1 Introduction

Intelligent Transportation Systems (ITS) are emerging in practice based on wireless communications, Global Navigation Satellite Systems (GNSS), the Internet, and sensor networks. The principal idea behind the development of ITS is to share and deliver useful information to all kinds of motorists, such as emergency vehicles, public and service vehicles, and civilian drivers, as well as cyclists and even pedestrians. The goal is to make driving safer, to facilitate medical assistance and law enforcement, to shorten driving time, and to contribute to a safer and greener environment. Several key issues are identified in enabling a successful deployment of ITS, including ITS architecture development, network support, communications-based technologies and application development [1]. Among these, communications-based issues arisen from the stringent requirements of safety applications and network scalability, such as channel congestion, play a significant role in holding the large-scale deployment of ITS back. As such, Cooperative ITS (C-ITS) with time-critical requirements utilize Vehicular Ad-hoc Networks (VANETs) that provide real-time wireless access with periodic channel traffic.

The performance of VANETs suffers from inefficient channel utilization, time-varying delays, and packet dropouts, due to the current wireless transmission mechanisms. These mechanisms are designed upon the layered architecture of the Dedicated Short Range Communications (DSRC) protocol stack. Under- and over-utilization of Vehicle-to-Vehicle (V2V) communications channels, specifically the Control Channel (CCH), must be avoided to enable important active safety applications to function efficiently in Cooperative Awareness Messaging (CAM) environments. The shared radio channels, especially the CCH, may possibly be saturated as more cooperative safety applications are adopted with the DSRC technology and periodic CAM become widely deployed, even though Carrier Sense Multiple Access with Collision Avoidance (CSMA/CA) is employed by IEEE 802.11p. It is understood from CSMA/CA-based wireless local area networks, such as Wi-Fi, that the communications performance of such networks drops significantly once the shared channel becomes saturated and its maximum capacity is exceeded [2]. To ensure stable system operations: (1) the channel load must not exceed a maximum threshold, and (2) the vehicular connectivity requirements imposed by safety applications must be guaranteed. Topology control protocols for sensor and wireless ad-hoc networks have been proposed to ensure network-wide connectivity through the dynamic adaptation of each node's transmission parameters [3], however, establishing stable vehicular networks is strongly challenged by the dynamic nature of vehicular networks and their harsh radio propagation environment.

VANETs rather require establishing and maintaining inter-vehicle communications links within each vehicle's local environment (based on the coverage requirements of safety applications adopted), to support cooperative safety applications and provide upper-layer protocols with accurate and updated data. The state information exchanged among vehicles can be modelled at the Application layer (APP) as neighboring context information for the use of awareness control protocols to ensure robust communications in local neighborhoods. This is achieved by dynamically adapting communications transmission parameters based on both the traffic conditions of the surrounding environment and the requirements of the safety applications being executed. However, the layered architecture of the DSRC protocol stack prevents information from being directly exchanged between nonadjacent layers, resulting in the inability of the protocol stack to provide rapid responses to any changes in the network state and/or channel condition [4].

The concept of Cross-Layer Design (CLD) has recently received much favorable empirical attention as an alternative solution to the layered network architecture. Several studies such as [5–9], although not targeting VANETs, are conducted to demonstrate the suitability of the CLD approach for improving the efficiency of cooperative channel utilization. The channel contention and packet delay requirements can be addressed by the design methodologies proposed jointly with the CLD technique [10–12]. DSRC can enjoy the benefits of a CLD approach to offer an improved performance in large-scale deployments. Although the existing research has rarely considered a CLD for DSRC, the Cross-Layer Designed DSRC (CLD-DSRC) has the potential to improve network congestion conditions and to promote the efficiency of channel utilization in large-scale VANETs. To this end, however, there is a lack of discussion on and understanding about how to better support vehicular DSRC with the CLD method. Various control measures, including transmit power, data rate, message rate, packet length and sensitivity control, can be used in combination to response to different stimuli such as a traffic jam or a highly demanding safety application requiring 10 Hz CAM to cover a wide area. Among them, the first three measures are strongly correlated to the success of cooperative safety applications in harsh fading environments. This paper provides an open discussion on how communications-based vehicular safety systems can be implemented using the CLD-DSRC methodology.

The rest of this paper is organized as follows. The results of an empirical study of DSRC channel conditions in various traffic scenarios are reported in Sect. 2. Section 3 provides an overview of the existing approaches in controlling the awareness and congestion in DSRC-based systems. Section 4 discusses the requirements of C-ITS safety mission applications, which are used along with the results represented in Sect. 2 to identify the most vital metrics affecting the DSRC channel condition. Also, a CLD for DSRC is proposed in Sect. 4 to efficiently address the awareness and congestion problems of VANETs. Section 5 represents complexity evaluation and performance verification of the proposed CLD-DSRC. Finally, this study is concluded in Sect. 6.

2   Empirical Study of V2V DSRC Performance

The necessity for optimal utilization of the DSRC medium, that is the CCH must be kept as accessible as possible to every user, is a serious consideration as: (1) a sender does not always know what type of data is important to receivers and hence the medium must be available to others to share essential data as well; (2) a sender does not know what data has been received by neighboring receivers and hence the medium must be available for retransmissions in case of errors; (3) the V2V radio frequency channel varies constantly and hence is unpredictable, so the noise level must be minimized. Using simulation results, this section analyzes the conditions of the

DSRC CCH to establish a relation between the control measures available and the channel conditions.

The simulation framework is set up in NS-2 and consists of two main blocks: (1) traffic scenarios and network topologies, and (2) simulation models for a fading radio propagation channel and adaptable MAC and PHY modules according to the IEEE 802.11p standard. For the NS-2 network settings, *Mac802_11Ext* and *WirelessPhyExt* modules of the NS-2 library are used to set the 802.11p parameters, and PBC is the agent module used to represent traffic sources. PBC agent is a broadcast frame generator that can define message generation frequency, the frame data modulation scheme and MAC frame payload size. Considering the literature, the Nakagami Propagation model is selected for the simulation of DSRC network. Table 1 provides the details of the configuration parameters used in the simulation studies.

Table 1. Simulation parameters

Parameter	Value
Noise floor	−99 dBm
Channel Clear Assessment (CCA) threshold	−95 dBm
CWmin	7
CWmax	1023
Data rate	6 Mbps
RF fading model	Nakagami, m = 1
Safety message size	378 Byte
Min/Max message exchange rate	1 Hz/10 Hz
Length of CBR channel monitoring period	1 s
Tx Range	1000 m

2.1 DSRC Channel Conditions in Various Traffic Scenarios

Channel Busy Ratio (CBR) was measured to analyze the DSRC channel condition in three different traffic scenarios. Scenario 1 considers a circular road with a radius of 954.93 m and a length of 6 km within which each node broadcasts safety messages of 378 bytes length at 10 Hz and a transmission power covering a 1 km range. Scenario 2 studies a topology configured as an intersection with 4 km of single lane for each road section leading to the intersection. Scenario 3 studies a bidirectional highway with 3 lanes of 4 km length each in each direction.

Figure 1 shows the changes in the channel congestion condition for topologically different scenarios with the number of vehicles travelling on the road as the variable. The channel congestion condition is measured against the CBR metric. Not surprisingly, as the density of vehicles in-range of one another increases the incremental trend of the CBR becomes more significant.

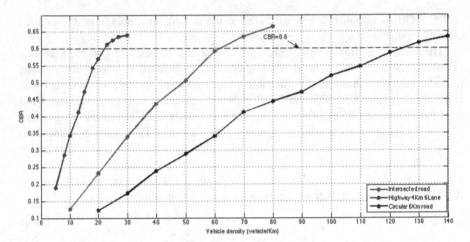

Fig. 1. DSRC channel condition

Previous studies show that the optimal value for the CBR, resulting in the maximum throughput, is between 60% and 70% [13–15]. Maintaining a relatively high CBR is suggested because (1) the dominant user of the shared channel is the Basic Safety Message (BSM), and (2) knowing when BSMs are needed by neighboring vehicles is inherently difficult for any host vehicle due to the unreliable nature of the DSRC wireless channel. Therefore, the strategies suggesting a significant portion of the channel capacity to be kept unused are harmful to safety operations of the system. The CBR value of 0.6 is considered as the target throughout this study. This means, the CBR must be kept below 60% to continuously maintain a non-congested channel. This condition places stringent requirements on the number of vehicles that can be within the transmission range of any host vehicle, depending on the types of the road and traffic scenarios. Figure 1 testifies that the combination of road types and traffic scenarios affects the channel condition differently based on the characteristics it possesses.

2.2   Performance of DSRC in Different Channel Congestion Conditions

To evaluate the channel congestion conditions, a highway scenario with different vehicle densities (imposing different CBRs) has been considered to firstly study the CBR metric for each density. Using the values derived for the CBR, the number of packets successfully received at different distances from the reference sender is calculated and shown in Fig. 2. The figure represents the average reliability of the DSRC wireless channel in different channel congestion scenarios for various separation distances between a pair of moving vehicles.

Since each safety application has a different requirement for its transmission range and a minimum CAM rate, and the reliability of the DSRC wireless channel is a factor of both the communications range and the CBR, this paper argues that the awareness

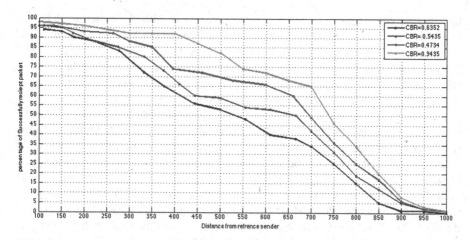

Fig. 2. DSRC performance in different channel conditions

control mechanisms must account for the reliability rate of the communications links. This means, if an application necessitates transmitting a message to a remote location and/or in a more crowded network, the message should be sent more frequently than if a closer area in a less busy network is the transmission target [16].

Figures 1 and 2 collectively represent that V2V DSRC reliability greatly depends on the characteristics of both the traveling road and the present traffic. The results by Ansari et al. [16] also disclose that the (relative) speed of the communicating nodes has a direct impact on the reliability of the DSRC channel, regardless of the positions of vehicles in relation to each other.

3   Existing Approaches to DSRC Congestion Control

The focus of this context is on awareness-based congestion-control techniques with application-driven adaptation of transmit power, CAM frequency and channel access contention window size. Various approaches and performance evaluations have been contributed to control the load on radio channels, however the requirements of the safety applications are seldom considered in the design policies proposed to guarantee the communications capacity of each vehicle within its local neighborhood. This section reviews different approaches targeting the issues of channel congestion control and awareness control.

The CCH is the most important channel of the DSRC band, due to being the only candidate to support safety missions, so the efficient use of this channel is critical. 200 µs or less is the recommended transmission time on the CCH. So, as per the recommendations of the US Federal Communications Commission (FCC), a service channel must be used for messages that take longer than 200 µs to transmit [17]. Hence, collisions in preamble transmissions cause a high waste of resources due to tight timing constraints. This is even more susceptible with the presence of hidden terminals. This effect considerably reduces the performance of VANETs. So, the MAC algorithms that determine which Mobile Station (MS) has the right to utilize the shared communications channel are vitally important for achieving predictable delays. In this regard, MAC schemes schedule all channel access aiming to keep interference incidents as low as possible at all transmission periods.

Standard multi-access schemes such as Time Division Multiple Access (TDMA), Frequency Division Multiple Access (FDMA), and Code Division Multiple Access (CDMA) are ineffective as DSRC MAC protocols, due to the dynamic nature of VANETs [17]. The reason for their inefficiency is that centrally coordinated time-slots, channels, or codes must be dynamically allocated to DSRC stations, which is extremely difficult to achieve in networks with highly mobile nodes [18]. Likewise, the Point Coordination Function (PCF) MAC protocol, which is the contention-free protocol of the IEEE 802.11 standard, requires a central node to access the medium for scheduling the transmission of stations and therefore is inapplicable to VANETs [17]. Hence, contention-based Wireless Random Access (WRA) mechanisms are often used by modern wireless access network protocols [19]. However, although the Distributed Coordination Function (DCF) employing Carrier Sense Multiple Access with Collision Avoidance (CSMA/CA) is the fundamental MAC technique of IEEE 802.11p, it is argued in the literature, such as [20, 21], that the 802.11p MAC method does not guarantee real-time communications because channel access is not guaranteed before a finite deadline. Accordingly, several different mechanisms have been proposed to increase the overall performance of real-time data transmission/reception, such as Self-organizing TDMA (STDMA). STDMA [20], a decentralized MAC scheme, aims to guarantee an efficient, reliable and timely delivery of safety critical messages by utilizing a GNSS for synchronization and time-slot sharing purposes. A comprehensive survey classifying and analyzing 34 different MAC layer protocols proposed for wireless ad-hoc networks within industry standards and/or research proposals is given in [22]. Furthermore, Booysen et al. [23] provide a summary of recently proposed MAC protocols for VANETs including STDMA. However, in the design of the CLD-DSRC, this paper grants the fundamental technique of CSMA/CA to be the sole governing technique of the IEEE 802.11p MAC sub-layer.

CSMA/CA utilizes a random back-off time following an unsuccessful medium access. The back-off mechanism employs a time counter to compute and to decrease the back-off interval based on a Contention Window (CW) – CW is the window size. Given that the channel is sensed idle, the counter is decremented. The counter, however, is stopped as soon as a transmission is sensed on the channel, and is reactivated when the channel becomes idle again for a period more than the DCF Inter-Frame Space (DIFS). The node starts to transmit packets as soon as the back-off time counter reaches zero. The initial back-off time for each transmission is uniformly chosen in the interval $[0, CW-1]$, where $CW \in [CWmin, CWmax]$. The back-off stage j, $j \in \mathbb{N}$, is increased after each unsuccessful transmission up to a maximum value. The value of CW is doubled in each step, to the maximum of CWmax, as j is increased.

3.1 Channel Congestion Control

Using field measurements and simulation studies, it is reported that the communications performance of DSRC degrades significantly in high vehicle density environments [24]. For example, the packet error rate in a VANET with 360 nodes with the transmission rate of 10 safety messages per second was about 71.1% [25]. The ability of vehicles to perform critical safety-of-live missions in such environments with high packet error rate levels is significantly impaired. One key factor, in addition to densely overlapped transmission areas and excessive CAM on the CCH, that contributes to the severe local throughput degradation when traffic density increases is that the initial value of CWmin in current VANET systems is set without considering the local density, which is often set too low for the number of vehicles presented in the area [26]. Beyond industry standards such as BSM Scheduling and Congestion Control (BSMCONGCTRL) of SAE J2945.1 [27] that deals with minimum performance requirements, how to control channel congestion in VANET is an active research topic.

Two types of congestion control techniques, proactive and reactive, are already widely under development and evaluations. The state information of the surrounding nodes available at the APP layer, and data generation patterns are collectively used by proactive techniques to satisfy the required application-level performance; these may be known as feedforward control mechanisms as well. The reactive techniques, however, use the channel congestion status to decide whether the transmission parameters need adaptations; these may be also known as feedback control mechanisms.

A distributed power-control congestion mitigation scheme with fair transmit is studied in [28], where optimal transmit power is calculated by each sender based on the position information of all its neighbors. The adaptation of transmit power is also used in [29] to control congestion. A distributed algorithm is proposed in [25] to adjust messaging rates by which the channel load is controlled and maintained at a target. This algorithm uses binary feedback and an Additive Increase Multiplicative Decrease (AIMD) mechanism. Ansari et al. [16] also suggest the adaptation of messaging rates based on the relative position of target neighbors. Another message-rate controller focusing on global fairness is proposed in [14], which adapts using AIMD and disseminates congestion information over multiple hops to achieve global fairness. The LInear MEssage Rate Integrated Control (LIMERIC) algorithm using a linear rate adaptation mechanism is proposed in [30], and the weighted-LIMERIC algorithm converging to weighted-fair message rates is further proposed in [15].

3.2 Awareness Control

The congestion-control philosophy advocating the maximization of each vehicle's awareness by maximizing channel throughput is preferred to the philosophy of transmitting only those safety messages thought to be needed [15]. The connectivity requirements imposed by the implemented safety applications, in addition to minimizing the channel load level, must be ensured among vehicles for stable system operations. Awareness control protocols need: (1) to have direct controls on each vehicle's communications range by adapting the transmit power to successfully communicate safety messages to a given distance (cover the necessary number of neighbors), (2) to adapt the packet generation rate to satisfy the required number of messages to be received at vehicles in-rage during a given time window, and (3) to set CW values based on local traffic conditions for improved channel throughputs. To optimize each vehicle's awareness of its neighbors, the number of safety messages received from each neighbor must be maximized [15]. Awareness control mechanisms must consider the requirements of C-ITS safety applications as they are different from one to another. The goal of safety mission applications is to maximize awareness. Awareness control mechanisms can be seen as topology controllers [2].

4   Cross-Layer Design for DSRC

4.1   Requirements of C-ITS Safety Applications

C-ITS enable a great number of applications to enhance driving safety and traffic efficiency based on the types of vehicular communications systems supported. These applications are categorized based on their roles within ITS. Intelligent transportation applications, from the most abstract viewpoint, are classified as safety (public) applications and non-safety (efficiency and infotainment) applications [31, 32]. The focus of most of the safety projects has been on the development of the six vital V2V safety applications represented in Table 2 [32–34].

Table 2. Requirements of C-ITS safety applications

Application name	Application requirements					
	CAM range[a]	Absolute positioning accuracy	Relative positioning accuracy	CAM rate	CAM period	CAM latency
		95% confidence level				
Extended/Emergency Electronic Brake Light (EEBL)	300 m	<0.7 m	<1 m	>10 Hz	100 ms	0.01–0.1 s
		Where-in-lane-level granularity				
Forward Collision Warning (FCW)	150 m	<0.7 m	<1 m	>10 Hz	100 ms	0.01–0.1 s
		Where-in-lane-level granularity				
Intersection Movement Assist (IMA)	300 m	<0.7 m	<1 m	>10 Hz	100 ms	0.01–0.1 s
		Where-in-lane-level granularity				
Blind Spot Warning + Lane Change Warning (BSW + LCW)	150 m	<1.1 m	<2 m	10 Hz	100 ms	0.1–1 s
		Lane-level granularity				
Do Not Pass Warning (DNPW)	150 m	<1.1 m	<2 m	10 Hz	100 ms	0.1–1 s
		Lane-level granularity				
Control Loss Warning (CLW)	300 m	<0.7 m	<1 m	>10 Hz	100 ms	0.01–0.1 s
		Where-in-lane-level granularity				

[a]300 m corresponds to 6 cars per lane in front and 6 cars per lane at rear @ 60 km/h.
150 m corresponds to 3 cars per lane in front and 3 cars per lane at rear @ 60 km/h.

Cooperative safety applications rely on the knowledge about the states of collaborating vehicles and time intervals between events and corresponding reactions. The applications represented in Table 2 are ad hoc based with high priority at the data link and stringent time requirements (V2V APP layer delays) to enhance transportation safety. Essentially all of them rely on CAM at received beacon rates of at least 10 Hz. These safety applications have the most stringent latency requirements and demand a relatively small communications range corresponding to small inter-vehicle distances. The recommended CAM ranges and rates for each application can be beneficial in light traffic scenarios where the traffic flow does not change frequently in a short time and all vehicles could keep their velocities accordingly. As such the CAM range and rate of applications may be determined based on the speeds of connected vehicles and the number (density) of vehicles travelling with the host vehicle.

The CAM range field specified in Table 2 is indicative and needs to be adjusted based on various factors including the condition and speed of the road that the vehicle travels on. Hence it is more reasonable to express the CAM range by the number of vehicles that must be covered by the message. Let's assume the values represented in Table 2 as CAM ranges correspond to the road speed of 60 km/h, with the fact that a three-second gap must be kept between each pair of following cars to allow for safe response to hazards or unexpected events; the three-second gap is equivalent to the safe distance of 50 m at 60 km/h. The minimum number of vehicles to be covered with the 300 m range requirement is then 6 cars per lane in front and 6 cars per lane at rear, and with the 150 m range requirement is 3 cars per lane in front and 3 cars per lane at rear of each host vehicle. These two requirements (either the coverage of at least 12 cars per lane or of at least 6 cars per lane) can ensure awareness among platoons of vehicles travelling together in various traffic scenarios. This, however, demands the precise position of each platoon's central vehicle to be known by all vehicles of the platoon.

Safety applications are the key factor for determining the most stringent requirements of C-ITS such as positioning needs in terms of both accuracy and reliability. Accuracy required for fault-free operations of these applications depends on various factors such as speeds of connected vehicles and spatial distances between them. Requirements of 0.5 m and 10 Hz are reported in [35, 36] for positioning accuracy and the position update rate of C-ITS applications respectively. Assisted GNSS-based positioning technologies and communications-based collaborative positioning methods can offer the required lane-level vehicle navigation and positioning between vehicles and infrastructure access points (road-side units). Because both approaches have some drawbacks due to limitations in visible satellites or communications bandwidth, a combination of different techniques may be needed under harsh scenarios. The channel capacity requirements for collaborative positioning in those scenarios are discussed in [37]. In addition to V2X communications and positioning technologies, enhanced digital road maps are required to support many of C-ITS applications, as maps provide location information of road entities and geometry preview of the road.

The above discussion reveals the relation between the requirements of communications, of networking and of positioning, with those of CAM by safety mission applications. Therefore, the live requirements of safety applications depend on the speeds of connected vehicles, spatial distances between them, and the CBR and the number (density) of vehicles travelling with the host vehicle, as well as the type of road (e.g. suburban street, highway, or intersections). This information is available at the APP layer of the DSRC protocol stack through feedback from cross layers, and hence, to best support the channel congestion control mechanisms, there must be an adaptation mechanism at the APP layer to feedforward the adaptive parameters to the PHY layer.

4.2   Cross-Layer Design Approach

The rationale behind the development of the CLD-DSRC is to satisfy the timeliness requirement of periodic communications when the DSRC medium of VANETs is congested, and to efficiently utilize the medium resources, e.g. channel bandwidth, otherwise. Deterministic metrics must be established to quantify the conditions of both communications and road traffic networks so that the changes in the status of either network can be detected. Such metrics can be employed by an adjustment controller within an Adaptation sub-layer to control parameters for message generation and exchange optimization based on the timeliness requirements of safety applications. The introduction of the Adaptation sub-layer in the DSRC protocol stack as the hub of CLD means additional codes for the PHY, MAC and APP layers must be implemented. Although, the execution of additional cross layer codes may adversely affect the protocol stack's internal throughput and endanger the integrity of individual protocols, an Operating System (OS) independent architecture ensures the integrity, efficiency and maintainability of the CLD stack. This necessitates the implementation of the Adaptation sub-layer using generic data-structures for multi-platform CLD optimization.

Because ACK mechanism is not activated in DSRC, the CLD-DSRC only has access to data measurable by each radio unit itself or data received via BSMs. The communications network status, conforming to the CBR or the rate of packets dropped (outdated) in the local queue, is available as feedback from the MAC layer in IEEE 802.11-based networks. Other information identified earlier as vital input data for the awareness and congestion controller, e.g. speed of vehicles, separation distances between vehicles, density of vehicles and the type of road, is accessible as feedback from the APP layer using BSMs, GPS data and digital maps. This information can then be passed on as feedforward to other layers such as the PHY, MAC or APP layer using one of the three implementation designs categorized by Srivastava and Motani [38], including direct communication between layers, indirect communication through a shared database, and the new abstractions using heaps instead of stacks. To allow for a multi-platform, non-OS-specific CLD implementation, we advocate the idea of a shared database for the freedom it offers for generic implementation of controls and data-structures.

Given that maintaining the CBR within the level of 60%–70% is the target of awareness and channel congestion control mechanisms, an adaptive transmission controller is inevitable. Many candidates have been identified in the literature including transmit power, messaging rate, bit rate, packet length, and sensitivity control [15]. We advocate a controller based on transmit power and message-rate controls, because their primary feature is a predictable, topology-independent correlation with the CBR metric. To receive feedforward values in the CLD-DSRC, the PHY, MAC and APP layers register with the Adaptation sub-layer for information about events that triggers adjustments to their parameters. Feedback values are processed at the Adaptation sub-layer and event information is feedforwarded to the registered layer via APIs to adjust its action accordingly. Each layer decides what optimizing action to take based on the feedforward values it receives. Figure 3 represents a schematic diagram for the CLD-DSRC. The Adaptation sub-layer combines the requirements of different simultaneous applications with the live conditions of the wireless channel to derive values

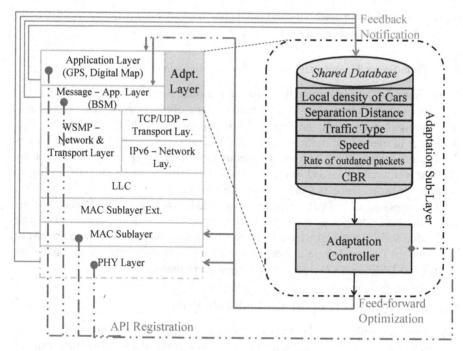

Fig. 3. CLD-DSRC protocol stack

for the parameters requiring adjustment. The Adaptation sub-layer must also ensure that appropriate controls of the OS are invoked and correct data-structures of targeted layers are updated.

5 Evaluation of CLD-DSRC Complexity

The CLD-DSRC is essentially a modification to the DSRC stack and requires minimal modification to the protocol stack that is integral to the OS of DSRC-enabled radios. This section identifies the metrics for evaluating the CLD-DSRC and evaluates its complexity by discussing the runtime overhead introduced by the CLD-DSRC design.

5.1 Evaluation Metrics

The CLD-DSRC is proposed to enhance the performance of VANETs by sharing information among the DSRC stack layers. However, this entails additional codes and APIs be implemented into the stack protocols. Two metrics, namely time-space complexity, and complexity of stack-database crossing and data path delay can be used to evaluate the efficiency of the proposed design. These are specified in the so-called Big O-notation for the evaluation of the intensity of resource utilization (O is Landau's symbol). The analysis is done for a problem of size n that is the number of changes in the conditions of communications and road traffic networks that mandate an adjustment in one of the transmission parameters at any given time.

5.2   Time-Space Complexity

If only one layer would receive feedforward at a time, because the choice of the next parameter on which to perform an adjustment is one of few possibilities, i.e., transmit power or message intervals, the time complexity of the CLD-DSRC was $O(log\ n)$. This is the case in sparse road traffic scenarios that is a good performance. However, due to the dynamic nature of VANETs simultaneous feedforward values can be received by different registered layers and hence the time complexity of the CLD-DSRC in highly dynamic, crowded traffic is $O(n)$ that is a fair factor.

The proposed CLD-DSRC requires a bounded (fixed) amount of space for the shared database which does not depend on the conditions of the communications and road traffic networks. For any condition, the CLD-DSRC will take the same amount of space and the occupied space is independent of the input, hence the space complexity of the CLD-DSRC is $O(1)$ that is an excellent performance.

5.3   Stack-Database Crossing and Data Path Delay

Layers register with the Adaptation sub-layer and feedforward is invoked on every change in every element of the database that a layer is registered for. The complexity of APIs depends on the number of registrations for feedforward and the changes in the conditions of communications and road traffic networks. The number of registrations is constant while the changes in the networks is in the order of n, and hence stack-database API crossing has an order of $O(n)$ complexity. On the other hand, dispatching feedforward values is asynchronous to receiving feedback values and hence data send and receive functions of the Adaptation sub-layer do not impact the data paths of the stack layers.

6   Discussion and Conclusions

An existing significant challenge in the deployment of DSRC-based V2V safety systems is wireless channel congestion and awareness control. This article discussed the development of a distributed cross-layer design approach to address the DSRC congestion and awareness control to maximize the channel throughput. Simulations have been used to study the attributes of the DSRC wireless channel. Then, the requirements of safety mission applications were studied to determine the parameters affecting the DSRC channel condition. The paper argued that in addition to the adaptation of messaging rate, other transmission behaviors such as transmit power and channel access contention window size must be adapted per the conditions of both communications and road traffic networks to provide the adaptive controller with stability, convergence, and fairness properties. The complexity verification and analysis showed the proposed controller is an efficient and fair design with $O(n)$ being the worst-case complexity for the proposed CLD-DSRC, where n is the number of changes in the communications and road traffic networks requiring an adjustment in one of the transmission parameters at any given time. The study of the proposed controller in more details to derive an optimal trade-off between transmit power, message intervals and channel access parameters as well as to investigate the controller's stability, convergence, and fairness properties is still valid and within our future research agenda.

References

1. Ansari, K.: Development of an inter-vehicle communications & positioning platform for transport safety applications. Doctor of Philosophy (PhD) Thesis. School of Electrical Engineering & Computer Science: Queensland University of Technology (2014)
2. Sepulcre, M., et al.: Congestion and awareness control in cooperative vehicular systems. Proc. IEEE **99**(7), 1260–1279 (2011)
3. Santi, P.: Topology control in wireless ad hoc and sensor networks. ACM Comput. Surv. **37**(2), 164–194 (2005)
4. Raisinghani, V.T., Iyer, S.: Cross-layer feedback architecture for mobile device protocol stacks. IEEE Commun. Mag. **44**(1), 85–92 (2006)
5. Hirai, T., Ohzahata, S., Kawashima, K.: A TCP congestion control method for real-time communication based on channel occupancy of a wireless LAN. In: 16th Asia-Pacific Conference on Communications (APCC) (2010)
6. Liu, J., et al.: An adaptive cross-layer mechanism of multi-channel multi-interface wireless networks for real-time video streaming. In: 7th International Conference on Ubiquitous Intelligence & Computing and 7th International Conference on Autonomic & Trusted Computing (UIC/ATC) (2010)
7. Cheng, R.-S., Lin, H.-T.: A cross-layer design for TCP end-to-end performance improvement in multi-hop wireless networks. Comput. Commun. **31**(14), 3145–3152 (2008)
8. Meddour, D.-E., et al.: A cross layer architecture for multicast and unicast video transmission in mobile broadband networks. J. Netw. Comput. Appl. **35**(5), 1377–1391 (2012)
9. Chen, Y.-L., et al.: Cross-layer design for traffic management in wireless networked control systems. In: IEEE 9th Conference on Industrial Electronics and Applications (ICIEA) (2014)
10. Bai, J., et al.: Optimal cross-layer design of sampling rate adaptation and network scheduling for wireless networked control systems. In: 2012 IEEE/ACM Third International Conference on Cyber-Physical Systems (ICCPS) (2012)
11. Israr, N., Scanlon, W.G., Irwin, G.W.: A cross-layer communication framework for wireless networked control systems. In: 1st International Conference on Wireless Communication, Vehicular Technology, Information Theory and Aerospace & Electronic Systems Technology, pp. 577–581 (2009)
12. Trivellato, M., Benvenuto, N.: Cross-layer design of networked control systems. In: IEEE International Conference on Communications, pp. 1–5 (2009)
13. Fallah, Y.P., et al.: Analysis of information dissemination in vehicular ad-hoc networks with application to cooperative vehicle safety systems. IEEE Trans. Veh. Technol. **60**(1), 233–247 (2011)
14. Tielert, T., et al.: Design methodology and evaluation of rate adaptation based congestion control for vehicle safety communications. In: 2011 IEEE Vehicular Networking Conference (VNC) (2011)
15. Bansal, G., Kenney, J.B.: Controlling congestion in safety-message transmissions: a philosophy for vehicular DSRC systems. IEEE Veh. Technol. Mag. **8**(4), 20–26 (2013)

16. Ansari, K., Wang, C., Feng, Y.: Exploring dependencies of 5.9 GHz DSRC throughput and reliability on safety applications. In: Proceedings of the 10th IEEE VTS Asia Pacific Wireless Communications Symposium (IEEE VTS APWCS 2013). Seoul National University, Seoul (2013)

17. Guo, J., Balon, N.: Vehicular ad hoc networks and dedicated shortrange communication. University of Michigan, Dearborn (2006)

18. Xu, Q., et al.: Vehicle-to-vehicle safety messaging in DSRC. In: Proceedings of the 1st ACM Workshop on Vehicular Ad hoc Networks (VANET 2004), pp. 19–28. ACM, Philadelphia (2004)

19. Karouit, A., et al.: A team study of a multiple-power wireless random channel access mechanism with capture effect. Math. Probl. Eng. **2013**, 16 (2013)

20. Bilstrup, K., et al.: On the ability of the 802.11p MAC method and STDMA to support real-time vehicle-to-vehicle communication. EURASIP J. Wirel. Commun. Netw. **2009**, 5:1–5:13 (2009)

21. Khairnar, V.D., Kotecha, K.: Performance of vehicle-to-vehicle communication using IEEE 802.11p in vehicular ad-hoc network environment. Int. J. Netw. Secur. Appl. (IJNSA), **5**(2), 143–170 (2013)

22. Jurdak, R., Lopes, C.V., Baldi, P.: A survey, classification and comparative analysis of medium access control protocols for ad hoc networks. IEEE Commun. Surv. Tutor. **6**(1), 2–16 (2004)

23. Booysen, M.J., Zeadally, S., van Rooyen, G.J.: Survey of media access control protocols for vehicular ad hoc networks. IET Commun. **5**(11), 1619–1631 (2011)

24. USDOT, Vehicle safety communications-applications (VSC-A), Final Report (2011)

25. Weinfield, A., Kenney, J., Bansal, G.: An adaptive DSRC message transmission interval control algorithm. In: Proceedings of 18th ITS World Congress 2011 (2011)

26. Ito, R., Nobayashi, D., Ikenaga, T.: Adaptive contention window control scheme for dense IEEE 802.11 wireless LANs. In: 2015 IEEE Pacific Rim Conference on Communications, Computers and Signal Processing (PACRIM) (2015)

27. SAE-International, On-Board System Requirements for V2V Safety Communications, in J2945/1 (2016)

28. Torrent-Moreno, M., et al.: Vehicle-to-vehicle communication: fair transmit power control for safety-critical information. IEEE Trans. Veh. Technol. **58**(7), 3684–3703 (2009)

29. Huang, C.-L., et al.: Adaptive intervehicle communication control for cooperative safety systems. IEEE Netw. **24**(1), 6–13 (2010)

30. Kenney, J.B., Bansal, G., Rohrs, C.E.: LIMERIC: a linear message rate control algorithm for vehicular DSRC systems. In: Proceedings of the Eighth ACM International Workshop on Vehicular Inter-Networking. ACM, Las Vegas (2011)

31. Dar, K., et al.: Wireless communication technologies for ITS applications. IEEE Commun. Mag. **48**(5), 156–162 (2010)

32. Papadimitratos, P., et al.: Vehicular communication systems: enabling technologies, applications, and future outlook on intelligent transportation. IEEE Commun. Mag. **47**(11), 84–95 (2009)

33. ARRB-Project-Team, Vehicle Positioning for C-ITS in Australia (Background Document). In: Green, D., et al. (ed.) Austroads Research Report, 2013, Austroads Ltd. Austroads Project No. NT1632, Austroads Publication No. APR431-13, p. 88 (2013)

34. Kenney, J.B.: Dedicated short-range communications (DSRC) standards in the United States. Proc. IEEE **99**(7), 1162–1182 (2011)

35. Shladover, S.E., Tan, S.-K.: Analysis of vehicle positioning accuracy requirements for communication-based cooperative collision warning. J. Intell. Transp. Syst. Technol. Plan. Oper. **10**(3), 131–140 (2006)

36. Ansari, K., Feng, Y.: Design of an integration platform for V2X wireless communications and positioning supporting C-ITS safety applications. J. Global Position. Syst. **12**(1), 38–52 (2013)
37. Efatmaneshnik, M., Balaei, A.T., Dempster, A.G.: A channel capacity perspective on cooperative positioning algorithms for VANET. In: ION-GNSS. 2009, pp. 3423–3430. Institute of Navigation, Curran, Red Hook (2009)
38. Srivastava, V., Motani, M.: Cross-layer design: a survey and the road ahead. IEEE Commun. Mag. **43**(12), 112–119 (2005)

Technique Stages for Efficient Wideband Spectrum Sensing Based on Compressive Sensing

Evelio Astaiza[1], Héctor Bermudez[1],
and Octavio J. Salcedo Parra[2,3(✉)]

[1] Universidad del Quindío, Quindío, Colombia
{eastaiza, hfbermudez}@uniquindio.edu.co
[2] Universidad Nacional de Colombia, Bogotá D.C., Colombia
ojsalcedop@unal.edu.co
[3] Internet Inteligente Research Group,
Universidad Distrital Francisco José de Caldas, Bogotá D.C., Colombia
osalcedo@udistrital.edu.co

Abstract. In this paper, the problems related on spectrum sensing in Cognitive Radio (CR) devices are discussed. In this context, the conventional mechanisms require that the operation signal sampling would be performed at least at the Nyquist rate and also allowing only narrowband sensing operation or wideband sensing limited by sensing continuous narrowband channels. Therefore, this problem is approached from the Compressive Sensing (CS) approach, which is a proposal that reduces the dimensionality of the signals, and therefore can be applied to sub-Nyquist sampling allowing the wideband spectrum sensing operation. In this context, it is proposed to use Signal representation, coding signal (sampling) and reconstruction, in this way signal representation is performed by hard thresholding, sampling the wideband signal is performed using the random demodulator and reconstruction through implementation reconstruction algorithm based on modified orthogonal matching pursuit (OMP). As a whole, the wideband spectrum sensing mechanism proposed verifies the methodological steps are valid and applicable to this type of scenario, and also allows to check the advantages and disadvantages of the sampling mechanism used as the reconstruction algorithm implemented.

Keywords: Compressive sensing · Convex programming · Sampling · Spectrum sensing · Random demodulator

1 Introduction

Currently, the demand for wireless communication services has grown exponentially, this has generated some overcrowded band [1], because they are used by commercial systems. However, there are frequencies bands which are sub-used [2], like TV Bands, those band offer a great opportunity to solve this problem. Therefore, there are spectral holes that are permanent in some cases and in others, occur at certain times on some frequency bands; which implies a dilemma, because users from some services such as

© Springer International Publishing AG 2017
S. Bouzefrane et al. (Eds.): MSPN 2017, LNCS 10566, pp. 138–154, 2017.
DOI: 10.1007/978-3-319-67807-8_11

mobile, do not have enough spectrum to transmit, but on the other hand, some spectral bands are not completely used. This happens due to the current static spectrum allocation strategy, and consequently dynamic spectrum access (DSA) is proposed as a solution strategy.

So, the technology which can help to implement devices with DSA capabilities is Cognitive Radio. This technology allows changing the parameters of the devices and the network itself in order to establish an efficient communication in terms of radio resource use, but this communication must not interfere with the users who have a legal concession of the band. CR devices have 3 steps to work and do the dynamic channel's assignment which are: Spectrum sensing, Radio Environment analysis and Transmission Parameters adjustment. Spectrum sensing is known as the CR enabler and it must be done continuously in the CR for giving key data such as traffic and noise statistics, channel state, White Spaces information, and so on, to finally do the transmission parameter adjustment, and doing so allowing the CR to adapt the environment

However, spectrum sensing is a task that involves significant challenges from the perspective of the computational resources required, and to implement this function using traditional methods such as the energy detector [3, 4], sensing per adapted filters [4, 5] sensed by cyclo-stationary characteristics [4, 6] and a wavelet detector [7, 8] among others, involves sampling the broadband spectrum at rates above the Nyquist rate; this is the reason why the new paradigm implemented called Compressive Sensing (CS) [9, 10] is so appealing; it provides an efficient way to sample and process sparse signals or signals that can be adequately approximated by sparse signals, in other words, those which can be approximated by an expansion in terms of a suitable base, that only has a few significant terms. Therefore, to solve the problems of spectrum sensing it is necessary to establish a set of methodological steps for the developing of sub-Nyquist sampling sensing in wideband signals. In addition, proposing an approximation with sensing algorithms for wideband signals is key to solve the sampling problem in rates below the Nyquist rate, and doing so improving the processing capacity requirements, which are proportional to the number of samples to process. In the same way, an alternative solution for solving this problem will be generated, which compared with the traditional spectrum techniques, it will allow to sense narrowband signals and wideband signals in sequential way.

Then, using the frequency domain sparse property of the wireless signals in outdoor scenarios [11], it is proposed a methodology for the use of CS in CR to solve spectrum sensing problem in wideband signals. The band of interest is divided into a finite number of spectral bands, in which the presence or absence of carriers through the reconstruction of the sampled spectrum is examined. The sampling process is performed with a random demodulator proposed in [11], and the reconstruction of the same for the identification the occupied bands by means of identifying the presence or absence of carrier is performed with the convex relaxation algorithm based on minimizing the norm ℓ_1.

This paper is organized as follows: In Sect. 2 the reference framework is described, then in Sect. 3 the methodology based on the proposed steps is defined in Sect. 4 the results are shown, and finally in Sect. 5 the conclusions of the study are shown.

2 Reference Framework

In the compressive sensing paradigm [14], it is assumed that a signal $z \in \mathbb{R}^n$ is formed by samples taken at the Nyquist rate; this signal, in turn, can be represented by an sparse approximation in a transformed domain, wherein, denoting by Φ the matrix of size $n \times n$ which represents the transformation between the original signal domain and the domain in which the signal is sparse, and assuming that in the transformed domain, the signal $x \in \mathbb{R}^n$ is described as $x = \Phi z$ and has significant components only, where $k << n$ and the remaining components are approximately zero. Therefore it is said that the signal $x \in \mathbb{R}^n$ is k-sparse, which is represented as $\|x\|_0 \leq k$, where the operator $\|x\|_p$ denotes vector norm ℓ_p of x when $p = 0$, and is not according with triangular inequality then $\|x\|_0 := |supp|$ and represent cardinality of x vector support, and the ℓ_p rule is defined as shown in Eq. 1.

$$\|x\|_p = \begin{cases} |supp(x)| & para\, p = 0 \\ \left(\sum_{i=1}^{n} |x_i|^p\right)^{\frac{1}{p}} & para\, p \in [1, \infty) \\ \max_{i=1,2,3,\ldots,n} |x_i| & para\, p = \infty \end{cases} \tag{1}$$

It may be interpreted manner not so precise, but highly illustrative, that compressive sensing allows sampling at the Nyquist rate followed by a sub-sampling performed by a matrix A of size $m \times n$, where $m < n$, therefore, the process of making m linear measurement by an acquisition system, can be represented mathematically as indicated by Eq. 2.

$$y = Ax \tag{2}$$

Where $y \in \mathbb{R}^m$ is the measurements vector.

To ensure the recovery of only the original signal from the linear measurements y, the sensing matrix A must satisfy, generally, the restricted isometry property (RIP) [14], which is illustrated in the following definition.

Definition 1. A matrix A satisfies the restricted isometry property of order k, if a $\delta_k \in (0, 1)$ such that

$$(1 - \delta_k)\|x\|_2^2 \leq \|Ax\|_2^2 \leq (1 + \delta_k)\|x\|_2^2 \tag{3}$$

For all $x \in S_k$, where S_k is the set of all k-sparse signals.

If a matrix A satisfies the restricted isometry property of order $2k$, then from Eq. 3 it can be interpreted that the matrix A preserves the distance of any pair of k-sparse vectors.

The problem of reconstructing the signal $x \in \mathbb{R}^n$ from the measurement vector $y \in \mathbb{R}^m$, can be done using algorithms based on convex relaxation which are a key focus of the sparse approach; they replace the combinatorial function ℓ_0 with the convex function ℓ_1, which converts the combinatorial problem in a convex optimization problem [13], the ℓ_1 norm is the convex function which is most approximated to the ℓ_0 function. The natural approach, from which the sparse approximation problem addressed, is to find the sparse solution $y = Ax$, by solving the optimization problem

$$\min_x \|x\|_0 \quad subject\ to \quad y = Ax \tag{4}$$

However the problem posed in Eq. 4 is a combinatorial problem which in general is NP-Hard [14], and the simple fact of working with all media cardinality k becomes an intractable computational problem, by replacing the ℓ_0 norm with the ℓ_1 standard the problem becomes the one raised in Eq. 5.

$$\min_x \|x\|_1 \quad subject\ to \quad y = Ax \tag{5}$$

When dealing with imperfectly sparse measurements (measurements contaminated by noise), the sensing model given by Eq. 6 is considered.

$$y = Ax + w \tag{6}$$

Where A is the sensing matrix of size $m \times n$, $y \in \mathbb{R}^m$ is the measurement vector and $w \in \mathbb{R}^m$ is the noise vector, therefore, inputs from y are the measurements from x contaminated by noise, therefore the optimization problem of Eq. 5 becomes

$$\min_x \|x\|_1 \quad subject\ to \quad \|Ax - y\|_2 \leq \in \tag{7}$$

Or equivalently

$$\min_x \left(\|x\|_1 + \frac{\mu}{2} \|Ax - y\|_2^2 \right) \tag{8}$$

The two programs are equivalent in the sense that the solution of a problem is also the solution of the other provided that the parameters $\in$ and μ are properly established; however, the correspondence between $\in$ and μ is not known beforehand; depending on the application and the information available, one of the two may be easier to obtain, which makes one of the two problems stated in Eqs. 7 and 8 preferred over the other. Properly selecting $\in$ or μ is a problem that is very important in practice, therefore, general principles for selection include:

- Perform statistical assumptions about w and x and interpret Eqs. 7 or 8 as e.g. maximum a posteriori estimates.
- Cross validation (perform reconstruction from a subset of the recovery action and validate on another subset of steps)
- Find the best values of the parameters on a test data set and use these parameters on current data with appropriate adjustments to compensate for differences in scale, dynamic range, sparsity and noise.

3   Proposed Methodological Approach

Next, the methodological stages to be covered in the process of developing an efficient spectrum-sensing algorithm are defined by the particular functionality of the observation phase defined in the cognitive cycle proposed by Mitola [15]. In this phase of observation, the following can be defined as objectives associated with spectrum sensing: (1) Identification of Blank Spaces, (2) Identification of radio technology, modulation, coding or characteristics of the signal present in the channel; (3) Identification of the quality or condition of the channel; Considering these objectives, the proposed methodological stages are:

3.1   Pre-processing and Digitizing the RF Signal

At this stage, it must be decided that the alternative of digitizing the Radio Frequency (RF) signal present in the radio environment is more convenient according to the objectives set for the spectrum sensing operation. In this phase, the major challenges are presented in the aspects related to the hardware components required for the acquisition of the signal, such as Digital Analog Converters (ADC), Low Noise Filters and Amplifiers (LNA); with respect to the digitization process, in the scenario in which broadband spectrum sensing is sought, ideally, the CR should be supported by fully radio software hardware, in which the RF signal is directly digitized. However, there are fundamental physical limits to be exceeded according to the operating bandwidths, operating frequencies and number of bits required in the resolution of the conversion; in addition, it is relevant to consider in this scenario the number of measurements generated in the process of digitizing the RF signal since, depending on it, more or less processing capacities will be required in the later phases. As for the characteristics required in the filters, an important aspect is related to the bandwidths and low ripple of the passing band, small transition bands and levels in the attenuated band which involves complex and high-order filters that require components with important restrictions in their frequency response, finally with respect to the amplification of the received signal when it is broadband. The amplifier is required to operate in its linear region, which is a major challenge given the frequency response required by the amplifier components.

According to the aforementioned, it is important to decide which sampler to use according to the specific objective that is sought with the spectrum sensing, in this sense, the possibilities to consider are the Nyquist Sampling or the Sub-Nyquist Sampling. If the objectives of the spectrum sensing are (1) or (3) it is convenient to perform a sub-nyquist sampling because of the low computational complexity associated with the pre-processing stage associated with the selected sampler, this because in order to achieve these sensing targets do not require a perfect reconstruction of the signal; if the objective of the spectrum sensing is (2) It is advisable to perform a Nyquist sampling since perfect reconstruction of the signal is required. The above is shown in the decision diagram of the proposed methodological approach, which is illustrated in Fig. 1.

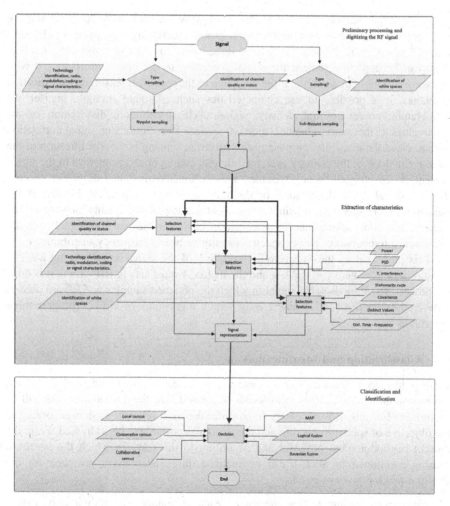

Fig. 1. Proposed methodological approach

In this sense, since the objective of sensing is the identification of blanks, it is proposed to use sub-nyquist sampling based on compressive sensing, covering the stage of digitalization of signal by means of a dispersed representation of the multiband signal and obtaining sub samples -nyquist using the analog converter - information called Random Demodulator [10].

3.2 Extraction of Characteristics

Once digitized measurements of the RF signal present in the channel are taken, these measurements must be processed to obtain adequate representation for classification and identification purposes. This is a very delicate stage since the different spaces of characteristics lead to different representations of the signal. Therefore, the feature space used must be strictly related to the sensing objective.

Some of the characteristics related to the objectives associated to spectrum sensing are signal power, interference temperature, power spectral density, cycle - stationary, time - frequency distribution, eigenvalue distribution, signal covariance, etc. Each of them can be used to represent the signal according to the objective associated with spectrum sensing. For example, if the objective of the spectrum sensing is identification of blanks, it is possible to use characteristics such as signal strength, interference temperature, power spectral density, signal cycle distribution, distribution of the eigenvalues of the matrix channel, time - frequency distributions or signal correlation matrix. Nevertheless, if the purpose of the spectrum sensing is the identification of the radio technology of the primary user, modulation, coding or characteristics of the signal present in the channel, it is advisable to use characteristics such as power spectral density, signal cycle distribution or distributions time - frequency. Finally, if the objective of the spectrum sensing is the identification of the quality or state of the channel, it is most appropriate to make use of characteristics such as signal strength, interference temperature, power spectral density or time - frequency distributions.

This process does the Sub-Nyquist sampling of the signal $x \in \mathbb{R}^n$, using a set of samples $y \in \mathbb{R}^m$ where $y = Ax + w$ and the matrix A must satisfy RIP. Then, it is done the processing of the disperse signal in which the obtained samples $y \in \mathbb{R}^m$ are used to recover the signal $x \in \mathbb{R}^n$ using greedy search algorithms or convex programming algorithms [9].

3.3   Classification and Identification

Once it has been defined, which feature or feature sets are to be used for signal representation, it is necessary to establish where and how the decision process will be performed. For this, it is necessary to consider the most relevant aspects according to the objective of spectrum sensing and the particular problem to be addressed. From the present methodological proposal and according to the ways in which the spectrum sensing mentioned in Sect. 1 can be realized, three alternatives are seen for the decision-making process in CR.

(1) Spectrum Sensing: In this alternative, each secondary user, individually, makes the decisions according to the established sensing objective, based on locally available measurements.

(2) Cooperative Spectrum Sensing (Centralized): In this alternative, all secondary users who share a geographic area or radius of influence environment send the decisions taken locally to a central entity. Which exploits all available knowledge to make the decision in accordance with the goal of established senses.

(3) Collaborative Spectrum Sensing (Distributed): In this alternative, all secondary users who share a geographic area or radius of influence environment send decisions made locally to all other collaborating members in the radio environment. Where each secondary user individually exploits all available knowledge, and makes decisions according to the goal of established senses.

For each alternative of spectrum sensing, it is necessary to define the rule or set of decision rules to be used, which is why, for the case of local spectrum sensing, the decision rule to be used par excellence is the rule of maximum a (MAP) [16], and for cooperative and collaborative spectrum sensing, the decision rules to be used may be rules of logical fusion [17] such as AND, OR or XOR, or Bayesian fusion rules [18]. There are other learning-based decision mechanisms such as Neural Networks [19], Vector Support Machines [20], Self-Organized Maps [21], Q-Learning [22] and Genetic Algorithms [23]. Leave to the discretion of the reader, as they are addressed in the learning phase defined in the cognitive cycle proposed by Mitola [15]. In general, the proposed methodological approach is summarized as illustrated in Fig. 1 at the end of the article.

4 Methodology Validation

Considering a single-antenna CR device that operates over a multiband (licenced) with a total bandwidth of $B\ Hz$, which is divided into non-overlapping k sub-bands of equal bandwidth b, equivalent to $B/k\ Hz$ per channel, as shown in Fig. 2

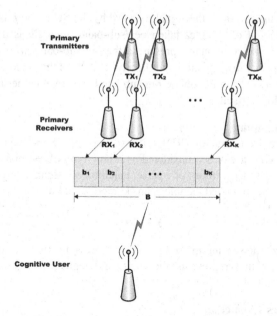

Fig. 2. Wideband spectrum sensing scenario

Assuming that the multiband signal samples are independent random variables that follow a normal distribution of zero mean and σ_s variance ($\mathcal{N}(0, \sigma_s)$), a presumption that is valid for any multiband signal in which each carrier of a sub-band is modulated independently by data-streams; and that noise samples in each antenna are random variables normally distributed, independent, of zero mean and σ_n variance ($\mathcal{N}(0, \sigma_n)$), la signal received in the antenna of the CR device can be expressed as indicated in Eq. (9).

$$x_j(n) = h_j s_j(n) + w_j(n) \tag{9}$$

where $x_j(n)$ is the n-[th] component of the signal received by the SU in the j-[th] sub-band with $j = 1, 2, .., k$, h_j represents the channel response in the j-[th] sub-band, $s_j(n)$ is the n-[th] component of the signal transmitted by the j-[th] PU on the j-[th] sub-band and received by the SU antenna and $w_j(n)$ is the n-[th] noise component in the j-[th] sub-band. The spectrum sensing problem in the j-[th] sub-band can be formulated as a statistical hypothesis testing problem in which a selection must be made between the hypothesis $\mathcal{H}_{0,j}$ which indicates that the j-[th] sub-band is available, and hypothesis $\mathcal{H}_{1,j}$ which indicates that the j-[th] sub-band is occupied; the aforementioned can be expressed according to Eq. (10).

$$\begin{cases} \mathcal{H}_{0,j} : x_j = w_j \\ \mathcal{H}_{1,j} : x_j = h_j s_j + w_j \end{cases} \tag{10}$$

Where $x_j \in \mathbb{R}^p$ is the vector of the signal received by the SU in the j-th sub-band, with p equal to the amount of samples taken per sub-band; $w_j \in \mathbb{R}^p$ is the vector representing the white noise components present in the j-th sub-band; $h_j \in [0, 1]$ represents the channel response in the j-th sub-band; finally, $s_j \in \mathbb{R}^p$ is the vector representing the signal transmitted by the j-th PU on the j-th sub-band. To develop the spectrum sensing we define the following stages.

A. SubNyquist Sampling

With the Random Demodulator (RD) [10] we performs Sub-Nyquist Sampling of multiband signal $\mathbf{x}(t)$, it can be considered as a new type of sampling system, which can be used for the acquisition of sparse bandlimited signals. From sub-Nyquist sampling process, the obtained samples can be represented as:

$$\mathbf{y} = \mathbf{A}\mathbf{x} \tag{11}$$

where $\mathbf{A} \in \mathbb{R}^{m \times n}$ is the sensing matrix, $\mathbf{y} \in \mathbb{R}^m$ the measurements vector and $\mathbf{x} \in \mathbb{R}^n$ is the k-sparse vector that represents the multiband signal, therefore, $\mathbf{y}$ entries are sub-Nyquist samples of $\mathbf{x}$.

B. Characteristics Extraction

From (3) we can see that, by the calculation of the samples covariance matrix of $\mathbf{y}$, results the following relation:

$$\mathbf{R}_y = \mathbf{A}\mathbf{R}_x\mathbf{A}^T \tag{12}$$

where $\mathbf{R}_x \in \mathbb{R}^{n \times n}$ is the signal covariance matrix and $\mathbf{R}_y \in \mathbb{R}^{m \times m}$ is the samples covariance matrix.

Therefore, it is possible from the samples covariance matrix to obtain the signal covariance matrix, and with it the performance of the wideband spectrum sensing operation identifying the energy in each of the k sub-bands.

To obtain the signal covariance matrix R_x from samples covariance matrix R_y, we must solve the optimization problem (13).

$$\min \|R_x\|_1 \, subject \, to \, R_y = AR_XA^T \tag{13}$$

The proposed solution to (13) is a modification of the OMP (Orthogonal Matching Pursuit) algorithm [25] which does not work with vectors, and the Kronecker product is not used, instead it works directly in matrix form as illustrated in the next section.

C. Clasification and Identification

Identification of the occupation or not of each sub-band is done in two stages: (1) decide on the preliminary occupation or not in function of the energy present in each sub-band of the signal estimated in antenna. (2) Decide on the final occupation of the multiband according to the occupation average associated to the preliminary decisions obtained for each sub-band. The spectrum sensing function is possible to complete by identifying the values in the main diagonal of the estimated signal covariance matrix R_x, doing $diag(R_x) = \widehat{X}[f]$. Then, to perform energy detection for each sub-band (stage 1), the energy of the signal received is compared to a detection threshold, thus, deciding the occupation or not of a sub-band. Thereby, the energy present in each sub-band can be calculated according to Eq. (14).

$$\varepsilon_j(f) = |h_j|^2 \sum\nolimits_{Sb_j} \left| \widehat{X}[f] \right|^2 \tag{14}$$

Where ε_j represents energy in the j-[th] sub-band over a sequence of N samples, Sb_j represents the j-[th] sub-band, h_j represents the channel response in the j-[th] sub-band, and $\widehat{X}[f]$ represents the signal estimated in the multiband. Then, if the energy in the j-[th] sub-band is higher than the $T_h(\varepsilon_j > T_{h_j})$ decision threshold, the decision made is $\mathcal{H}_{1,j}$ (occupied sub-band); on the contrary, the decision is $\mathcal{H}_{0,j}$ (free sub-band - WS).

Detection probabilities, P_{d_j}, miss detection probability, P_{md_j}, and false alarm probability, P_{f_j}, in the j-[th] sub-band are defined as indicated in Eqs. (15), (16) and (17).

$$P_{d_j} = P(\mathcal{H}_{1,j}|\mathcal{H}_{1,j}) \tag{15}$$

$$P_{md_j} = P(\mathcal{H}_{0,j}|\mathcal{H}_{1,j}) = 1 - P_{d_j} \tag{16}$$

$$P_{f_j} = P(\mathcal{H}_{1,j}|\mathcal{H}_{0,j}) \tag{17}$$

According to the central limit theorem [24], if the number of samples is sufficiently large (≥ 10 in practice), the test statistics (mean and variance) of ε_j associated to hypotheses $\mathcal{H}_{0,j}$ and $\mathcal{H}_{1,j}$ are normally distributed asymptotically and given by Eqs. (18) and (19).

$$E(\varepsilon_j) = \begin{cases} 2N\sigma_{nj}^2 : \mathcal{H}_{0,j} \\ (SNR_j + N)\sigma_{n_j}^2 : \mathcal{H}_{1,j} \end{cases} \tag{18}$$

$$Var(\varepsilon_j) = \begin{cases} 2N\sigma_{nj}^4 : \mathcal{H}_{0,j} \\ 2(2SNR_j + N)\sigma_{n_j}^4 : \mathcal{H}_{1,j} \end{cases} \tag{19}$$

With $\sigma_{n_j}^2$, noise energy is denoted in the j-th sub-band and SNR_j denotes the signal to noise ratio in the j-th sub-band.

Then, the detection probabilities and false alarm in the j-th sub-band can be expressed, as indicated in Eqs. (20) and (21).

$$P_{d_j} = Q\left[\frac{T_{h_j} - E(\varepsilon_j|\mathcal{H}_{1,j})}{\sqrt[2]{Var(\varepsilon_j|\mathcal{H}_{1,j})}}\right] = Q\left[\frac{T_{h_j} - (SNR_j + N)\sigma_{n_j}^2}{\sqrt[2]{2(2SNR_j + N)\sigma_{n_j}^4}}\right] \tag{20}$$

$$P_{f_j} = Q\left[\frac{T_{h_j} - E(\varepsilon_j|\mathcal{H}_{0,j})}{\sqrt[2]{Var(\varepsilon_j|\mathcal{H}_{0,j})}}\right] = Q\left[\frac{T_{h_j} - 2N\sigma_{n_j}^2}{\sqrt[2]{2N\sigma_{n_j}^4}}\right] \tag{21}$$

Where

$$Q(x) = \frac{1}{\sqrt{2\pi}}\int_x^\infty e^{-\frac{t^2}{2}}dt \tag{22}$$

Thereby, the decision threshold T_{h_j} for a specific value of P_{f_j} is given by (23).

$$T_{h_j} = Q^{-1}(P_{f_j})\sqrt[2]{2N\sigma_{n_j}^4} + 2N\sigma_{n_j}^2 \tag{23}$$

Finally, the detection probabilities, P_d, miss detection probability, P_{md}, and false alarm probability, P_f, of the multiband are calculated according to Eqs. (24), (25), and (26).

$$P_d = \frac{1}{K}\sum_{j=1}^{K}\left\{Q\left[\frac{T_{h_j} - (SNR_j + N)\sigma_{n_j}^2}{\sqrt[2]{2(2SNR_j + N)\sigma_{n_j}^4}}\right]\right\} \tag{24}$$

$$P_{md} = \frac{1}{K}\sum_{j=1}^{K}\left\{1 - Q\left[\frac{T_{h_j} - (SNR_j + N)\sigma_{n_j}^2}{\sqrt[2]{2(2SNR_j + N)\sigma_{n_j}^4}}\right]\right\} \tag{25}$$

$$P_f = \frac{1}{K} \sum_{j=1}^{K} \left\{ Q \left[\frac{T_{h_j} - 2N\sigma_{n_j}^2}{\sqrt[2]{2N\sigma_{n_j}^4}} \right] \right\} \tag{26}$$

5 Wideband Spectrum Sensing Algorithm

The idea is to reconstruct the covariance matrix, R_x, from the representation of the covariance matrix, R_y, as the weighted sum of the lowest amount possible of external products of the columns of matrix A. To perform the estimate of the covariance matrix of the signal it is important to calculate the K amount of significant components of the multiband signal that permit conducting a correct detection with probability above or equal to 0.95; this amount of significant components represents the amount of iterations the covariance estimation algorithm must perform. Experimental results permit establishing the relation existing between the number of significant components of the multiband signal and the bandwidth total of the multi-band B, the bandwidth of each sub-band (channel) b and the sub-sampling n/m factor, as indicated in (27)

$$K = \left(\frac{n}{m}\right) B/b \tag{27}$$

A. Covariance Estimation Algorithm

Let $X \in \mathbb{R}^n$ be the representation in the frequency domain of signal x, and $\Psi \in \mathbb{R}^{n \times n}$ the Fourier discrete transformation matrix, such that $X = \mathcal{F}(x) = \Psi x$ where X presents only $k \ll n$ significant values (inputs different from zero); upon sampling X with the sampling matrix $\varphi \in \mathbb{R}^{m \times n}$ where $k < m < n$ to obtain $y = \varphi X = \varphi \Psi x = Ax$; if φ fulfills the restricted isometry property (RIP) in the k order [14] and has low coherence with Ψ, then X may be effectively recovered from y. To carry out the estimation process of the signal's covariance matrix in the channel and solve the problem posed in Eq. (13), we need to use two auxiliary variables. The first of these (i,j) to avoid re-selecting external products, coordinates (i,j) keep the indices of the external products that can be selected. The second $\mathbf{R} \in \mathbb{R}^{m \times n}$ to store the remainders produced upon removing the external products selected from R_y. Initially, $\mathbf{R}$ is equal to R_y and variable (i,j) starts with all the possible combinations of indices of external products of the columns of the sensing matrix $(i,j) \leftarrow \{(1,1),(1,2),\ldots,(n,n)\}$; then the external product is selected that best adapts to the remainder through

$$(i_t, j_t) \leftarrow \arg\_\max_{(i',j') \in (i,j)} \frac{\left| \left\langle \mathbf{R}, \mathbf{P}_{i'j'} \right\rangle \right|}{\left\| \mathbf{P}_{i'j'} \right\|_2}, \text{ excluding from the indices those corresponding}$$

to the external product selected and calculating the weights associated to each external product selected through least squares $\hat{u} \leftarrow \arg\_\min_u \left\| R_y - \sum_{t'=1}^{t} u_{t'} \mathbf{P}_{i'j'} \right\|_2$; then the remainder is updated, according to the external products selected and associated weights $\mathbf{R} \leftarrow R_y - \sum_{t'=1}^{t} \hat{u}_{t'} \mathbf{P}_{i'j'}$. The process is carried out on K occasions to obtain the estimated covariance matrix, $\widehat{R}_x$, in which all its inputs are zero, except in the K inputs that correspond to the external products selected, inputs assigned the calculated weighted values.

B. Wideband Spectrum Sensing Algorithm

To implement the spectrum sensing function, the algorithm illustrated in Fig. 3 is proposed, where the input parameters of the proposed algorithm are: sensing matrix $\mathbf{A}$, samples vector $\mathbf{y}$, the total bandwidth of the multiband B, the bandwidth of each sub-band b, the size m of samples vector and sample size signal vector n at Nyquist rate (line 1). The proposed algorithm returns occupied and available sub-bands vector in the multiband denoted by ch (line 2); two auxiliary variables are used, Psb to store the energy per sub-band in all multiband (line 3) and Pc (line 4) which stores the energy of each signal component. The spectrum sensing process starts calculating the sub-bands that are in the multiband (line 7) and the amount of significant components of the multiband (line 8). Then, the signal covariance matrix $\mathbf{R}_x$ is estimated by *Covariance_Estimation* function (line 9). Next, the main diagonal vector of $\mathbf{R}_x$ is obtained (line 11) and it contains the estimated energy signal components. The sub-band energy is calculated (line 13), and finally the presence or absence of signal in each sub-band is estimated (lines 14 to 17).

	Algorihtm: Compressive Wideband Spectrum Sensing
1	Input: A, y, m, n, B, b
2	Output: ch
3	Var: Psb % Sub-band Energy
4	Pc % Signal Componets Energy
5	Begin
6	$Cont = 0$
7	$k = B/b$
8	$K = \left(\frac{m}{n}\right)k$
9	$\mathbf{R}_x \leftarrow$ *Covariance_Estimation* (A, y, K)
10	For $i = 1$ to n
11	$Pc(i) \leftarrow \mathbf{R}_x(i, i)$
12	For $j = 1$ to k
13	$Psb(j) \leftarrow sum(Pc\left(Cont * \frac{n}{k}\right)$ to $Pc((Cont + 1) * n/k))$
14	If $Psb(j) > 0$ Then
15	$ch(j) \leftarrow 1$
16	Else
17	$ch(j) \leftarrow 0$
18	End If
19	$Cont = Cont + 1$
20	End For
21	End For
22	Return ch

Fig. 3. Compressive wideband spectrum sensing algorithm

6 Performance Evaluation

In this section, the performance of the proposed algorithm is analyzed in a multiband signal scenario composed of six sub-bands (channels) of 3.3 MHz bandwidth each, which have a random occupation. To evaluate the performance of the proposed spectrum sensing algorithm, there are used as metrics the detection probability and Receiver Operating Characteristic compared to the metrics obtained from the sequential energy detection algorithm [26] and CS based algorithms [27–30]; the obtained results are shown in Figs. 4 and 5. In Fig. 4 the performance of the proposed algorithm is observed versus the performance of the other algorithms listed above; in the figure, it can be seen that the performance of the algorithms in [26–30] is lower than the performance achieved by the proposed algorithm. Figure 3 shows that the detection probability of the proposed algorithm is approximately equal to 1 for values of SNR greater than 0 dB, while other algorithms reach this detection probability for higher values of SNR.

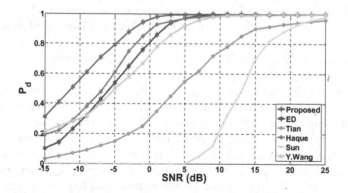

Fig. 4. Compressive wideband spectrum sensing algorithm

Figure 5 reveals that the best performance in terms of ROC curves corresponds to the algorithm proposed; this is because the area below the curve of the algorithm proposed is the biggest, indicating the capacity of the algorithm proposed to identify correctly the WS. As also noted in Fig. 5, the algorithm with the worst performance is that proposed by Sun [29], given that the ROC curve indicates a probability of 0.5 of correctly detecting the WS. Considering that the results illustrated in Fig. 5 correspond to the ROC curves of the five algorithms contrasted to an SNR of 1 dB, it is further evidence that the algorithm proposed improves significantly the performance of the other algorithms under low SNR conditions.

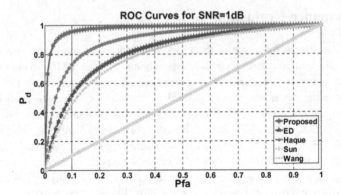

Fig. 5. ROC curves for SNR = 1 dB

7   Conclusions

This article presents a methodological stages to perform spectrum sensing based on compressive sensing, where the validity of the proposal is demonstrated, at same time, is presented a bandwidth spectrum sensing algorithm based on CS, which allows successful signal recovery and identify occupied bands and white spaces reaching a superior performance than sequential energy detector.

The proposed algorithm presents superior performance at SNR values below 5 dB using sub-Nyquist sampling in comparison with sequential energy detector which uses Nyquist sampling rate, at SNR values above 5 dB performance is same.

Similarly, the success of the proposed model based on compressive sensing for spectrum sensing in Cognitive Radio systems, which it can be evidenced, that the proposed model successfully performs the operation of spectrum sensing, but it also makes evident the deficiency in the comprehensive sampling mechanism called a random modulator; the restriction that the ratio n/m be a whole number, makes the number of samples to be taken from the sparse signal be much higher than the estimated theoretical, in which the one proposed for the simulation scenario would be 36.

References

1. Negrete, J.F., Páez, E., Sánchez, G.I., Bravo, J.: Spectrum Crunch a la Vuelta de la Esquina, MediaTelecom, Technical report, May 2013
2. McHenry, M.A., McCloskey, D., Roberson, D., McDonald, J.T.: Spectrum occupancy measurements Chicago, Illinois. Technical report, November 2005. Urkowitz, H.: Energy detection of unknown deterministic signals. Proc. IEEE **55**(4), 523–531 (1967)
3. Verma, P.K., Taluja, S., Dua, R.L.: Performance analysis of Energy detection, Matched filter detection & cyclostationary feature detection Spectrum Sensing Techniques. Int. J. Comput. Eng. Res. **2**(5), 1296–1301 (2012)
4. Sahai, A., Hoven, N., Tandra, R.: Some fundamental limits in cognitive radio. In: Proceedings of Allerton Conference Communication Control Computing (2004)

5. Ghozzi, M., Marx, F., Dohler, M., Palicot, J.: Cyclostatilonarilty-based test for detection of vacant frequency bands. In: Proceedings of 2nd International Conference on Cognitive Radio Oriented Wireless Network and Communications, Mykonos Island (2006)
6. Tian, Z., Giannakis, G.B.: A wavelet approach to wideband spectrum sensing for cognitive radios. In: Proceedings of IEEE International Conference on Cognitive Radio Oriented Wireless Networks and Commun. Mykonos Island (2006)
7. Lavanya, P.V., Sindhu Bargavi, R., Saravanan, R.: Wavelet and energy detection based spectrum sensing techniques in cognitive radio technology. MIT Int. J. Electron. Commun. Eng. **3**, 53–58 (2013)
8. Candès, E.J., Tao, J.T., Romberg, J.: Robust uncertainty principles: exact signal reconstruction from highly incomplete frequency information. IEEE Trans. Inform. Theory **52**, 489–509 (2006)
9. Donoho, D.L.: Compressed sensing. IEEE Trans. Inform. Theory **52**, 1289–1306 (2006)
10. Tropp, J.A., Laska, J.N., Duarte, M.F., Romberg, J.K., Baraniuk, R.G.: Beyond nyquist: efficient sampling of sparse bandlimited signals. IEEE Trans. Inform. Theory **56**, 520–544 (2010)
11. Candès, E., Tao, T.: Decoding by linear programming. IEEE Trans. Inform. Theory **51**(12), 4203–4215 (2005)
12. Natarajan, B.K.: Sparse approximate solutions to linear systems. SIAM J. Comput. **24**, 227–234 (1995)
13. Astaiza Hoyos, E., Jojoa Gómez, P.E., Bermúdez Orozco, H.F.: Compressive sensing: a methodological approach to an efficient signal processing, Revista DYNA, pp. 203–210, August 2015
14. Mitola, J.: Cognitive radio: An integrated agent architecture for software defined radio. Doctor of Technology, Royal Inst. Technol. (KTH), Stockholm, Sweden (2000)
15. Trees, H.V.: Detection, Estimation and Modulation Theory. Willey, New York (1968)
16. Varshney, P.: Distibuted Detection and Data Fusion, 1st edn. Springer, New York (1996)
17. Da Silva, C., Choi, B., Kim, K.: Distributed spectrum sensing for cognitive radio systems. In: Information Theory and Applications Workshop, pp. 120–123 (2007)
18. Haykin, S.: Neural Networks: A Comprehensive Foundation. Prentice Hall, New York (1994)
19. Shawe, J., Cristianini, N.: Support Vector Machinesand Other Kernel Based Learning Methods. Cambridge University Press, Cambridge (2000)
20. Kohonen, T.: The Self Organizing Map. IEEE Proc. **78**(9), 1464–1480 (1990)
21. Hosey, N., Bergin, S., Macaluso, I., O'Donohue, D.: Q-learning for cognitive radios. In: Proceedings of China – Ireland Information and Communications Technologies Conference (2009)
22. Goldberg, D.E.: Genetic Algorithms in Search, Optimization and Machine Learning. Addison-Wesley Longman Publishing Co. Inc., Boston (1989)
23. Gendenko, B.V., Kolmogorov, A.N.: Limit Distributions for Sums of Independent Random Variables. Addison-Wesley, Reading (1954)
24. Tropp, J., Gilbert, A.: Signal recovery from random measurements via orthogonal matching pursuit. IEEE Trans. Inform. Theory **53**(12), 4655–4666 (2007)
25. Olabiyi, O., Annamalai, A.: Extending the capability of energy detector for sensing of heterogeneous wideband spectrum. In: IEEE Consumer Communications and Networking Conference (CCNC), pp. 454–458 (2012)
26. Olabiyi, O., Annamalai, A.: Parallel multi-channel detection: a practical solution to energy detection of heterogeneous wideband spectrum. In: IEEE Sarnoff Symposium (SARNOFF), pp. 1–5 (2012)

27. Haque, T., Yazicigil, R.T., Pan, K.J., Wright, J., Kinget, P.R.: Theory and design of a quadrature analog-to-information converter for energy-efficient wideband spectrum sensing. IEEE Trans. Circ. Syst. **62**(2), 527–535 (2015)
28. Sun, W., Huang, Z., Wang, F., Wang, X.: Compressive wideband spectrum sensing based on single channel. IEEE Electron. Lett. **51**(9), 693–695 (2015)
29. Wang, Y., Guo, C., Sun, X., Feng, C.: Time-efficient wideband spectrum sensing based on compressive sampling. In: IEEE 81 Vehicular Technology Conference, pp. 1–5 (2015)

Predicting Response Time-Related Quality-of-Service Outages of PaaS Cloud Applications by Machine Learning

Angela Schedel and Philipp Brune[✉]

University of Applied Sciences Neu-Ulm, Wileystraße 1, 89231 Neu-Ulm, Germany
Angela.Schedel@student.hs-neu-ulm.de, Philipp.Brune@hs-neu-ulm.de
http://www.hs-neu-ulm.de

Abstract. For customers running their applications on Platform-as-a-Service (PaaS) cloud environments it is important to ensure the Quality-of-Service (QoS) of their applications. Knowing in advance if and when a potential problem is likely to occur allows the application owner to take appropriate countermeasures. Therefore, predictive analytics using machine learning could allow to be alerted in advance about potential upcoming QoS outages. In this context, mainly Infrastructure-as-a-Service (IaaS) or Software-as-a-Service (SaaS) have been studied in the literature so far. Studies about predicting QoS outages for the Platform-as-a-Service (PaaS) service model are sparse. Therefore, in this paper an approach for predicting response-time-related QoS outages of web services running in a PaaS cloud environment is presented. The proposed solution uses the open source Apache Spark platform in combination with MLib and binary classification by the naive Bayes algorithm. The approach is evaluated by using test data from a social app backend web service. The results indicate that it is feasible in practice.

Keywords: Cloud computing · PaaS · Quality-of-Service · Predictive analytics · Machine learning · Apache spark

1 Introduction

Cloud computing [14] has become increasingly popular in recent years. While many authors discuss the use of predictive analytics to help ensuring the Quality-of-Service (QoS) of cloud services [2,6,10,18], they focus mainly on its internal use by the providers of Infrastructure-as-a-Service (IaaS) or Software-as-a-Service (SaaS) cloud services [14].

However, in the case of Platform-as-a-Service (PaaS) [14] cloud providers, also their customers come in to play, as these run and maintain applications on the PaaS platforms for which they have to ensure the QoS to their customers or users again. And due to the cloud characteristic of on-demand self-service [14], the PaaS customers also have the ability to impact the resource allocation of their service.

S. Bouzefrane et al. (Eds.): MSPN 2017, LNCS 10566, pp. 155–165, 2017.
DOI: 10.1007/978-3-319-67807-8_12

For cloud services, in particular the availability is crucial for the users who depend on a stable running system [6]. To avoid negative impact on the availability of their cloud-hosted applications, PaaS customers need the ability to forecast strong or sudden changes in the resource utilization of their applications and to react and induce an adjustment or switch resources if necessary [3]. Despite this, so far only few authors have focused on the possibility that PaaS customers may want to make their own predictions independent of the PaaS providers about the resource utilization of the service they use [19].

Therefore, in this paper the possibility to use machine learning to forecast exceptional peaks in the response time of a PaaS-hosted web service implementation is studied from the PaaS customer's perspective (aka the developer or maintainer of the web service). Apache Spark as an Open Source platform is used, which offers supervised as well as unsupervised machine learning algorithms through its machine learning library (MLlib)[1]. From MLib, the naive Bayes classifier (a supervised learning method) was selected and evaluated for the intended purpose. The results indicate the practical feasibility of the proposed approach.

The rest of this paper is organized as follows: Sect. 2 analyzes the related work in detail. In Sect. 3 design of the prediction approach is described, while Sect. 4 outlines the respective proof-of-concept implementation. In Sect. 5, the evaluation and results are presented. We conclude with a summary of our findings.

2   Related Work

Despite that the methods and tools of predictive analytics evolved from data mining [8], the two concepts are not identical [16]. While data mining searches for patterns in or correlations between different data sets, predictive analytics uses data mining techniques to analyze collected historical data so that predictions about future events are possible [16]. Based on this forecasting, suggestions for future actions could be made [16].

Predictive analytics are getting more and more important in all kinds of business areas [4,10,11,20,22]. There usage in marketing [11], Social Web mining for public health, environmental and national security surveillance [4] or supply chain management [22] are just a few examples.

The prediction of the availability of IT systems has also been widely discussed in the literature [7,9,12,23,24]. With respect to cloud computing [14], ensuring the availability of their services is crucial for cloud providers, as it is considered as one of the big advantages by their customers [6,15]. By using current as well as historical data, the future availability as well as capacity needs for specific reappearing time frames, e.g. high service utilization at certain daytimes, can be forecasted [2,6]. Predictive analytics is especially important for the cloud provider, who has to guarantee the QoS and the fulfillment of his Service Level Agreements (SLA) to its customers [2,15]. The availability of cloud

---

[1] http://spark.apache.org.

resources typically will depend on unpredictable factors such as user behavior or current events as well as predictable periodic demand variations such as growing e-commerce short before specific holidays like Halloween or Christmas [3]. Only few attempts have been made to take the influence of users' behaviour and spontaneous decisions for predicting system workloads into account [17,18].

Most important for predictive analytics is the usage of high quality data [8]. Only by using accurate data, models could identify hidden relations between different variables [8]. For predictions of cloud computing availability mainly historical log data of e.g. CPU or memory utilization is used to predict upcoming changes [17–19].

A variety of popular Open Source tools are currently discussed, which also could be used for predictive analytics: First, the R platform for statistical computing and graphics which is written in the corresponding R programming language and is able to include extensions written in C, C++ or Fortran[2]. Second, the KNIME environment[3], written in Java and based on the Eclipse integrated development environment (IDE)[4]. It also supports the Predictive Model Markup Language (PMML), a standard that allows easy exchange of analytical models between different applications [10]. Third, Apache Spark, a system for high-volume cluster data processing[5]. It offers the possibility to write applications in Java, Scala, Python or R and with MLlib provides a library for machine learning.

While R is mainly a programming language for statistical modeling accompanied by an extendible software environment, KNIME provides an end-to-end analytics platform, where the user is able to read, transform, analyze and generate data. In contrast, the main purpose of Apache Spark is to provide a high-speed, cluster-based execution environment for high-volume data processing applications [21]. By in-memory computing, Spark offers a fast approach for processing data queries [21]. Because of these features and the advantages from a developers perspective [21], Apache Spark was selected for the work presented in this paper.

Most of the existing approaches focus mainly on the perspective of the cloud provider and the SaaS and IaaS service models only. Here, it is the provider's duty to always meet the QoS guaranteed in the SLA. And for these cloud service models, usually only the provider could foresee upcoming changes in utilization due to the historical data logs which are collected, saved and used for predictive analytics. For the customer it is complicated to forecast those changes especially for SaaS applications, since he has no control of the underlying software or infrastructure. In case of PaaS and IaaS, the user has more control over the infrastructure and it should be possible to collect log data in order to use it for prediction purposes independently of the cloud service provider. However, so far only few authors have discussed the management of cloud services from the cloud provider's customers' (aka users') perspective [19]. And the latter work only focuses on the mathematical and methodical side of using predictive analytics to forecast run-time behavior [19].

---

[2] https://www.r-project.org.

[3] https://www.knime.org.

[4] http://www.eclipse.org.

[5] http://spark.apache.org/.

Therefore, in this paper the question is addressed how response time-related QoS outages could be predicted from log data using machine learning and the open source Apache Spark platform by PaaS cloud customers.

3   Design of the Prediction Approach

To design and evaluate the proposed prediction approach, a test data set with measured response times of a web service was used. This log data set was obtained during a previous load test of a web service backend for a social mobile app using a simulated workload [5].

The respective service backend consists of RESTful web services implemented using Java Enterprise Edition (EE) JAX-RS API, Java Persistence API (JPA) for object-relational mapping, a PostgreSQL database and running on the Heroku Platform-as-a-Service (PaaS) cloud environment[6] [5]. The response times in this data set were measured within the server only, thus neglecting network latencies. The black curve in the diagram in Fig. 1 shows these data, covering, a time interval of 378000 ms (378 s), in which the response times vary between regular values and a few exceptional, clearly visible peaks. These peaks are now considered as indicators of potential QoS violations, since the web service would respond too slow to the corresponding request in this case.

The proposed approach now is based on the hypothesis that the occurence of such peaks in the near future could be predicted from the pattern of measured response times, i.e. that the response time pattern in the *TestInterval* is a characteristic precursor to the occurence of a peak in the subsequent future *PeakInterval* after a certain *Delay* time, as illustrated by the respective interval bars in Fig. 1.

For a given, fixed set of values for TestInterval, Delay and PeakInterval, this interval triplet is now "shifted" in time over the full data set while classifying each response time pattern by 0 or 1, depending if an extraordinary peak occurs in its subsequent PeakInterval (1) or not (0), respectively. This is illustrated in Fig. 1, denoted by 1st round, 2nd round and so on to denote the "shifting". Following this procedure, a data set consisting of labeled patterns of measured values from each TimeInterval is produced, with one labeled pattern per point in time. This resulting data set now can be used to train a binary classification algorithm [13].

Different algorithms have been proposed for binary classification. Besides the naive Bayes classifier, logistic regression, decision trees or random forests are some of the methods supported by Apache Spark's MLlib[7]. Since the naive Bayes classifier "is a simple, multiclass classification algorithm with the assumption of independence between every pair of features" [1] and "can be trained very efficiently" [1], it was selected in the present approach.

---

[6] http://www.heroku.com.
[7] https://spark.apache.org/docs/2.0.2/ml-guide.html.

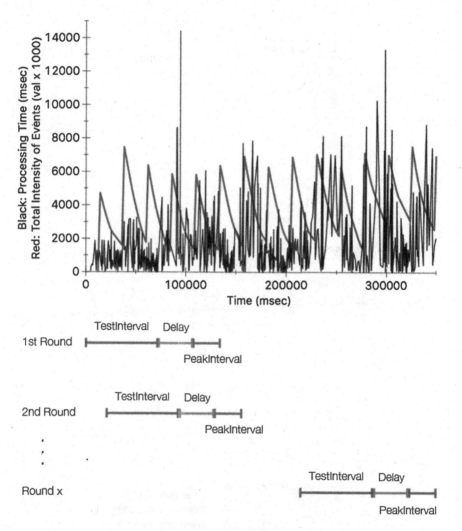

Fig. 1. Diagram (top) of the measured response times per time stamp (black line) of the log data set of a web service used for design and evaluation of the present approach (taken from [5]). Illustration of the TestInterval, PeakInterval and Delay time spans and their "shift" through the data (bottom).

4   Proof-of-Concept Implementation

"A classifier is a function that assigns a class label to an example" [25], with an example being a tuple of n values $E = (x_1, x_2, ..., x_n)$ [25]. In the present case, there are two class labels, $c = 1$ corresponding the occurence of a critical peak in the PeakInterval, and $c = 0$ to no occurence of such a peak. An example E here is given by the measured response-time values x_i of a TestInterval.

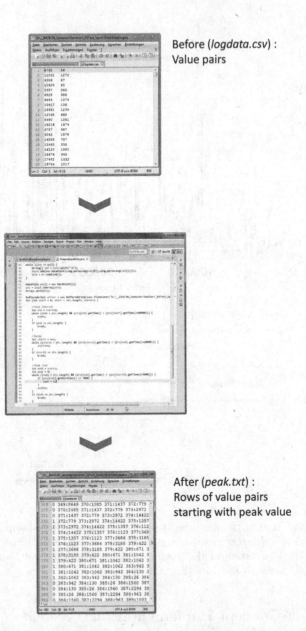

Before (*logdata.csv*) :
Value pairs

After (*peak.txt*) :
Rows of value pairs
starting with peak value

Fig. 2. Schematic illustration of the log data pre-processing to prepare the input for Apache Spark and the naive Bayes classifier. The Java program PrepareInputData.java shown in the middle in the Eclipse IDE window reads the logdata.csv file containing log data value pairs as input and converts it to the output file peaks.txt for loading the data into Apache Spark.

Every example is classified to be in class $c = 1$, if

$$f_b(E) = \frac{p(1|E)}{p(0|E)} \geq 1, \tag{1}$$

with $p(c|E)$ being the probability of E belonging to class c, and the function $f_b(E)$ a Bayesian classifier [25]. Under the assumption of conditional independence of the values x_n, this classifier is given by the naive Bayes classifier [25]

$$f_{nb}(E) = \frac{p(1)}{p(0)} \prod_{i=1}^{n} \frac{p(x_i|1)}{p(x_i|0)}. \tag{2}$$

The total probability $p(c)$ of class c as well as the probability $p(x_i|c)$ of a measured value x_i being in class c can now be obtained from the training data set and then allow to classify further data sets [1,25].

Despite its simplicity, it delivers very good prediction results in many scenarios, even compared to other more sophisticated classification algorithms [25]. However, this "good performance of naive Bayes is surprising because it makes an assumption that is almost always violated in realworld applications: given the class value, all attributes are independent" [25]. Also in the present case, it is obvious that the measured response-time values within a TestInterval could not be assumed to be conditionally independent, since they all depend on the internal state of the web server. So it is interesting to see if the naive Bayes classifier performs well in this case.

First, the log data recorded (a CSV text file named *logdata.csv* in this case) needs to be pre-processed and converted to a file format suitable for the naive Bayes implementation of Apache Spark. While the input log data shown in Fig. 1 comes as a text file containing a list of unsorted x-y-value pairs (measured response time for a timestamp, both in milliseconds, one per line), the data format required as input for the naive Bayes classifier requires a class label for the PeakInterval (0 or 1) at the beginning of each line, followed by a sorted list of index-value pairs (the values x_i), separated by white space and representing the pattern of the measured values of the corresponding TestInterval. Therefore, each line of the resulting data file is of the form

```
0 1:47 2:66 3:360 4:487 5:386  ... .
```

A PeakInterval is classified to contain a critical peak if it contains at least one response time value exceeding a lower bound of 7000 ms. If this value exceeded, the PeakInterval and thus also the corresponding response time pattern in the TestInterval (corresponding to a line of the output file) will be labeled by 1, otherwise by 0.

Therefore, a Java program was developed using the Eclipse Luna IDE[8] to preprocess the data accordingly for a given set of input values for the TestInterval, Delay and PeakInterval. This pre-processing is illustrated schematically in Fig. 2.

---

[8] http://www.eclipse.org.

Here, the output file of the pre-processor and subsequent input file to the naive Bayes classifier is labeled as *peak.txt*.

For the present evaluation, since this input file to Apache Spark is well structured and comparably small in case of the test data set used, Apache Spark was used on a single computing node and in standalone mode without underlying Hadoop. However, due to the built-in capabilities of Spark, the presented approach could be easily scaled to run on a cluster and process very large input data sets as well.

For this work, Apache Spark version 2.0.2 (November 14, 2016) has been used, running on a Windows PC. To use Spark, in general Scala, Python and the hadoop-winutils need to be installed first. However, since only Java is used as a programming language in the present case, the installation of the other two programming languages was not necessary.

For using the naive Bayes classifier, the `JavaNaiveBayesExample.java` example program provided in the Spark MLib documentation [1] only had to be slightly adapted in the present case.

Spark uses resilient distributed datasets (RDDs), which enable a program to operate in parallel on a set of values partitioned across cluster nodes. The *peak.txt* input file generated by the pre-processor is loaded into such a JavaRDD. The program then splits it randomly into two RDDs with a 60/40 ratio. 60% of the original RDD are used to train the naive Bayes classifier. The other 40% go into a test RDD, which is used to measure the accuracy of the predictions by the classifier. The obtained accuracies are then written as output to another text file named *accuracy.txt* for further analysis.

5   Evaluation and Results

The Proof-of-Concept (PoC) implementation was evaluated using the test data set illustrated in Fig. 1 for different values of TestInterval, Delay and PeakInterval.

In practice, the delay needs to be long enough to enable a system to react to the potential exceptional response time peak in advance, e.g. a loadbalancer to direct upcoming requests to another server. So 10000 ms were chosen during the evaluation, which seems already a conservative choice to this respect. To analyze the impact of the Delay value on the accuracy, the evaluation was performed for different values of PeakInterval and TestInterval and with a Delay value of 0 and 10000 ms. The results of the test runs are shown in Table 1.

The prediction accuracy with the finite delay is slightly lower then without one, which corresponds with the general observation that long-range predictions in time are usually harder to achieve then short-range ones. In both cases, the highest accuracy was obtained for a test interval of 50000 ms and a peak interval of 5000 ms (marked in red in Table 1), which seems to be specific for the sample. In this case, the occurrence of an exceptional peak is predicted with an accuracy of over 80%.

Even though the test data set used is rather small, these results are promising with respect to the practical usability of the approach. To be able to predict that

Table 1. Prediction accuracies obtained with the naive Bayes classifier and the test data set for different choices of the time and peak intervals without (top) and with a delay of 10000 ms (bottom). The highest prediction accuracies achieved are marked in red.

Test Interval length (ms)	Peak Interval length(ms)	Delay (ms)	Accuracy
60000	6000	0	0.7946
60000	5000	0	0.8082
60000	4500	0	0.7596
50000	8000	0	0.7379
50000	6000	0	0.7737
50000	5100	0	0.7727
50000	5000	0	**0.8365**
50000	4500	0	0.8113

Test Interval length (ms)	Peak Interval length(ms)	Delay (ms)	Accuracy
60000	6000	10000	0.6630
60000	5000	10000	0.6777
60000	4500	10000	0.6177
50000	8000	10000	0.7849
50000	5100	10000	0.7793
50000	5000	10000	**0.8075**
50000	4500	10000	0.7963
50000	3000	10000	0.6766

a critical peak is likely to occur in about 10 s with a probability of over 80% would already be sufficient for a loadbalancer to route requests to another server.

However, it remains to be evaluated if this holds true or even improves for further, larger log data sets from different applications and servers as well.

6 Conclusion

In conclusion, in this paper the possibility to forecast exceptional peaks in the response time of a PaaS-hosted web service implementation has been studied from the customer's perspective. Therefore, a predictive analytics approach using machine learning with the naive Bayes classifier and the Apache Spark open source framework has been proposed and evaluated using one log data set. The obtained results are promising with respect to the practical feasibility and benefits of the approach.

However, the influences on the quality of the prediction results of the selected algorithm, the input values for the time intervals as well as the log data set itself need to be studied in more detail. Therefore, further research is needed to collect and analyze more and larger data sets from different applications and comparatively evaluate other machine learning algorithms then the naive Bayes classifier.

References

1. https://spark.apache.org/docs/2.0.2/mllib-naive-bayes.html. Accessed 26 Apr 2017
2. Adegboyega, A.: An adaptive resource provisioning scheme for effective QoS maintenance in the IAAS cloud. In: Proceedings of the International Workshop on Virtualization Technologies (VT 2015), NY, USA, pp. 2:1–2:6 (2011). http://doi.acm.org/10.1145/2835075.2835078
3. Armbrust, M., Fox, A., Griffith, R., Joseph, A.D., Katz, R., Konwinski, A., Lee, G., Patterson, D., Rabkin, A., Stoica, I., Zaharia, M.: A view of cloud computing. Commun. ACM **53**(4), 50–58 (2010). http://doi.acm.org/10.1145/1721654.1721672
4. Boulos, M.N.K., Sanfilippo, A.P., Corley, C.D., Wheeler, S.: Social web mining and exploitation for serious applications: technosocial predictive analytics and related technologies for public health, environmental and national security surveillance. Comput. Methods Prog. Biomed. **100**(1), 16–23 (2010)
5. Brune, P.: Simulating user interactions: a model and tool for semi-realistic load testing of social app. backend web services. In: Proceedings of the 13th International Conference on Web Information Systems and Technologies (WEBIST 2017), pp. 235–242. SCITEPRESS (2017)
6. Chaczko, Z., Mahadevan, V., Aslanzadeh, S., Mcdermid, C.: Availability and load balancing in cloud computing. In: International Conference on Computer and Software Modeling, Singapore, vol. 14 (2011)
7. Danninger, M., Robles, E., Takayama, L., Wang, Q.Y., Kluge, T., Stiefelhagen, R., Nass, C.: The connector service-predicting availability in mobile contexts. In: Renals, S., Bengio, S., Fiscus, J.G. (eds.) MLMI 2006. LNCS, vol. 4299, pp. 129–141. Springer, Heidelberg (2006). doi:10.1007/11965152_12
8. Eckerson, W.W.: Predictive analytics. Extending the Value of Your Data Warehousing Investment. TDWI Best Practices Report 1, pp. 1–36 (2007)
9. Grünbaum, D.: Predicting availability to consumers of spatially and temporally variable resources. Hydrobiologia **480**(1), 175–191 (2002)
10. Guazzelli, A., Stathatos, K., Zeller, M.: Efficient deployment of predictive analytics through open standards and cloud computing. SIGKDD Explor. Newsl. **11**(1), 32–38 (2009). http://doi.acm.org/10.1145/1656274.1656281
11. Hair Jr., J.F.: Knowledge creation in marketing: the role of predictive analytics. Eur. Bus. Rev. **19**(4), 303–315 (2007)

12. Houmb, S.H., Georg, G., France, R., Reddy, R., Bieman, J.: Predicting availability of systems using BBN in aspect-oriented risk-driven development (AORDD). In: Proceedings of the 9th World Multi-Conference on Systemics, Cybernetics and Informatics, vol. 10, pp. 396–403 (2005)
13. Kraipeerapun, P.: Neural network classification based on quantification of uncertainty. Ph.D. thesis, Murdoch University (2009)
14. Mell, P.M., Grance, T.: SP 800–145. The NIST definition of cloud computing (2011)
15. Menascé, D.A., Ngo, P.: Understanding cloud computing: experimentation and capacity planning. In: International CMG Conference (2009)
16. Mishra, N., Silakari, S.: Predictive analytics: a survey, trends, applications, oppurtunities & challenges. Int. J. Comput. Sci. Inf. Technol. 3(3), 4434–4438 (2012)
17. Ramezani, F.: Autonomic system for optimal resource management in cloud environments. Ph.D. thesis, University of Technology Sydney (2016)
18. Ramezani, F., Lu, J., Hussain, F.: A fuzzy predictable load balancing approach in cloud computing. In: Proceedings of the International Conference on Grid Computing and Applications (GCA), p. 108. The Steering Committee of The World Congress in Computer Science, Computer Engineering and Applied Computing (WorldComp) (2013)
19. ur Rehman, Z., Hussain, O.K., Hussain, F.K., Chang, E., Dillon, T.: User-side QoS forecasting and management of cloud services. World Wide Web 18(6), 1677–1716 (2015)
20. Shmueli, G., Koppius, O.R.: Predictive analytics in information systems research. Mis Q. 35, 553–572 (2011)
21. Shoro, A.G., Soomro, T.R.: Big data analysis: apache spark perspective. Global J. Comput. Sci. Technol. 15(1) (2015)
22. Waller, M.A., Fawcett, S.E.: Data science, predictive analytics, and big data: a revolution that will transform supply chain design and management. J. Bus. Logist. 34(2), 77–84 (2013)
23. Ward, S.A., Gittens, M.: A real-time application to predict and notify students about the present and future availability of workspaces on a university campus. In: Proceedings of the 2015 ACM Annual Conference on SIGUCCS, pp. 67–74. ACM (2015)
24. Wolski, R., Spring, N., Hayes, J.: Predicting the CPU availability of time-shared unix systems on the computational grid. Cluster Comput. 3(4), 293–301 (2000)
25. Zhang, H.: The optimality of naive bayes. AA 1(2), 3 (2004)

Intelligent Road Design Using Artificial Intelligence Techniques

Camilo Isaza Fonseca[1], Octavio J. Salcedo Parra[1,2(✉)],
and Brayan S. Reyes Daza[2]

[1] Universidad Nacional de Colombia, Bogotá, Colombia
{caisazafo,ojsalcedop}@unal.edu.co
[2] Universidad Distrital "Francisco José de Caldas", Bogotá, Colombia
osalcedo@udistrital.edu.co, bsreyesd@correo.udistrital.edu.co

Abstract. In the biggest and principal world cities exist departments dedicated exclusively to handle and organize an intelligent road system that would permit to optimize the times of the trajectories that are utilized by their users. The opposite case happens in cities of underdeveloped countries, as if it is Bogota's case in Colombia, where technics that would permit to realize an optimal administration of road and transit sector are not introduced. That means that is important to develop a model that would permit to implement a solution that makes use of the new technologies of the biggest world cities. One of these is the use of intelligent traffic lights that could be operated from a distance making use of the design presented in this work and which one will be test under conditions that allow to measure its yield in contrast with other previous works.

Keywords: Artificial intelligence · Fuzzy logic · Graph · Intelligent traffic lights · Optimization · Traffic system

1 Introduction

The TSP problem is one of the most commonly encountered when computing is being talked about, this is a problem that consists of finding the shortest routes between two points that are distant from n sub-points that must be part of the route. This type of problem has many postulated solutions (as expected), although in general, for the case of this work should be sought the most optimal solution that allows finding the indicated routes in the shortest possible time. For this, a Research to determine the main needs of a city with a population of more than 5,000,000 inhabitants making use of new cutting-edge technologies applying artificial intelligence techniques. That provide an optimal solution that transport to the cities to improve their paths Vials (in terms of technology) with traffic lights and traffic regulators that contribute to the improvement of people's quality of life and the development of a clean and self-sustaining ecosystem.

© Springer International Publishing AG 2017
S. Bouzefrane et al. (Eds.): MSPN 2017, LNCS 10566, pp. 166–177, 2017.
DOI: 10.1007/978-3-319-67807-8_13

2   Hypothesis

For a city with a high population density and in which approximately half a
million vehicles circulate [1] it is essential to propose tools that optimize mobility
and contribute to economic and cultural development through the modification
of the archaisms that have been marking the Methodologies that have been used
in the design of roadways and traffic manipulation models. For a city such as
Bogotá, a design can be proposed that modifies the use of traffic controls that
have been used for ever traffic lights. That is why to apply techniques, which
intervene directly and in real time in the times of Transit and stop of these
can represent a solution. That provides a remarkable improvement around the
average waiting times per traffic light, decreasing them by at least 10%. It is
also expected to obtain improvement in the number of vehicles that are stopped
to wait in each cycle of the semaphore decreasing this amount in at least a 60%
reflected with the data obtained in the work of O. Salcedo [2]. In addition, it is
also expected to be able to obtain a benefit in terms of the average speed of the
vehicles that transit in the way object by at least 40%. Which could obtain a real
and direct benefit compared to the models previously proposed and that were
proposed in this work, as it is, for example, the ANFIS model of O. Salcedo [2].

3   Methodology

Artificial intelligence techniques have undoubtedly represented the most important and convenient paradigm in solving problems requiring real-time assistance.
Among the most outstanding and most used methodologies, we can find models
of fuzzy logic in which parameters intervene that are obtained through measurement elements that are strategically located as required so that a timely response
can be offered to the needs that it demands the problem. In addition, fuzzy logic
has been closely related to the problem solving of vehicular traffic detection and
manipulation, as was already observed in the work of O. Salcedo [2]. Moreover, in
the work of K. Jena [3], a tool developed using fuzzy logic techniques can be used
to control a vehicle remotely as a cruise control. For purposes of this work will be
used one of the most modern artificial intelligence techniques, simulation based
on intelligent agents. They interact with their closest similes (cellular automata),
with this will develop systems that manipulate traffic lights as they have the ability to act as independent entities and in society in a multi-agent design. This is
a solution that promises to effectively meet the waiting times improvement and
also provides the ability to mutate against unexpected changes and also provides
the possibility to act differently depending on the date, time and climatic situation. To carry out the programming of the fundamental software of the design
will be used a language of high level (Python) that will provide the necessary
tools and that also provide to the sufficient support to be executed in any class
of machine independent of its operating system. Implementing this solution in
the object of study can be expensive and risky, that is why a state-of-the-art
simulator is used in which we can implement a tool that allows emulating the

behavior of different road paths that have traffic lights and other elements that are part of real life and that will be programmed through the Transmodeler interface. This allows us to construct a scale-based design of the object that will be taken for the study (explained later) and will allow implementing the result of this work in order to obtain the result and analyze them with the original version of the model. In order to obtain the data on which it is going to work, it is possible to choose to use magnetic loop sensors (as was previously done in [2]). Because these provide true and accurate information without giving way to the mistakes that may be made by human agents in the performance of this work. In addition, these sensors allow us to obtain the information at any time of the day and in almost any climatic condition, although, in order to obtain an initial sample to check the effectiveness of the model, we opt for a manual data collection. In the work of the modular implementation of the traffic, controllers will be used techniques based on automata with independent behaviors oriented to the behavior in neighborhoods. Simulating the behavior of the cellular automata but obtaining the benefits of the techniques of diffuse logic, which will define a hybrid interleaving of technologies, which, as expected, provide a solution that meets the objectives proposed in the present work. Specifically, in the city of Bogota, a system of 15 traffic lights that in certain conditions seem not to work optimally, these crosses correspond to the four that are included between Carrera 97 between streets 24 and 24C and Carrera 100 between streets 24 And 24C, this can be seen in Fig. 1 These crossings control all traffic from the town

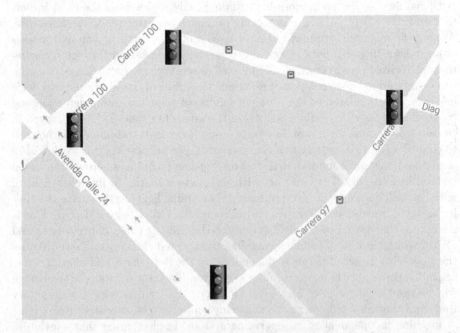

Fig. 1. Map corresponding to the area to be analyzed and to which the simulation is applied. Source: Google Maps.

of Fontibón to 26th and 24th Street (Avenida Esperanza), which represents a bottleneck that would affect the mobility of users by lengthening waiting times and reducing average speed considerably. For the purposes of data collection, a checker shall be assigned at each junction to take the corresponding information, in addition to waiting times at traffic lights in a peak hour (5:30 p.m.) and 1 h (10:00 a.m.) with in order to obtain information that will be verified as the case may be. This will later be loaded in the simulator to perform the verification with the intelligent system running and thus be able to obtain information about the changes that are presented with this.

4 Design

High-level programming greatly facilitates the work of programmers; in particular, Python, which will be the main language of this work, provides a special facility in developing robust tools that can offer greater guarantees to users, has a variety of libraries that provide very good utilities to the software developed in this. To structure a fuzzy logic the first thing we must do is to define the main element to be measured and to establish parameters that allow to quantify with ordinality a certain amount of these elements taking as reference an initial measure. This means that for the specific case, the first thing to be done is to make an average vehicle measurement at each of the traffic lights to be studied and this value will be assigned to above average value. The values will then be assigned by adding or decreasing (depending on the case) between 3 and 5 vehicles, an example illustrating this situation is presented below:

$$i = number\ of\ vehicles\ observed\ in\ the\ initial\ sampling$$

The quantification would be done as follows: $None = 0\ vehicles\ Few = x - 5$ $vehicles\ Some = x\ vehicles\ Many = x + 5\ vehicles\ Full = x + 10\ vehicles$

With the above, if we had a traffic light in which initially 10 vehicles were observed, the quantification would be:

$$None = 0\ vehicles$$

$$Few = 5\ vehicles$$

$$Some = 10\ vehicles$$

$$Many = 15\ vehicles$$

$$Full = 20\ vehicles$$

Now, another important aspect of fuzzy logic you see the answer to be obtained according to the parameter that has been observed. A response should be prepared to level the vehicles. For the example above, if the semaphore is calibrated to authorize passage for and seconds, the ratio between the time to increase and the number of vehicles to be passed is directly proportional. That is to say, the greater number of vehicles, the longer the time must be increased to the standard time of the traffic light, for example:

$$ValueObtained = full, time = y + n$$

Where n is a contingency value that must be modified over time in order to find a balance that allows to obtain a value between few and many for the next data acquisition. This contingency value will not change over time as follows.

Execution 1: We get a full traffic, the traffic light time is, and then we assign a random value between 5 and 10 which will be the contingency value. Therefore, the value of the semaphore time for the next execution is: $time = n + random\,(5, 10)$.

Execution 2: This execution is divided in two cases:

Case 1: We get a full traffic value.

In this case, we will add a random contingency value between 1 and 5 as follows: $time = time + random\,(1, 5)$.

Case 2: We get a traffic value less than many.

In this case, we will reduce the contingency value but this time to a lesser extent in order not to re-saturate the traffic at this traffic light as follows: $time = time - random\,(3, 8)$.

Execution 3: This execution is divided into 2 cases:

Case 1: We continue with a full value.

In this case we should simply wait for the traffic to decrease without changing the time because this will cause traffic at the complementary traffic light to increase.

Case 2: We get a value less than many.

In this case we will reset the time of the traffic light to the time with which it would operate normally: $time = time - period$.

Special execution: In the event that in a run we find a traffic light with traffic equivalent to none the traffic light time will correspond to 5 s that will allow pedestrians to cross at complementary traffic lights. With the above, we would have a fuzzy logic design capable of operating on a simple network of traffic lights. For purposes of a large city, it is necessary to choose to couple all these intersections in a system that allows establishing a connection between them so that the control of the traffic is complete and allows working together and in this way obtaining a real and verifiable benefit. To satisfy this need will be used a unidirectional graph that allows obtaining information about the nearby traffic lights in order to provide a timely response. The implementation in python for this system will use a `semaphore` type element which will act as a node, this lead to I get a dictionary-like element that will have content to the predecessor nodes, or in other words, earlier traffic lights. The implementation will then be a recursive, so, being in any node, we can reach the first **semaphore** of the road and we can get information about the traffic at this point. The Algorithm 1.1, which is responsible for establishing a path between two traffic lights, is shown below.

Algorithm 1.1. Development of a graph in Python using dictionaries. Source: Authors

```
def set_child(G, u, v): #G is current
graph, u is current node, v is next
node
        if u not in G:
                G[u]={}
        if v not in G:
                G[v]={}
        G[u][v]=1 # u and v are now
        connected
        links[v]+=1
        return G
```

A new need that arises from the implementation of these dictionaries is that, according to the characteristics of these in python, we must assign a unique identifier for each of these, be it a number, name, code, address or other key element That allows us to locate them quickly in the dictionary (in constant time). Therefore, it could be suggested to establish a coding according to the sector in which the semaphore is located, which would have advantage over other systems because a remote coding could be performed with only the information of the location of the semaphore. Otherwise, it would be if, for example, we used the signal of the traffic light, in cities where this information does not rest on any document, a specialized firm should be hired to go all over the city, checking traffic lights after traffic lights. This would greatly increase the costs of implementing such a solution especially where the geographic territory is too large. For the answer according to the values obtained in the traffic valuation at each semaphore a special method was designed, which would work with the logic that was already proposed in both types, numerical and with our quantitative organization. The Algorithm 1.2 shows the code used for this.

Algorithm 1.2. Development of the fuzzy system in Python. Source: Authors

```
x=10 #mean value of cars
s_time = 15 #Standar time value
current_time = s_time #Actual time
def get_time(xx): #xx is the current value
        of cars
        if (xx==0):
                return 5
        elif (xx<=x):
                print" few_or_mean_cars_
at_" + time.strftime("%H:_%M:_%S")+" in_
" + id_return s_time
        elif (xx<=x+5):
                print "many_cars_at_" +
time.strftime("%H:_%M:_%S")+" in_" + id_
                return current_time
        else:
                print "full_cars_at_" +
time.strftime("%H:_%M:_%S") + "in_" + id_
                if (current_time - s_time
>=20): \# Ejecution 3 with full
                        return current_time
                if (current_time - s_time
>=8):\# Ejecution 2 with full
                        return current_time
+ random (1,5)
                else:
\# Ejecution 1 with full
                        return current_time
+ random (5,10)
xx=get_traffic()
current_time = get_time(xx)
```

The previous code also generates a console report on the traffic conditions at a traffic light and provides the time and its identification to obtain real-time traffic information in the city. Note the implementation for each of the cases that were previously proposed for fuzzy logic.

In terms of data collection and determination of important system variables, a roadmap was established that would be used to avoid obtaining information that does not correspond or that is not valid. Specifically, the methodology for this data collection focuses on a resource that was delivered to the observers at the site to take the information through a manual timer. This sheet consists of a table in which to take the arrival time of 30 vehicles, the time in green of the traffic light, the red time of the traffic light, the average arrival of vehicles and the number of vehicles remaining in the Traffic waiting for the junction.

The design will be presented later in the implementations where the data taken for the 15 traffic lights of our test or initial sampling will be attached.

To simulate the behavior of vehicles and traffic lights, a simulation based on discrete events is used to connect directly to the TransModeler platform through a pipe provided by the operating system. This simulation is designed in layers like this:

Layer 1: Simulator in Python, is responsible for controlling the timing and storing the main structure of intersections.

Layer 2: Intersection class, this layer being a class responsible for handling the traffic lights of each intersection, that is, for a system with n intersections, instances of the intersection class will be used.

Layer 3: Traffic light class, this being an innerclass of the intersection class, this being the one in charge of obtaining information about traffic and also provide information about the time it needs to evacuate traffic.

Each layer is part of the previous one, an image describing this structure can be seen in Fig. 2.

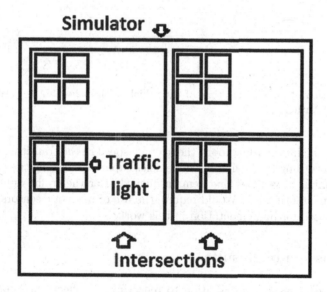

Fig. 2. Structure designed for a simulator with four intersections and each of them with four independent traffic lights. Source: Authors.

Another important aspect for the design of the project was to find a balance that would give validity to the time of departure of the vehicles, clearly these should have a waiting time according to their position in the queue that is done at the traffic light. This time was calculated manually from the reaction of the first driver, performing the test with a manual transmission vehicle, the start time circulates around the 3.0 s. In addition, starting a vehicle that is in position x and if you have correct visibility of vehicles ahead, would have a duration of:
$$S(x) = 3.0 + 0.7x.$$

Where x is the position that the vehicle has in the tail. In the Fig. 3 shows the function for the first 10 cars in the queue.

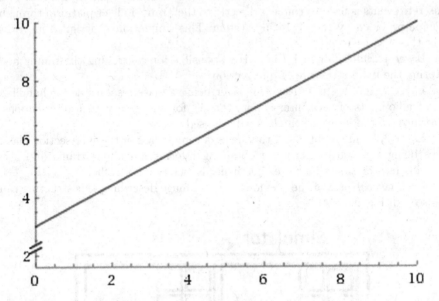

Fig. 3. Function of the starting time of the vehicle with respect to its position in the tail. Source: Authors.

Finally, the information about the average speed of the transiting vehicles is estimated according to the number of vehicles capable of leaving the traffic light and the number of vehicles that remain queued after the traffic light, in order to obtain this information. Would require the use of magnetic sensors but these will not be used for implementation in this work.

5   Discussion of Results

The results of a project, in addition to reflecting the effectiveness of an alternative, serve to open a field of research that allows other interested people to go deeper into the subject. For example, if the results of this project become unfavorable, other researchers who read this article may choose to present an improvement. A modification or simply, they might discover that studying this topic has no relevance because it has already been shown that this technique does not work with the field of study.

As already mentioned, a simulation was carried out on a main sample. The 15 traffic lights included between carrera 100 and carrera 97 at the height of Avenida Esperanza and 24C Street, main departures from Fontibon to the East of The city, in these was obtained a quite favorable result; The execution of the algorithm to load the traffic lights demonstrated a strong advantage over the traditional system. With a notable improvement in vehicle density at the sector, intersection and traffic light levels, which is around 60% in a low number of executions and 98% in a remarkably high number of executions, the results can be seen in Fig. 4.

Percent Effectiveness

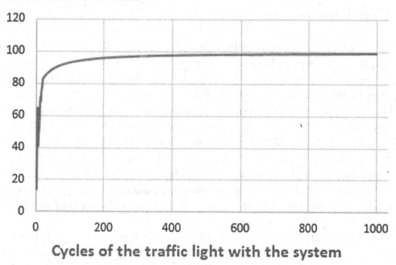

Cycles of the traffic light with the system

Fig. 4. Effectiveness of the algorithm on a structure designed for a simulator with four intersections and each of them with four independent traffic lights.

In contrast to the work of O. Salcedo [2], the algorithm presented in this paper, with an execution such as that given by Salcedo for his ANFIS model, shows an improvement in traffic between 68% and 72%. That compared to ANFIS would mean an improvement of 10% on average. This would demonstrate that there is a viable way to optimize the ANFIS model in order to improve its results. For the other values that are evaluated in [2] would require the use of a magnetic loop sensor to allow us to obtain information about it.

As for one of the most robust works in terms of traffic redirection and traffic relief, the work of Z. Cao [4], which operates under the techniques of traffic light control and vehicle re-addressing In the work of Z. Cao [4] in the Grid sector, an improvement of 35% can be seen in the Travel times. While in the CityHall sector, a 20% improvement can be observed using only the traffic light modification technique, because Cao's work is much more efficient when using his combined techniques. The above allows us to show that the work presented here has the conditions to operate with greater efficiency than that of Cao. Even if it is evaluated in the same road corridors (if you take the model that modifies the traffic lights, LCO, only).

Finally, as we can see, when the diffuse algorithm is executed in a balanced system like the one proposed in this work, a very considerable improvement can be observed in a sudden case of vehicular chaos. Moreover, if the execution were extended to infinity, the traffic would improve completely in the sector with an observable result of up to 98%, which positions a diffuse system like this in a position that would allow it to be part of the future solutions for the traffic of a city.

6   Conclusions

The TSP Traveler Salesman Problem is a rather exotic source of study as you can find important information from a large number of sources. As well as historical references that can serve as guidance in choosing the technologies and strategies that will be used to solve instances of this problem over time.

The security and veracity of the information is an important point to take into account since we will have at our disposal tools that will be working in real time and that can directly affect the integrity, health and life of the people [5].

In the coming years, the internet of things will take over the behavior of the technological media that we know today, gaining a direct influence on the tools that are used daily and in community. Likewise as in the decisions, that are made regarding the implementation of new technologies that are part of the common and daily life of societies.

With the solution presented in this work, we are giving the world a new alternative to reduce traffic in big cities. As well as optimizing people's time and improving the environment by reducing the pollution of vehicles and the time, they last lit up in the streets. In addition, we are delivering to the big cities a tool they can use to improve the quality of life of their inhabitants, without a doubt, by taking advantage of this work, the beneficiaries can be millions. We are giving an opportunity to new technologies to emerge and we can make the most of their benefits.

Undoubtedly, fuzzy logic is a key tool that we can take advantage of traffic regulators, has a very good performance and a low cost implementation, in addition, provides a very good performance in terms of the solution be concerned. To conclude, traffic is a colossus that we must combat and the best way is to make use of the technological means that we have at hand applying the techniques of networks, interconnection and artificial intelligence that allow us to recognize and identify adaptive patterns to predict and control The excessive growth of agents involved in this problem.

References

1. Baraya Rubiano, A.: El Runt Tiene la Realidad del 'CENSO' Automotor en Colombia: Hay Más de 11 Millones de Vehículos (2015) http://www.motor.com.co/actualidad/tecnologia/runt-realidad-censo-automotor-colombia-hay-11-millones-vehiculos/21229
2. Salcedo Parra, O., Pedraza Martínez, L., Hernández Surez, C.: Modelo de Semaforización Inteligente para la Ciudad de Bogotá. Ingeniería **22**, 61–69 (2006)

3. Swarup Jena, K., Arockia Vijay, J., Ranjan Senapati, P.: Fuzzy logic based approach for controlling of a vehicle in its longitudinal motion. Middle-East J. Sci. Res. **S1**, 346–352 (2017)
4. Cao, Z., Jiang, S., Zhang, J.: A unified framework for vehicle rerouting and traffic light control to reduce traffic congestion. IEEE Trans. Intell. Transp. Syst. **18**, 1958–1973 (2017)
5. Bell, M.: Hyperstar: a multi-path astar algorithm for risk averse vehicle navigation. Transp. Res. Part B: Methodol. **43**, 97–107 (2009)

Mobility Prediction in Vehicular Networks: An Approach Through Hybrid Neural Networks Under Uncertainty

Soumya Banerjee[1]([⊠]), Samia Bouzefrane[2],
and Paul Mühlethaler[3]

[1] Birla Institute of Technology, Mesra, Jharkhand, India
soumyabanerjee@bitmesra.ac.in
[2] Conservatoire National des Arts et Metiers, Paris Cedex 03, France
[3] Eva Team, Inria, 2 Rue Simone IFF, 75012 Paris, France

Abstract. Conventionally, the exposure regarding knowledge of the inter vehicle link duration is a significant parameter in *Vehicular Networks* to estimate the delay during the failure of a specific link during the transmission. However, the mobility and dynamics of the nodes is considerably higher in a smart city than on highways and thus could emerge a complex random pattern for the investigation of the link duration, referring all sorts of uncertain conditions. There are existing link duration estimation models, which perform linear operations under linear relationships without imprecise conditions. Anticipating, the requirement to tackle the uncertain conditions in *Vehicular Networks*, this paper presents a hybrid neural network-driven mobility prediction model. The proposed hybrid neural network comprises a *Fuzzy Constrained Boltzmann machine (FCBM)*, which allows the random patterns of several vehicles in a single time stamp to be learned. The several dynamic parameters, which may make the contexts of *Vehicular Networks* uncertain, could be vehicle speed at the moment of prediction, the number of leading vehicles, the average speed of the leading vehicle, the distance to the subsequent intersection of traffic roadways and the number of lanes in a road segment. In this paper, a novel method of hybrid intelligence is initiated to tackle such uncertainty. Here, *the Fuzzy Constrained Boltzmann Machine (FCBM)* is a stochastic graph model that can learn joint probability distribution over its visible units (say n) and hidden feature units (say m). It is evident that there must be a prime driving parameter of the holistic network, which will monitor the interconnection of weights and biases of *the Vehicular Network* for all these features. The highlight of this paper is that the prime driving parameter to control the learning process should be a fuzzy number, as fuzzy logic is used to represent the vague and uncertain parameters. Therefore, if uncertainty exists due to the random patterns caused by vehicle mobility, the proposed Fuzzy Constrained Boltzmann Machine could remove the noise from the data representation. Thus, the proposed model will be able to

Soumya Banerjee is Visiting Professor at Le Conservatoire National des Arts et Métiers, CNAM Paris, France.

© Springer International Publishing AG 2017
S. Bouzefrane et al. (Eds.): MSPN 2017, LNCS 10566, pp. 178–194, 2017.
DOI: 10.1007/978-3-319-67807-8_14

predict robustly the mobility in VANET, referring any instance of link failure under *Vehicular Network* paradigm.

Keywords: Vehicular network · Mobility prediction · Link failure · Fuzzy Constrained Boltzmann Machine · VANET · Uncertainty

1   Introduction

With the increase of wireless networks and the growing trends towards *the Internet of Things (IoT)*, vehicular communication is being viewed from different perspectives. These include the road safety and traffic management [1]. However, scenarios of vehicular networks are becoming more complex as several dynamic parameters of vehicles are being introduced: vehicle speed at the moment of prediction, number of leading vehicles, average speed of the leading vehicles, the distance to the subsequent intersection and the numbers of lanes in a road segment. The problem is thus more realistic and several research initiatives are already being accomplished, by considering the data obtained relating short-term vehicle movement [2,3]. The reliability of contexts, variables in different road intersections, different traffic scenarios and inter-vehicle link duration offer challenges to formulate the prediction model [4]. In addition to, a substantial number of research initiatives concern probabilistic modeling of vehicles which infer immediate future locations. Even so, it has been observed that to configure a robust and intelligent vehicular networks [5], each tiny parameter such as road intersection problem parameters can be handled with an effective group scheduling of vehicles. Thus those intelligent neuro-fuzzy (neural-network and fuzzy logic driven) models becoming more adaptive to suit different traffic conditions [6]. Inspired by such models [7,8], this paper proposes a *Fuzzy Constrained Boltzmann Machine (FCBM)*. This is a stochastic graph model and can learn joint probability distributions over certain time units with many existing as well as hidden features of different vehicular network environments. The relevance of proposed approach is two fold: firstly, the class of Boltzmann machine is a specialized class of deep learning algorithm and no such model currently exists. Moreover, conventional deep learning models are being controlled with visible and hidden features of problem domain. In this case, an uncertain relationship is represented with these inherent uncertainty as a fuzzy number. Thus, the constraints of relationships between the features should be driven by fuzzy logic and this could serve to train the Boltzmann machine to infer smarter decision about mobility predictions in vehicular networks. We develop the simulation and experimental model and test it with the corresponding data set. Several interesting observations have been obtained. The analysis shows that a hybrid intelligent model is required, where uncertainty and non-linear optimal conditions persist. The remaining part of the paper has been organized as follows: Sect. 2 briefly mentions the most relevant intelligent models deployed for vehicular networks under different conditions. Section 3 develops a mathematical formulation of the proposed approach, and outlines the role of auxiliary functions for modeling fuzzy logic in Boltzmann scheme in Sect. 3.1. Section 4 provides a short introduction to the highlights conventional Boltzmann machine and its relevance to hybrid neural networks. Section 4.1 gives details of simulation and the corresponding results comparing them to the available data set. Finally, Sect. 5 highlights about the contributions and mentions future research directions in the field.

2   Related Work

Very few core research implementations are available using different computational intelligence schemes in vehicular networks for mobility prediction. Most approaches (e.g. fuzzy logic and rough set) use clustering or classifications of vehicles according to their location even in boundary regions [12,13]. However specific intersection control problems in smart cities are being treated with neuro-fuzzy learning from real traffic conditions [14]. Traffic and vehicle speed prediction have also been developed using neural networks and hidden Markov models [6]. Inspite of all the existing models, sensing techniques and prediction of mobility in vehicular networks have raised substantial research challenges. This is primarily because, none of the intelligent models could encompass diversified uncertain parameters of vehicular networks and making the predictions unrealistic. Inspired by recent studies of deep learning and machine learning approaches [15], this paper adopts a basic Boltzmann machine approach. The model is trained through fuzzy numbers, which represents different non-linear features of vehicular network as well as network connectivity overheads. The proposed model is termed as hybrid neural network.

3   Mathematical Formulation of Proposed Model

The following parameters are being considered, while formulating the proposed model:

- Vehicle speed S_m at the moment of prediction
- Number of leading vehicles
- Average speed of leading vehicles
- Distance (optional) to the next intersection
- Number of lanes in the road segment (R_s)

These parameters are non-deterministic and lead to major concerns of uncertainty in vehicular networks. In addition, these parameters and their associated contexts can contain uncertainties. They are listed as:

- Change of vehicle Speed
- Different driving habits and road conditions
- Density of traffic
- Position of traffic lights

Therefore a specific objective function can be formulated (Table. 1).

Table 1. List of prime variables

Parameters/Variables	Semantics
$i \in I$	Time interval between vehicles ->I = {1,2,......m}
$j \in J$	Index of different access points (AP), where J = {1,2,.....n}
γ^{a}	Vehicle departure ratio from source
M_{ij}	Rate of mobility from i to j
L_i	Length of time interval
x_{ij}	Mobility prediction decision variable for the points i to j
P_s	Prediction Scenario with respect to the parameters mentioned for Vehicular Network
α	time interval

[a]This is used to represent the auxiliary function β and indicates weight bias of fuzzy

The objective function is described, the objective function can train the proposed Boltzmann Machine through symmetric triangular Fuzzy Numbers. The inclusion of fuzzy factor sis to tackle uncertain parameters and their contexts mentioned in the previous description. We divide the approach into two major parts:

a. Initially, optimal control of the delay for vehicle:

The total vehicle delay time for whole network is:

$$MinV_D = [min \sum_{j\in J}\sum_{k=1}^{P_S}\sum_{i\in R_s}[V_i^j(k) - M_{ij}(k)]\alpha] \tag{1}$$

where $V_i^j(k)$ is the number of vehicles for point i for road section R_s at the time instance k and α is the sampling interval period for complete network coverage.

b. For this part, we assume that there must exist a non-linear optimal control of mobility, where, for training with the uncertain parameters of the vehicular network, a fuzzy number is introduced in triangular form (it signifies that the core function can represent at least three values of membership or certainty factor: for example: road traffic could be moderately normal, medium, strongly adequate etc.). We also observe that there could be different trends of mobility for two communicating vehicles before the communication may fail due to the predicted enhancement in the intermediate distance. Therefore, this non-linear factor can be represented with another form of exponentiation function. Thus, if the minimum value of vehicle delay under non-linear/uncertain factors is being considered, then

$$MinV_D = [min \sum_{j\in J}\sum_{k=1}^{P_S}\sum_{i\in R_s}[V_i^j(k) - exp(\beta_0^j(k)]\alpha] \tag{2}$$

Here, P_s the prediction scenario, parameter $\beta_0^j(k)$ and $V_i^j(k)$ is the result of an auxiliary function, this will be essentially to formulate a final value of the training function for the Boltzmann Machine. In practice, Boltzmann machines are comprised of visible units, (say V), and hidden units. The visible units are those which receive information from the 'environment' (in this case it could be the traffic conditions from the road and other features derived from the traffic contexts), i.e. the training set is a set of binary vectors over the set V. The distribution over the training set is denoted as a continuous function $P^+(V)$. Moreover the machine has an energy reference, which is modified through the positioning of interconnected weights of features during the operation. The machine may stop learning correctly, when it is scaled up to anything larger than a trivial value. There are two phases involved in Boltzmann machine training, and we switch iteratively between both of them. One is the positive phase, where the visible units' states are clamped to a particular binary state vector sampled from the training set (according to P^+). The other is the negative phase, where the network is allowed to run freely. Therefore, the reference energy level of the machine should be discrete out of uncertainty factors and this switching effect from positive to negative must encompass all the membership values of uncertainty [9,10]. As in this case, the hidden features in random or urban traffic conditions are free from external interference, and their values are unknown to us. Hence, we cannot update their weights. Thus, the more membership or certainty values of hidden feature vectors are introduced, the more precise prediction can be.

In the next subsection, the structure of the auxiliary function is derived.

3.1   Structure of the Auxiliary Function in a Vehicular Network

Here, we refer to the structure of $\beta_0^j(k)$:

$$\delta_0^J(k) = \left\{ k[\gamma_0^j(k) \oplus \gamma_0^j(k+1)] \right\} \tag{3}$$

if $(1 \leqslant k \leqslant P_s - 1)$ and subsequently as the value of $\delta_0^J(k)$ could be treated as a fuzzy number trivially with 3 values; if k = 0, then $\delta_0^J(k) = 0$, if k = P_s then $\delta_0^J(k) = P_s$. The construction of Right hand side of the expression with γ_0^j indicates the weight bias of fuzzy nmber which is additive with the instances of values k. That means, k and (k+1) instances are considered here for formulating auxillary function and thus β_0^j.

For implementation, we also investigate the learning features of vehicular networks and it could be either simple sample function or a multiple sample function for error estimation in the final value of the training function in the Boltzmann Machine. It is known that better scaling and an error free representation will make the network learn better for the prediction of the vehicles movement. Considering all the listed parameters, multiple sample features will be suitable to make the training of the network more error free. Assuming, the multiple sample features, the final training function, say X(w), where w is the edge weight of the features connected in the Boltzmann Machine, can be expressed as [10]:

$$T(w) = \frac{1}{2} \sum_{i=1}^{n} \sum_{i=1}^{m} (f_c(x^i) - y_c^i)^2 \qquad (4)$$

It is clear that two terms i.e. $f_c(x^i)$ and y_c^i in the expressions related to T(w) are the coefficients of the training function to be operated on feature vectors taken from vehicular network paradigm. The first one depends on the network edge weight w where the second one is independent of w. Therefore, a partial derivative is derived for the final training weight $w_{Ps_j}^k$ for all k and j.

4 Proposed High Level Description of the Hybrid Neural Network

The term hybrid neural network was coined from the concept that a neural network in its core form can be modified with the supporting mode of computational intelligence like fuzzy logic, specially to for the training purposes. Prior to describing the proposed model, a brief background is presented on conventional Boltzmann Machines (Fig. 1). They were one of the first examples of a neural network capable of learning internal representations, and are able to represent and (given sufficient time) solve difficult combinatoric problems [9]. The structure comprises of some visible and some hidden units. A graphical representation of an example of a Boltzmann machine is shown in Fig. 1. Each undirected edge represents dependency. In this example there are 3 hidden units and 4 visible units.

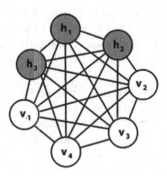

Fig. 1. Basic structure of Boltzmann machine network

Structurally, the network can learn by the adjustment of weights and hence it finally culminates with an energy function E [9,10]:

$$E = -(\sum_{i<j} w_{ij} s_i s_j + \sum_{i} \theta_i s_i)$$

Algorithm 1. *Hybrid Boltzmann machine*

Given: a training set of feature vectors (n) of a vehicular network at a random condition
        Assume visible neurons 10, hidden feature neuron: 625 and a standard random
number function;
    t = 0:
                    While termination condition can't be satisfied
                        for all features to n **do**
                        end for
Assign the function value as eq. (1) & (2)
Formulate T(w) following eq. (4)
                        for all fuzzy numbers weight w **do**
                        initiate final T(w)
                        end for
                        t = t+1;
                        end while

---

where, w_{ij} is the connection strength between unit j and unit i . s_i is the state, $s_i \in \{0, 1\}$ of unit i,

θ_i is the bias of unit i in the global energy function. ($-\theta_i$ is the activation threshold for the unit).

Normally, Boltzmann machines are made of two layers of neurons, with connections only between different layers and no connections within the same layer. The bottom layer (i.e. the visible one) is denoted further by a binary vector v = $[v_1, v_2, .., v_{n_v}]$, in which each unit v_i is a binary unit, and where n_v is the size of v (i.e. the number of neurons of the visible layer). The top layer (i.e. the hidden one) is represented by the binary vector h = $[h_1, h_2, .., h_{n_h}]$, in which each element h_j is binary, and where n_h is the size of h. Furthermore, each neuron from the visible layer has associated bias. The biases of the visible neurons are grouped in a vector a = $[a1, a2, .., an_v]$. Similarly, hidden layer neurons have biases, collected in vector b = $[b1, b2, .., bn_h]$. The broad high level description is presented in:

In this paper, the implementations of the algorithm is done in Visual C++. In all the settings, the momentum was set to 0.5, the learning rate to 0.05. We assume 10 visible and around 625 hidden (under uncertain conditions) neurons, to be trained with a fuzzy triangular function.

4.1 Results and Analysis

The above *Fuzzy Constrained Boltzmann Machine (FCBM) algorithm* is simulated in VC++ 5.0 with MFC (Microsoft Foundation class) support and the algorithm is tested an available data set [11]. The VC++ code uses two threads that read and write from the synthesized vehicular network with the function getVecMessage ( ) and sendVecMessage( ) from the library predefined as <msn.h>. Prior to developing the desired simulation, the following propositions are made to support the simulation across the interconnected device network

- Nodes: A node is an instance of an executable and can be a sensor, actuator, processing or monitoring algorithm.
- Messages: A message is a typed data structure made up of primitive types like integer, floating point, boolean, etc., arrays of primitives and constants. Nodes communicate with each other by passing messages.
- Context of Topic: A Context of Topic is an asynchronous data transport system based on a subscribe/publish system and is identified by a name. One or more nodes are able to publish data (messages) to a topic and one or more nodes can read data on that context of topic. Data is exchanged asynchronously by means of a topic and via a service. This process will help to identify more vehicular network features. Finally, this will produce a training set of vectors
- Services: A services allows nodes to communicate with each other through a synchronously communication. The service nodes are able to send a request and receive a response.

The following observation in values of weights (Fuzzy numbers) are done following the prediction scenario P_s:

The different intermediate states of the vehicular network have been demonstrated with the different weight values and there are substantial changes from weight mark iterations from 0-7. The prediction scenario P_s is also different with time stamps from 20–130 ms as shown in Fig. 2. It is shown that a Fuzzy driven Boltzmann machine with different vehicle tracks and having same network overheads can predict the movement of vehicles.

The network processing overhead increases proportionally with an increase in vehicle density for all types of highway road/tracks as shown in Fig. 2. The network processing overhead in the scheme is higher because of the additional features incurred for the tasks such as accident zone identification, travel direction identification, risk factor assignment and prioritization of emergency vehicles like fire services or ambulances.

Prediction is more accurate after the first two tracks (red and blue) are being for training following the weight values shown in Table 2. The green and blue curve of the track shows certain steady value with all the features, however for prediction scenario P_s the red track diminished after certain iterations.

Table 2. Analysis of Prediction Scenario with different time stamps and feature weights

Wt. w	0	2	3	4	5	6	7
$P_s = 20$	.5 1 .86	.4 0 1	.3 .6 1	0 0 1	0 0 1	0 0 1	0 0 1
	1 .6 1	1 1 0.8	1 1 1	1 1 .5	1 1 .5	0 1 .7	0 1 1
	0 1 .7	1 0 1	1 .8 1	.8 0 1	1 0 1	0 0 1	1 0 1
$P_s = 130$	.5 0 1	.6 0 0	0 0 0	0 0 1	0 0 1	0 0 1	0 0 1
	0 1 0	0 1 1	0 1 1	1 .4 .6	1 .6 .4	0 0 1	0 0 1
	1 .9 1	1 .9 1	1 1 1	.9 0 1	1 0 1	1 0 1	1 1 1

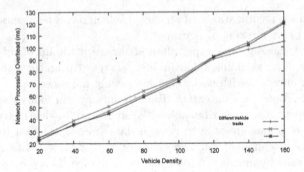

Fig. 2. Movement track

Following the data set in [11], the second part of the simulation is shown. In this case, to identify the different types of vehicles, the simulation time differs depending on the weighted feature w. However, the average vehicle density alters considerably, with respect to average connectivity distance. The other part of simulation is also done with the number and types of vehicles. The impact is one of the important parameter to understand the prediction error analysis.

The plots shown in Fig. 3 are closely analogous to the parameters studied: acceleration of 12 similar vehicles are being considered and the simulation time is calculated. The simulation code developed for the Boltzmann machine with fuzzy numbers as constraints, is shown in appendix, and following the code, the RMS value of the simulation performed on the data set [11] is given in terms of

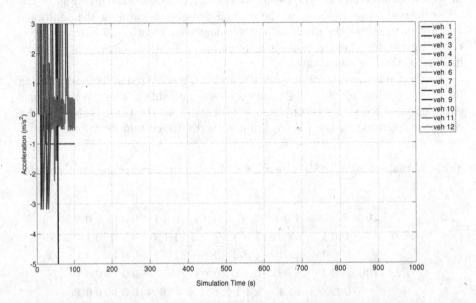

Fig. 3. Impact of vehicle acceleration and simulation time for prediction

vehicle mobility predictions. The values collected for the phases of delivery and acknowledgement and the total time of the iteration have also been presented. For the acknowledgment phase, there are the minimum and maximum time used for the message and the number of conditional variables of the messages for vehicles through FCBM are also given. We also observe that the phases of configuring the Boltzmann machine with 10 visible and 625 hidden units can be kept as maximum to train the network. When more than 625 uncertain features from traffic conditions exist, the prediction time differs randomly, even after successful training with fuzzy triangular values.

In the Fig. 4, a plot is shown for 12 vehicles of different types, with an intermediate gap and distance between them. The plot has been restricted with iterations of simulation and it is found that, if the intermediate gap of all 12 types of vehicles are considered, then with available training scheme only vehicle number 12, 8 and 10 can be referred for effective prediction. The other vehicles cannot be considered with this training function, as the intermediate gaps are uncertain and random. The curve shows in the plot are also not smooth and it becomes more stiffer for the best convergence of vehicle 12.

We demonstrate final results as statistical comparisons. It is the impact of vehicle density and average connectivity distance. We assume statistical Rayleigh fading with superimposed log normal scale. The results show that both vehicle density and average connectivity increases as the average vehicle density increases. Further, as shadow fading occurs, therefore, standard deviation value increases for both these parameters. This means that the average vehicle density required to satisfy a given value of average connectivity distance decreases, whenever the value of standard deviation increases. Three vehicles 12, 8 and 10

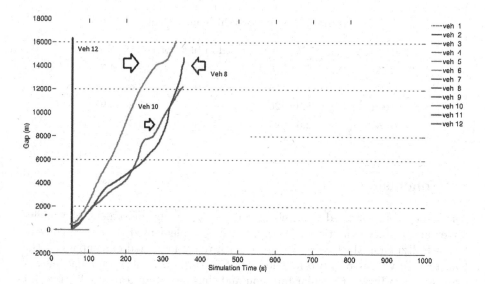

Fig. 4. Restricted vehicles with uncertain gap

are considered to test the convergence of decision in uncertainty, and the lower red curve demonstrates minimum deviation, but with minimum fuzzy training value (Fig. 5).

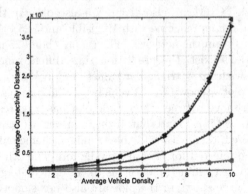

Fig. 5. Optimal vehicle density & connectivity

For immediate reference, we present a snapshot of the results as in Table 3: all pairs of iterations with acknowledgment and delivery of movement prediction are shown and minimum error should correspond to greater precision. It should be mentioned that, we performed a single partial derivative to obtain the final training function $T(w)$ with the auxiliary function shown in Sect. 3.1. A higher order and more iterations of partial derivative will lead to better precision and could reduce the error value in prediction.

Table 3. Results for vehicle movement

Iteration	Min	Max	Val. passed in function	RMS	Err.
Ackn.	2.1	2.6	05	32.7	4.7
Delv.	1.0	7.9	15	33.6	8.7
Ackn.	5.3	8.0	20	41.2	3.92
Delv.	2.4	2.6	25	34.3	2.1

5   Conclusion

The paper demonstrated a novel model to predict the movement of vehicles under uncertainty conditions. The approach is implemented through a conventional Boltzmann Machine and trained with fuzzy logic and encompassing the features of a vehicular network. The hidden features and their combinations are expressed as a fuzzy triangular function and thus a computationally lightweight application could be developed. However, while deploying the simulation, it was observed that as conventionally a Boltzmann machine is used for deep learning applications (principally pattern recognition), existing Python libraries are inadequate to support the simulation. The application can be well extended with more real life data instances and if the order of partial derivation could be higher when choosing final training function, better throughput and accuracy could be obtained. A greater numbers of intelligent optimization algorithms like different variants of swarms can be chosen to select the precise combinations of parameters. In addition, the complexity of the program may lead to a trade-off between accuracy of prediction and execution time.

APPENDIX

```
Code Segment:
 Communication Prototype Functions */
#include <mspnvehicle.h>
#include <killApp.h>
#include <boost/thread/thread.hpp>
void openNewTerminal();
bool notificationKilledProcess
(atv_acrosser::killApp::Request &req,
void receiveKillCommunication(int argc, char **argv);
boost::mutex mtxTerminal;
boost::mutex::scoped_lock lock (mtxTerminal);
boost::condition_variable condTerminal;
/* It proves the presence of
terminal window that execute the process
communication */
bool existTerminal = false;
/********************************************************************
* @function: openNewTerminal
* Thread opens a new terminal and executes the communication
* program. It also remains waiting status on the condition variable
* to launch again the process communication.
*********************************************************************/
void openNewTerminal()
{
int statusSystem = 0;
/*Open the first terminal with communication program*/
existTerminal = true;
statusSystem = system("gnome-terminal_-x_./communication");
printf("\nTERMINAL_OPENED_STATUS:_%d", statusSystem);
/* Infinite while, there will be always a condition variable
which wait a signal from a killed process.
When the the condition variable will be awake from a killed process,
it will open a new terminal and execute the communication
program and wait again another signal from a killed process */
while(1)
{/
*Condition variable, wait to be awake after the killed process */
while(existTerminal == true)condTerminal.wait(lock);
/*Open a new terminal and execute the communication process */
statusSystem = system("gnome-terminal_-x_./communication");
printf("\nTERMINAL_OPENED_STATUS:_%d", statusSystem);
if(statusSystem < 0)
 printf("\n_PROBLEM_TO_OPEN_THE_NEW_WINDOW_DURING_THE
RESTARTING_OF_THE_SOFTWARE_communication");
```

```
}}
*****************************************************************
* @function: receiveKillCommunication
* Thread waits the communication with communication process via
* ROS service in case the process communication needs to
* terminate. When receive the notice from the service the
* function notificationKilledProcess is called.
*****************************************************************/
void receiveKillCommunication(int argc, char **argv)
{
ros::init(argc, argv, "");
ros::NodeHandle n;
//Here the service called
"restartCommunication" is created and
//advertised over ROS.
ros::ServiceServer service = n.advertiseService
("restartCommunication", notificationKilledProcess);
 ros::spin();
}/
**********
**************************
***************************
* @function: notificationKilledProcess
* This function has called each time
that ROS service answers from
* the communication creating * a syncronization with it.
* The function will change in false
the value of the variable
* existTerminal and wake up the
* condition variable condTerminal
* with the scope of open a
new terminal and execute the process
* communication.
*****************************************************************/
bool notificationKilledProcess(atv_acrosser::killApp::Request &req,
atv_acrosser::killApp::Response &res)
{
 ROS_INFO("PID_KILLED_%ld", (long int)req.pid2Kill);
/* set to false the variable existTerminal, it means there are nt
open terminal with running communication */
existTerminal = false;
/* wake up the condition variable condTerminal */
 condTerminal.notify_one();
return true;
}
int main(int argc, char **argv)
{
boost::thread openNewTerminal_Thread(&openNewTerminal);
boost::thread receiveKillCommunication_Thread(
&receiveKillCommunication, argc, argv);
openNewTerminal_Thread.join();
receiveKillCommunication_Thread.join();
return 0;
 }
/* Boltzmann Prototype with Fuzzy training*/
#include <math.h>
#include <fstream>
#include <iostream>
#include <random> using namespace arma;using namespace
std;
```

```
#define elif else if
#define HIDDEN_SIZE 200
#define BATCH_SIZE 2000oncatenateMat(vector<mat> &vec){int
height = vec[0].n_rows;int width = vec[0].n_cols;
mat res = zeros<mat>(height * width, vec.size());
for(int i=0;
i<vec.size(); i++){mat img = vec[i];
img.reshape(height * width, 1);res.col(i) = img.col(0);}
res = res / 255.0;return
res;}int ReverseInt (int i){
unsigned char ch1, ch2, ch3, c
h4;ch1 = i & 255;c
h2 = (i >> 8) & 255;ch3 = (i >> 16) &
255;ch4 = (i >> 24) & 255;
return((int) ch1 << 24) +
((int)ch2 << 16) + ((int)ch3 << 8) + ch4;}
void read_Mnist(string
filename, vector<mat> &vec)
{ifstream file (filename, ios::binary);
if (file.is_open()){int magic_number = 0;int
number_of_images = 0;
int n_rows = 0;int n_cols = 0;
file.read((char*) &magic_number,
sizeof(magic_number));
magic_number = ReverseInt(magic_number);
file.read((char*)
&number_of_images,sizeof(number_of_images));
number_of_images = ReverseInt(number_of_images);
file.read((char*)
&n_rows, sizeof(n_rows));
n_rows = ReverseInt(n_rows);
file.read((char*) &n_cols, sizeof(n_cols));n_cols =
ReverseInt(n_cols);
for(int i = 0;
i < number_of_images; ++i){mat tp(n_rows, n_cols);
for(int r = 0; r < n_rows; ++r)
{for(int c = 0; c < n_cols; ++c)
{unsigned char temp = 0;file.read((char*)
&temp, sizeof(temp));tp(r, c) = (double)
temp;}} vec.push_back(tp);}}}
voidreadData(mat &x, string xpath)
{//read MNIST iamge into Arma Mat
vectorvector<mat> vec;read_Mnist(xpath, vec);
random_shuffle(vec.begin(), vec.end());
x = concatenateMat(vec);} mat
sigmoid(mat M){return 1.0 / (exp(-M) + 1.0);}
voidmatRandomInit(mat &m, int rows,
int cols, double scaler){m =
randn<mat>(rows, cols);m = m * scaler;
} matgetBernoulliMatrix(mat &prob)
{// randu builds a Uniformly distributed
matrixmat ran = randu<mat>
(prob.n_rows, prob.n_cols)
;mat res = zeros<mat>(prob.n_rows,
prob.n_cols);res.elem(find(prob > ran)).
ones();return res;}
voidsave2txt(mat &data, string str, int step){string s =
std::to_string(step);str += s;
str += ".txt";FILE *pOut = fopen(str.c_str(), "w");
for(int i=0; i<data.n_rows; i++){for(int
```

```
j=0; j<data.n_cols; j++)
{fprintf(pOut, "%lf", data(i, j));
if(j == data.n_cols - 1) fprintf(pOut, "\n");
else fprintf(pOut, "
");}}fclose(pOut);}
matFCBM_training(mat x, int hidSize,
int batchSize, int cd_k) /* Fuzzy Numbers*/
{int nfeatures = x.n_rows;
int nsamples = x.n_cols;
// b is hidden layer;// c is visible layermat
w, b, c;matRandomInit(w,
nfeatures, hidSize, 0.12);matRandomInit(b, hidSize, 1, 0);
matRandomInit(c, nfeatures, 1, 0);int counter = 0;double
lrateW = 0.01; //Learning rate fo
r weights double lrateC = 0.01; /
/Learning rate for biases of visible units double lrateB
= 0.01; //Learning rate for biases
of hidden units
double weightcost = 0.0002; double initialmomentum = 0.5;double
finalmomentum = 0.9;double
errsum = 0.0;double momentum;
mat incW = zeros(w.n_rows, w.n_cols);mat incB =
zeros(b.n_rows, b.n_cols);
mat incC = zeros(c.n_rows, c.n_cols);
while(1){// start positive phaseint randomNum =
((long)rand() + (long)rand()) %
(nsamples - batchSize)
;mat data = x.cols(randomNum, randomNum + batchSize -
1);data = getBernoulliMatrix(data);
mat poshidprobs = sigmoid(w.t() * data + repmat(b, 1,
batchSize));poshidprobs =
normalise(poshidprobs, 1, 0);
mat posprods = data * poshidprobs.t() /
batchSize;mat poshidact = sum(poshidprobs, 1) /
batchSize;mat posvisact = sum(data, 1)
/ batchSize;// end of positive
phasemat poshidprobs_temp = poshidprobs;mat
poshidstates, negdata;
// start negative phase//
CD-K algfor(int i = 0; i < cd_k; i++){poshidstates =
getBernoulliMatrix(poshidprobs_temp);
negdata = sigmoid(w * poshidstates + repmat(c, 1, batchSize));
negdata =getBernoulliMatrix(negdata);
poshidprobs_temp = sigmoid(w.t() * negdata + repmat(b, 1, batchSize));
poshidprobs_temp = normalise(poshidprobs_temp, 1, 0);}
mat neghidprobs = poshidprobs_temp;
mat negprods = negdata * neghidprobs.t() /
batchSize;mat neghidact = sum(neghidprobs, 1)
/ batchSize;mat negvisact = sum(negdata, 1) / batchSize;//end of
negative phasedouble err = accu(pow(mean(data - negdata, 1), 2.0));
//errsum = err + errsum;if(counter > 10) momentum
= finalmomentum;
else momentum = initialmomentum;
// update weights and biasesincW = momentum * incW + lrateW
* ((posprods - negprods) - weightcost * w);
incC = momentum * incC + lrateC * (posvisact - negvisact);
incB =
momentum * incB + lrateB * (poshidact - neghidact);
w += incW;c += incC;b += incB;cout<<"counter_=
"<<counter<<",_error_=_"<<err<<endl;
```

```
if(counter % 100 == 0){save2txt(w, "w/w_", counter / 100);
save2txt(b, "b/b_",
counter / 100);save2txt(c, "c/c_", counter / 100);}
if(counter >= 10000) break;++ counter;}
return w;}int main(int argc,
char** argv){long start, end;start = clock();
mat trainX;readData
(trainX, "mnist/train-images-idx3-ubyte");cout<<"Read
trainX_successfully,
including_"<<trainX.n_rows<<"
features_and_"<<trainX.n_cols<<"_samples."<<endl;// Finished
reading datamat
w = FCBM_training(trainX, HIDDEN_SIZE, BATCH_SIZE, 1);
end = clock();cout<<"Totally_used
time:_"<<((double)(end - start)) /
CLOCKS_PER_SEC<<"_second"<<endl;return 0;
```

References

1. Omar, H., Zhuang, W., Abdrabou, A., Li, L.: Performance evaluation of vemac supporting safety applications in vehicular networks. IEEE Trans. Emerg. Topics Comput. 1(1), 69–83 (2013)
2. Pack, S., Choi, Y.: Fast handoff scheme based on mobility prediction in public wireless LAN systems. IEEE Proc. Commun. 151(5), 489–495 (2004)
3. Yavas, G., Katsaros, D., Ulusoy, O., Manolopoulos, Y.: A data mining approach for location prediction in mobile environments. Data Knowl. Eng. 54(2), 121–146 (2005)
4. Wang, X., Wang, C., Cui, G., Yang, Q.: Practical link duration prediction model in vehicular ad hoc networks. Int. J. Dist. Sensor Networks, vol. 2015
5. Wu, W., Zhang, J., Luo, A., Cao, J.: Distributed mutual exclusion algorithms for intersection traffic control. IEEE Trans. Parallel Distrib. Syst. 26(1), 65–74 (2015)
6. Cheng, J., Wu, W., Cao, J., Li, K.: Fuzzy group-based intersection control via vehicular networks for smart transportations. IEEE Trans. Ind. Inform. 13(2), 751–758 (2017)
7. Alsharif, N., Aldubaikhy, K., Shen, X.: Link duration estimation using neural networks based mobility prediction in vehicular networks. In: IEEE Canadian Conference on Electrical and Computer Engineering (CCECE). IEEE Procdings (2016)
8. Jiang, B., Fei, Y.: Traffic and vehicle speed prediction with neural network and Hidden Markov model in vehicular networks. In: IEEE Intelligent Vehicles Symposium (IV) (2015)
9. Streubel, T., Hoffman, K.H.: Prediction of driver intended path at intersections. In: IEEE Intelligent Vehicles Symposium Proceedings (2014)
10. Hinton, G.E., Sejnowski, T.J., Rumelhart, D.E., McClelland, J.L. and the PDP Research Group, eds.: Learning and Relearning in Boltzmann Machines (1986)
11. Hinton, G.E., Osindero, S.: A fast learning algorithm for deep belief nets. Neural Comput. 18(7), 1527–1554 (2006)
12. Mahajan, R.: CRAWDAD dataset microsoft/vanlan (v. 2007-09-14), September 2007. downloaded from http://crawdad.org/microsoft/vanlan/20070914, https://doi.org/10.15783/C7FG6S
13. Tal, I., Muntean, G.M.: User oriented fuzzy logic based clustering scheme for vehicular Ad hoc networks. In: IEEE Vehicular Technology Conference (VTC Spring), pp. 1–5 (2013)

14. Jinila, B., Komathy: Rough set based fuzzy scheme for clustering and cluster head selection in VANET. Elektronika IR Elektrotechnika **21**(1) (2015). ISSN 1392-1215
15. Aoyagi, M.: Learning coefficient in Bayesian estimation of restricted Boltzmann machine. J. Algebraic Stat. **4**(1), 31–58 (2013)

Building of an Information Retrieval System Based on Genetic Algorithms

Badr Hssina[(✉)], Soukaina Lamkhantar, Mohammed Erritali,
Abdelkrim Merbouha, and Youness Madani

Faculty of Sciences and Technics, Sultan Moulay Slimane University,
Beni Mellal, Morocco
badr.hssina7@gmail.com

Abstract. In an information retrieval system (IRS) the query plays a very important role, so the user of an IRS must write his query well to have the expected result.

In this paper, we have developed a new genetic algorithm-based query optimization method on relevance feedback for information retrieval. By using this technique, we have designed a fitness function respecting the order in which the relevant documents are retrieved, the terms of the relevant documents, and the terms of the irrelevant documents.

Based on three benchmark test collections Cranfield, Medline and CACM, experiments have been carried out to compare our method with three well-known query optimization methods on relevance feedback. The experiments show that our method can achieve better results.

1 Introduction

Nowadays, we see an incessant development of information technologies. These technologies produce large volumes of information, which can exist in the form of different languages, making the retrieval of a specific information very difficult. To remedy this problem, the information retrieval domain provides us with the techniques and the tools necessary to easily find the looked-for information, called relevant information. These tools are called Information Retrieval Systems [16].

In an IRS, each document is represented by an intermediate representation called indexation, and to find the documents that are relevant to a user's information need, the user expresses his need by a query, and the choice of this query is a very important step in the search for relevant documents.

The first problem in an Information Retrieval System is represented in the formulation of the first request of the user. This explains the importance placed on current query optimization techniques, which allow the user to obtain his information needs. One of the most effective techniques is the relevance feedback. It uses the judgment provided by the user during the first search for information by the system to modify the second query. In fact, the application of the artificial intelligence techniques on the information science knew great progress, notably in information retrieval which is one of the principal lines of the research in

S. Bouzefrane et al. (Eds.): MSPN 2017, LNCS 10566, pp. 195–206, 2017.
DOI: 10.1007/978-3-319-67807-8_15

the artificial intelligence field. Among the evolutionary algorithms in the world of artificial intelligence that gives powerful results in the field of information retrieval, we cite the genetic algorithms.

The use of the Genetic Algorithms (GA) in the Information Retrieval System has grown greatly in recent years because it gives good results in the search for information that interests us from a large volume of information. GA is used in the different steps to perform an IRS, either in the phase of reformulation of the query, the indexing phase or the search phase.

In this paper, we will present a new genetic algorithm-based query optimization method based on relevance feedback for Information Retrieval System.

The reminder of the paper is organized as follows: In Sect. 2, we present some previous work of GA in an Information Retrieval System and some related work with ours. A detailed description of our work is presented and detailed in Sect. 3. In Sects. 4 and 5, we give some experimental results. Finally, we give a conclusion and some future works in Sect. 6.

2   Genetic Algorithm in Information Retrieval System

2.1   Information Retrieval System

An Information Retrieval System is defined as a system allowing to find the relevant documents to a users query written in a free language, from a voluminous documents database.

The search for information tries to solve the following problem: "Given a very large collection of objects (mostly documents), find those that respond to a need for information expressed by a user (request)". In the Information Retrieval System, we find a request and we want to find the objects (documents) that are relevant to it. The way to evaluate a document if it is relevant or not is to calculate the similarity between the request and that document.

After the calculation of the similarity, it is important to index all the documents and also the request, that is to make them in a presentation to facilitate its use. In our case, we use the vector representation [1], where each element of the vector represents the weight (frequency) of each term or concept in the document or query.

2.2   Genetic Algorithm

Genetic algorithms are stochastic optimization algorithms based on the mechanisms of natural selection and genetics [2]. Their operation is extremely simple. We leave with a population of potential solutions(chromosomes), initially selected arbitrarily. We evaluate their relative performance(fitness)and on the basis of these performances, a new population of potential solutions is created using simple evolutionary operators: selection, crossing and mutation. This cycle is repeated until a satisfactory solution is illustrated in Fig. 1.

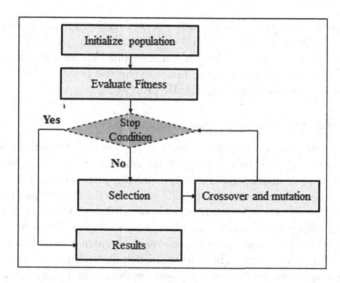

Fig. 1. General scheme of a genetic algorithm

There has been an increasing interest in the application of GA tools to IR in the last few years. Concretely, the machine learning paradigm, whose aim is the design of a system able to automatically acquire knowledge by itself, seems to be interesting in this topic.

The first thing in a genetic algorithm is the definition of the initial population (selection operator or evaluation) on which we will apply the treatment. In our case, we use the similarity calculation which plays an important role of fitness function as it enables us to decide whether an individual is going to be selected or not. There are lots of methods to make the selection such as the biased lottery, the elitist method or the selection by tournaments.

After applying the selection operator to the initial population, the second step is reproduction with the application of the crossing or crossover operation and the mutation operation.

In the literature, we find much of the work that apply genetic algorithms in the search for information, as in [3] the authors use in their Information Retrieval System the genetic algorithm to find the relevant documents for a user's query, using the vector representation to present the documents of the search base and the query. They have made comparisons with precision measurements and recall of the system using different fitness functions like cosine, Dice and Jaccard.

Vajitoru [4] also uses the Genetic Algorithms in the research of information. He proposed a new operation of crossing to improve the research with the genetic algorithm. For that, he made a comparison between his proposal and a classic GA, and the results shows the effectiveness of its proposal.

Sathya and Simon [5] use the genetic algorithms to improve an information retrieval system and make it effective for obtaining more pages relevant to the users query and optimize the search time.

In [6] the researchers present a new fitness function for approximate information retrieval which is very fast and very flexible than cosine similarity.

Fan et al. propose an algorithm for indexing function learning based on GA, whose aim is to obtain an indexing function for the key term weighting of a documentary collection to improve the IR process [7].

2.3   Genetic Algorithms in Query Optimization

In the literature, we find many works that use genetic algorithms for query optimization to improve the efficiency of Information Retrieval Systems. As in [8] the authors have utilised genetic algorithms for database query optimization for a large query. The Researchers of [9] use Genetic algorithms in Information retrieval in the area of optimizing a boolean query. They use Information Retrieval effectiveness measures, precision and recall as a fitness function. The goal of this work is to retrieve most relevant documents with less number of the non-relevant document. The authors conclude that the quality of initial population was important to have the best results of the genetic programming process, and the less quality of initial population caused worse results. To get good results, they choose parents depending on the recall fitness values than the precision fitness values.

The work of *Anubha Jain et al.* [10] reviews relevance of genetic algorithms to improve upon the user queries in the field of Information Retrieval. The results of the studies categorically prove the applicability of genetic optimization algorithms in improving the Information Retrieval process. The paper presents diverse proposals on the relevance of genetic algorithm in search query optimization which are promising and still developing areas of research.

As pointed out by Leroy et al. [11], the query optimization methods based on relevance feedback or genetic algorithms using dynamic query contexts could help users search the internet. From the study of Salton and Buckley [12], we know that, in a method, the calculation of traditional relevance feedback query optimization expression is simple, but the determination of its parameters is difficult. According to the study of Lopez-Pujalte et al. [13], the order information of the relevant documents is very useful to search an optimized solution for a genetic algorithm-based relevance feedback method.

In a genetic algorithm based query optimization method, the key work to consider is how to use the relevance feedback information to design its genetic operators and fitness function.

3   Genetic Algorithm Based Query Optimization Method

3.1   Document Vectorization and Relevance Feedback

We produce a dictionary $D = (t_1, t_2, ..., t_n)$, each document in the collection is described as an n-dimensional weight vector $w = (w_1, w_2, ..., w_n)$, where each weight w_i is calculated by the TF*IDF formula, and each query in the collection is also described as a weight vector $q = (u_1, u_2, ..., u_n)$, is calculated by the TF-method formula.

$$TF = \frac{f(t_i, d_j)}{N} \qquad (1)$$

$f(t_i, d_j)$ is the number of occurrences of the term t_i in the document d_j and N is the total number of terms in the document d_j.

$$IDF = \frac{log(f(t_i, d_j))}{M} \qquad (2)$$

$f(t_i, d_j)$ is the number of occurrences of the term t_i in the document d_j and M is the total number of documents in the corpus.

For each query, the top-15 documents retrieved based on the cosine similarity (ranking the values in a descending order) will be input to our GA as relevance feedback.

$$Sim_{cos}(X, Y) = \frac{\sum_{i=1}^{n} x.y}{\sqrt{(\sum_{i=1}^{n} x^2)}.\sqrt{(\sum_{i=1}^{n} y^2)}} \qquad (3)$$

3.2 Chromosomes and Population

A chromosome is represented as a weight vector $w = (w_1, w_2, ..., w_n)$, where w_i is a real number and denotes the weight of the keyword t_i for i = 1,2,. . .n .

Our GA receives an initial population P consisting of $| R_{rel} | +2$ chromosomes, including the original query vector q, the $| R_{rel} |$ relevant document vectors in R_{per} and the average-weight vector $q_{avg} = (avg_1, avg_2, ..., avg_n)$.

3.3 Fitness Function

In our GA, the definition of our fitness function consists of two parts: x and y. The x is relative to both the order of appearance of the relevant documents in feedback and the terms of relevant documents in feedback. The y is relative to the terms of the irrelevant documents in feedback.

For any chromosome $w = (w_1, w_2, ..., w_n)$ in the current population P, its fitness value is calculated by the formula:

$$F(w) = x + y \qquad (4)$$

The formula of x is:

$$\sum_{d_i \in R_{rel}} | Horng(w) - cosine(w, d_i) | \qquad (5)$$

The Horng and Yeh fitness function is defined as:

$$Horng(w) = \frac{1}{| R |} \sum_{i=1}^{|R|} \left[r(d_i) \sum_{j=1}^{|R|} \frac{1}{j} \right] \qquad (6)$$

Here, $| R |$ is the number of the documents in set R. $d_1, d_2, ..., d_{|R|}$ are the documents in R sorted by descending order of their cosine similarity values with the chromosome w. Function $r(d_i)$ gives the relevance of d_i, being unity if d_i belongs to R_{rel} and zero if d_i belongs to R_{irrel}.

The formula of y is:

$$y = \sum_{d_i \in R_{irrel}} Cosine(w, d_i) \tag{7}$$

$\sum$ counts for every document $d_i in R_{irrel}$, its cosine similarity with the chromosome w.

3.4   Genetic Operators

The formal definitions of the three genetic operators used in our GA can be described as follows:

Two-Point Crossover: Firstly, two integers i and j in $(1, 2, . . . , n)$ will be produced randomly, and we select two parents w and v, which are randomly selected using the fitness proportional selection from current population P. Suppose $1 \leq i \leq j \leq n$, and the two parents are:
$$w = (w_1, w_2, , w_{(i-1)}, | \; w_i, ..., w_j, | \; w_{(j+1)}, ..., w_n), v = (v_1, v_2, , v_{(i-1)}, |$$
$$v_i, ..., v_j, | \, v_{(j+1)}, ..., v_n)$$
then, two offspring w and v will be generated as below:
$$w' = (w_1, w_2, , w_{(i-1)}, | \; v_i, ..., v_j, | \; w_{(j+1)}, ..., w_n), v' = (v_1, v_2, , v_{(i-1)},$$
$$| \, w_i, ..., w_j, | \, v_{(j+1)}, ..., v_n)$$

Weight-Adjusting Mutation: This genetic operator is used to tune the weights of keywords (genes) in a chromosome. It can generate an offspring from a parent w, which is randomly selected using the fitness proportional selection from the current population P.

Firstly, an integer i in $(1, 2, ..., n)$ will be produced randomly, and then a real number w_i' between $MIN_i \; and \; MAX_i$ will be produced randomly. Finally, from the parent:

$$w = (w_i, w_2, ..., w_{(i-1)}, w_i, w_{i+1}, ..., w_n)$$

an offspring w' will be generated as below:

$$w' = (w_i, w_2, ..., w_{(i-1)}, w_i', w_{i+1}, ..., w_n)$$

Overturn Mutation: Firstly, an integer i in (1, 2, . . . , n) will be produced randomly, and then from the parent:

$$w = (w_i, w_2, ..., w_{(i-1)}, w_i, w_{i+1}, ..., w_n)$$

an offspring w' will be generated as below by executing a reversal operation between zero and non zero:

$$w' = (w_i, w_2, ..., w_{(i-1)}, w'_i, w_{i+1}, ..., w_n)$$

where w'_i will be $(MAX_i + MIN_i)/2$ if $w_i = 0$, otherwise it will be 0.

3.5   Next Generation

After the offspring have been produced by operating our three genetic operators given above with configurable probabilities, our fitness function is used to determine the chromosomes of the next generation.

Firstly, the offspring is added into current population P. Secondly, the fitness values of all chromosomes in P are calculated. Lastly, the $| R_{rel} | +2$ chromosomes with the smaller fitness values (i.e. better chromosomes) in P will be brought to the next generation.

3.6   Termination Criteria and Solution

The iterative procedure of our GA will be stopped by one of the following termination criteria:

- From a generation, its fitness value does not change for the rest of the iterations.
- From a generation, its fitness value changes but very weakly for the rest of the iterations.
- A threshold of the number of iterations is reached.

If one of these criteria is met then the value of the fitness function of the generation is defined as the best fitness value of all the current generations.

After stopping the iteration procedure, the chromosome with the lowest fitness value (the best chromosome) in the latest generation P will be selected as the optimized query produced by our genetic algorithm.

4   Experimental Results

4.1   Test Collections

Our experiments were carried out based on three benchmark test collections:

- Cranfield: contains 1400 documents on different aspects of aeronautical engineering.
- Medline: contains 1033 documents on medicine.
- CACM: contains 3204 documents on computing.

4.2   Experiments Preparation

Dictionaries: In our experiments, for the efficiency of converting the documents and queries in a test collection into the weight vectors in VSM, a dictionary of keywords was used for each test collection. The dictionary was formed with the following procedure:

1. Extract all the words from all documents in each collection.
2. Remove stop-words using the list of stop-words generated according to the frequency dictionary of Kucera and Francis [14].
3. Stem the rest of the words using the Porter Stemmer [16], which is the most commonly used stemmer in English.
4. Delete all irrelevant words to reduce the size of the weight vector, such as the words that appear before the text for each document.

As a result, the dictionary for Cranfield collection contains 3824 keywords; the dictionary for Medline collection contains 6985 keywords and the dictionary for CACM collection contains 719 keywords.

Description of Documents and Queries: In each collection, when using its dictionary to generate the keyword vector of each document, we need first to use the Porter Stemmer to stem the document, then to extract keywords from the document according to the dictionary, and last to calculate keyword weights with the TF*IDF-method.

In addition, for each request for a given collection, its term vector is treated in the same way as the documents, but the weight of the terms is calculated by the TF method.

4.3   Selection of Relevance Feedback

In our experiments, for each query in a collection, the first 15 documents (a = 15) extracted and sorted in descending order of the cosine similarity values with the query will be examined to determine their relevance. The first 15 documents will be used for the relevancy judgment, which will be used to optimize the query and includes the four query optimization methods that we will compare with our experiments.

4.4   Selection of Queries

For each collection, we have selected only the queries that result at least three relevant documents by the first 15 documents found, and do not extract at least five documents. Our experiments were carried out on these queries.

5   Explanation of Our Experiments

Based on the descriptions of the Dec-hi method, the Fitness9 and the Fitness10 in Lopez-Pujalte et al.'s experiments [12], we have realized the Ides traditional Dec-hi method [4], the Horng and Yehs GA-based method [15] and the Lopez-Pujalte et al.'s GA-based method [12]. Below, we use Dec-hi(Ide), Fitness9 (Horng) and Fitness10 (Pujalte) to represent respectively the three query optimization methods. As done in Lopez-Pujalte et al.'s experiments, in our experiments both Fitness9 and Fitness10 use the one-point crossover and the random mutation genetic operators.

5.1   Control Parameters

All the control parameters used in our genetic algorithm have been determined experimentally. The crossover probability c1 is 0.4. The mutation probabilities m1 and m2 are 0.3 and 0.3, respectively. The limit on the number of iterations is 2000, namely threshold $\beta = 2000$.

For Fitness 9 and Fitness10, the probabilities of the one-point crossover and random mutation genetic operators are 0.6 and 0.4, respectively. Their limits on the number of iterations are 2000 and 200, respectively, because from our experiments we have found that the fitness value of Fitness10 only varies in the first few iterations.

5.2   Evaluation and Experimental Plan

As done in Lopez-Pujalte et al.'s experiments, we evaluate the results of retrieval by the classical measures of recall and precision. The precision is calculated by interpolation at fixed recall intervals. We calculate the average precision for three recall values (0.25, 0.5, and 0.75, representing low, medium, and high recall, respectively) so as to be able to compare the different methods.

The experimental plan follows the following steps:

- Each query is compared with all documents belonging to a given collection, using the Cosine similarity measure. Therefore, a similarity list of each query with the other documents in the collection is obtained.
- This list is ranked in descending order of degree of similarity.
- The standardized document vectors corresponding to the first 15 documents in the list, with their degrees of similarity to the standardized query vector, will be the inputs of our genetic algorithm.
- The program produces a hidden file containing for each request all the documents that are not to be considered in the evaluation process, i.e. the first 15 documents used in the modification of the requests. This method is called the residual collection method, used by Salton and Buckley [16].

5.3 Experimental Results and Comparison

Comparison Between Our Genetic Algorithm and the Other Genetic Algorithms: Based on CACM, Medline and Cranfield collections, we have conducted three experiments to compare our method with the two other methods: Fitness9 (Horng) and Fitness10 (Pujalte). Our experiment results on three collections that are shown, respectively, in Figs. 2, 3 and 4.

From these figures, we can see that, by making comparison with the original query, fitness9 function, fitness10 function and our GA have increased the average accuracy, respectively, from 133.71 and 159.43 to 177.05 for the CACM collection, from 33.84 and 74.46 to 76.55 for the Medline collection, and from 66.95 and 118.41 to 120.97 for the Cranfield collection.

We can also see that, compared with the original query, Ide Dec-hi method and our GA the average accuracy have raised respectively from 150.61 to 177.05 on the CACM collection and from 105.47 to 120.97 on the Cranfield collection.

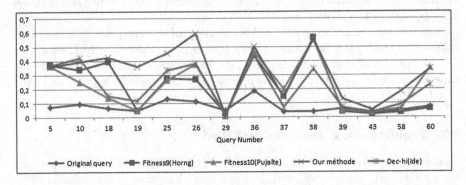

Fig. 2. Comparison of our GA, to other GAs and the Ide Dec-hi method (on CACM)

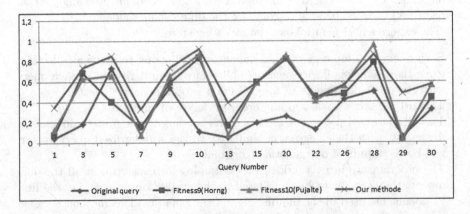

Fig. 3. Comparison of our genetic algorithm and other genetic algorithms (on Medline)

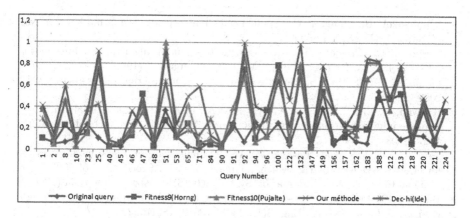

Fig. 4. Comparison of our GA, to other GAs and the Ide Dec-hi method (Cranfield)

6   Conclusion and Perspectives

In this work, we have presented our genetic algorithm for optimizing a query in order to improve the results of an Information Retrieval System by searching the optimal query that gives us the best results.

Based on three benchmark test collections: Cranfield, Medline and CACM, we have conducted three experiments to compare our GA-based method with three other well-known query optimization methods on relevance feedback: Horng method (Fitness 9), Lopez-Pujalte method (Fitness 10) and the traditional Ide Dec-hi method. The results of our experiments indicate that: First, based on the Cranfield, Medline and CACM collections, our GA-based method can get better results than both the Horng and Yehs GA and the Lopez-Pujalte et al.'s GA. Second, based on the Cranfield and CACM collections, our GA can also achieve better results than the traditional Ide Dec-hi method.

As Perspectives, We aim to consolidate the proposed approach by evaluating it on other larger collections such as the well-known collection called TREC, then work on languages other than English to prove the effectiveness of our method.

An other perspective of our work is to apply our method in an e-learning system for finding an optimal profile for a learner.

References

1. Salton, G.: Automatic Text Processing: The Transformation, Analysis, and Retrieval of Information by Computer. Addison- Wesley Publishing Co., Inc., New York (1989)
2. Alam, F., Saadi, H.S., Alam, M.S.: A novel comparative study between dual population genetic algorithm and artificial bee colony algorithm for function optimization. In: 19th International Conference on Computer and Information Technology (ICCIT) (2016)

3. Klabbankoh, B., Pinngern, O.: Applied genetic algorithms in information retrieval. IJCIM **7**(3) (December 1999)
4. Vrajitoru, D.: Crossover improvement for the genetic algorithm in information retrieval. Inform. Process. Manag. Int. J. **34**(4), 405–415 (1998)
5. Simon, P., Siva Sathya, S.: Genetic algorithm for information retrieval. In: IAMA 2009 (2009)
6. Radwan, A.A.A., Latef, B.A.A., Ali, A.M.A., et al.: Using genetic algorithm to improve information retrieval systems. World Acad. Sci. Eng. Technol. **17**, 1021–1027 (2008)
7. Fan, W., Gordon, M.D., Pathak, P.: AIJPersonalization of search engine services for effective retrieval and knowledge management, In: Proceedings of 2000 International Conference on Information Systems (ICIS), Brisbane, Australia (2000)
8. Butey, P.K., Meshram, S., Sonolikar, R.L.: Query optimization by genetic algorithm. J. Inform. Technol. Eng. **3**(1), 44–51 (2012) ISSN: 2229–7421
9. Owais, S.S.J., Kromer, P., Snasel, V.: Query optimization by genetic algorithms. In: Dateso 2005, pp. 125–137 (2005). ISBN 80-01-03204-3
10. Jain, A., Chande, S.V., Tiwari, P.: Relevance of genetic algorithm strategies in query optimization in information retrieval. Int. J. Comput. Sci. Inform. Technol. **5**(4), 5921–5927 (2014)
11. Leroy, G., Lally, A.M., Chen, H.: The use of dynamic contexts to improve casual Internet searching. ACM Trans. Inform. Syst. **21**(3), 229–253 (2003)
12. Lopez-Pujalte, C., Guerrero-Bote, V.P., Moya-Anegon, F.D.: A test of genetic algorithms in relevance feedback. Inform. Process. Manage. **38**, 793–805 (2002)
13. Cordon, O., Herrera-Viedma, E., Lopez Pujalte, C., Luque, M., Zarco, C.: A review on the application of evolutionary computation to information retrieval. Int. J. Approximate Reasoning **34**, 241–264 (2003)
14. Kucera, H., Francis, W.N.: Computational Analysis of Present-day American English. Brown University Press, Providence (1967)
15. Horng, J.-T., Yeh, C.-C.: Applying genetic algorithms to query optimization in document retrieval. Inform. Process. Manage. **36**, 737–759 (2000)
16. Buckley, C., Salton, G., Allan, J., Singhal, A.: Automatic query expansion using SMART: TREC 3. In: Proceedings of the Third Text Retrieval Conference, Gaithersburg, Maryland pp. 69–80 (1994)

A GRC-Centric Approach for Enhancing Management Process of IoT-Based Health Institution

Fouzi Lezzar[1], Djamel Benmerzoug[1], Kitouni Ilham[2(✉)],
and Aomar Osmani[3]

[1] LIRE Laboratory, Constantine 2-Abdelhamid Mehri University,
Constantine, Algeria
{fouzi.lezzar,djamel.benmerzoug}@univ-constantine2.dz
[2] MISC Laboratory, Constantine 2-Abdelhamid Mehri University,
Constantine, Algeria
ilham.kitouni@univ-constantine2.dz
[3] Galilée Institut, Paris 13 University, Villetaneuse, France
ao@lipn.univ-paris13.fr

Abstract. In hospital emergency wards, tasks are extremely complex to manage and pose serious health risks to patients. Related tasks, which are mainly focused around patient management, are achieved through conventional methods that lead generally to management breakdowns. Consequently, these latters that directly disrupt the patient's care chain and degrade their quality should be reduced with the exploration of efficient management approaches. In this paper, we will use Governance, Risk and Compliance approach (GRC) coupled with Internet of Things technology (IoT) we will call this new approach tGRC (things GRC). Such approach will provide a set of tools that may effectively address medical staff vital needs and improve the quality of patients' care. We wish to provide an effective support enabling by the way finer management features of the related tasks, providing an efficient data collection by using sensors and wearable devices and a real time awareness around the occurring events.

Keywords: Internet of Things · Governance-Risk-Compliance · Healthcare tasks management · Context-awareness

1 Introduction

Many healthcare institutions in Algeria suffer from multiple dysfunctions. Despite efforts made by authorities to improve the situation (new hospitals, rehabilitations of old ones, training of new physicians...), the problem persists and medical staff, patients and globally health system are severely affected.

Actually, the study that we led on this crucial question revealed various reasons that are principally linked to mismanagement of the related activities, equipment, human and material resources. In [29] authors determined the influence of human resource management on the improvement of healthcare delivery in public hospitals. This good

S. Bouzefrane et al. (Eds.): MSPN 2017, LNCS 10566, pp. 207–221, 2017.
DOI: 10.1007/978-3-319-67807-8_16

management leads to a better healthcare delivery quality. Numerous other studies confirmed this point [32, 33].

First, it is necessary to note that the artifacts used during work are essentially limited to Excel paper sheets, which are often not updated and sometimes even get lost between the different services. This situation is caused by the important work volume imposed on the personnel, which decreases the efficiency of work and healthcare delivery quality. While a primary aim of healthcare organizations is to provide cost effective, high quality, shared and seamless healthcare delivery, they also aim to reduce medical errors, safeguard patients' data and streamline clinical and administrative tasks [28]. The numerous studies that have been carried on this issue have almost all shown the importance of management [29] and management breakdowns among the medical staff members that inevitably have an impact on the quality of care provided to patients and put them in a potentially vulnerable and dangerous situation. Consequently, these management breakdowns that directly disrupt the patient's care chain and degrade their quality should be significantly reduced with the investigation of efficient management approaches.

In this paper, we will use Governance, Risk and Compliance approach (GRC) coupled with Internet of Things technology (IoT) called tGRC. Such approach will provide a set of tools that may effectively address medical staff vital needs and improve the quality of patients' care. We propose an effective support enabling management features of the related tasks as well as providing an efficient data collection in real time awareness around the occurring events; particularly those which constitute a priority in any health institution.

We led a study in an Algerian maternity ward to well understand the typical way with which medical activities are achieved by medical staff like midwives, gynecologists-obstetricians, nurses, anesthetists…; and to identify the principal used artifacts to manage and coordinate work. We started, therefore, by analyzing the way with which medical staff deal to collect information, operate with different medical cases, and how they manage the work. It was necessary also to identify different actors and their roles, all this information will certainly allow us to provide the most suitable IT proposition for the future system. It appears that the medical staffs need an efficient tool that takes in consideration the procedural, intellectual and social complexity of the management process. Indeed the huge volume of data should be collected and made available to the concerned persons rather than ignored until it becomes source of mistakes. Consequently, information displaying and notification should have a great attention form us and be targeted to facilitate decision-making process. This last has to be efficient and precise, because we operate in a high-risk environment that does not support a high rate of errors.

As a result of our analysis study in a maternity ward which is an organizations operating in high-risk, complex and dynamic work environments, in particular because they rely on collaboration among multiple groups of professionals and the high number of unexpected events, we noticed that providing health is a risky business and risks can have multiple sources: Patient, health care staff, Organization.

Organization of the paper: In Sect. 2, we present a domain model for IoT-based Health Institution applications. Section 3 is devoted to the proposed architecture based on GRC and IoT technologies, we discuss the two important notions: Internet of things and GRC and expose our conceptual methodology and motivate the choices made and we consider the details of the different architecture levels as well as the main supported functionalities. In Sect. 4 we recall the reference frame for integrated GRC, and we attempt to formalize the tGRC concepts. Our aim is to facilitate understanding the relationship between all concepts of the tGRC. In Sect. 5, we present some implementation aspects. Related works are presented in Sect. 6. Finally, we present the conclusion remarks in Sect. 7.

2 Domain Model for Health Institution Application Based on IoT

We propose a conceptual model for a health institution applications based on IoT. The model is based on previous work on advanced enterprise systems [4] and those of the IoT domain [5, 6].

Figure 1 shows the conceptual model which is composed of domain entities and the relationships that can exist between those entities.

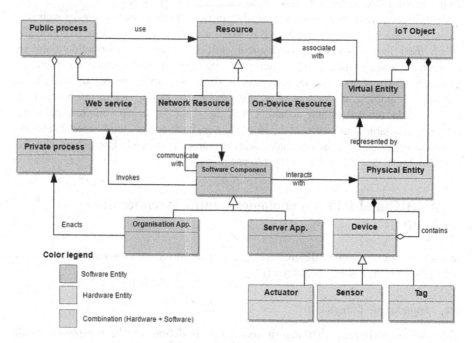

Fig. 1. Domain model of health institution application based on IoT

A public process is the aggregation of the private processes and/or Web services participating in it. Let us notice that private processes are considered as the set of processes of the organization itself and they are managed in an autonomous way to serve local needs. The public processes span organizational boundaries. They belong to the organizations involved in a collaboration relationship and have to be agreed and jointly managed by the different partners.

The most generic IoT scenario can be identified as that of a generic Agent (human or software component) needing to interact with a physical entity in the physical world. Physical entities are represented in the digital world by a virtual entity. An IoT object (or a thing) is the composition of a virtual entity and the physical entity it is associated to, in order to highlight the fact that these two concepts belong together.

In the physical environment, physical entity is the composition of one or more devices. This can be achieved by using devices of the same class, as in the case of certain similar kinds of body-area network nodes, or by using devices of different classes, as in the case of an RFID tag and reader.

In addition, it's important to realize that the device entity will often perform in a bi-directional manner with the "IoT object" at the edge of the network either acting as input devices (sensors) or output devices (actuators). Besides input and output devices, tags are used to identify physical entities, to which the tags are usually physically attached. The identification process is called "reading", and it is carried out by specific sensor devices, which are usually called readers. The primary purpose of tags is to facilitate and increase the accuracy of the identification process.

Public process (which is the aggregation of the private processes and/or web services participating in it) consumes resources. Resources are software components which used in the actuation on physical entities. There is a distinction between on-device resources and network resources. As the name indicates, on-device resources are hosted on devices (like software that is deployed locally on the device). They include executable code for accessing, processing, and storing sensor information, as well as code for controlling actuators. On the other hand, network resources are resources available some wherein the network, e.g., back-end or cloud-based databases. A virtual entity can also be associated with resources that enable interaction with the physical entity that the virtual entity represents.

3 A GRC and IOT Technologies Centric Architecture (tGRC)

In this section we present different concepts related to system process management particularly in the field of health care.

3.1 Internet of Things

The concept of Internet of things is recent and is defined as the integration of all devices that connect to the network, which can be managed from the web and in turn provide information in real time, to allow interaction with people they use it [25]. Internet of Things is becoming a reality thanks to many factors: low powers processors, improvements in wireless communication technologies, electronic devices, etc. [21].

One of the areas that can benefit from IoT solutions is e-health, which can be defined as the use of information and communications technologies and electronic devices in healthcare practice. IoT are used to monitor and observe physiological statues of patients inside or outside the health institution, using a set of sensors to collect their information and then sending it to remote centres for analysing and make suitable decisions. For example, Masimo Radical-7 monitors the patient's status remotely and reports that to a clinical staff [15].

Health monitoring applications are characterized by [1]: Gathering data from sensors, offering displays and user interfaces capabilities, durability, low power, robustness, accuracy and reliability and accessibility to infrastructural services throw a set of networks.

Economic growth of IoT-based services is also considerable for businesses. The whole annual economic impact caused by the IoT is estimated to be in range of $2.7 trillion to $6.2 trillion by 2025 [35]. Table 1 shows the projected market share of dominant IoT applications [35]. According to a Forbes magazine report, the market for IoT in healthcare will be more than $117 Billion by 2020 [9]. Many researchers think that IoT will have an important impact in healthcare domain. For an instance, Zhang and colleagues argue that Internets of Things and Cloud computing will be key in telemedicine and in Ambient Assisted Living applications [10–12]. This thought is based on several factors: reduced cost (Table 1) [8], better care, improving lifestyles of patients, improving medical staff working conditions [8].

Table 1. Health expenditure, total (% of GDP) by country [18]

Country	1995	2014
United States	13.1	17.1
Tuvalu	8.2	16.5
Sweden	8.0	11.9
Germany	9.4	11.3
Ecuador	3.4	9.2
Algeria	3.7	7.2
Bangladesh	3.2	2.8

3.2 Governance, Risk Management and Compliance

Recent growth in the number of standardizations such as Sarbanes-Oxley (SOX), ISO, and Basel III encouraged companies around the world to re-evaluate how they do business. The high costs of non-compliance mean that contemporary corporate executives have adopted thorough initiatives of Governance, Risk management and Compliance (GRC). Thus, most Fortunate companies list the GRC approach as the primary goal in the development of their business. The first company that proposed an integrated GRC is MetricStream[1]. This integration began in 2002 and it was only after the crisis of 2008 that the market began to integrate them: some large companies felt the need to control risks and above all to have a way of checking compliance with regulation when making large strategic decisions. The Enterprise Governance, Risk, and

---

[1] http://www.metricstream.com/.

Compliance (eGRC) market size is estimated to grow from USD 19.42 Billion in 2016 to USD 38.00 Billion by 2021 [22].

The GRC is an integrated approach for managing Governance, Risk and Compliance, enabling organizations to manage risk and regulatory issues across the organization. It provides a set of essential services and functional components that encompass various areas of risk and compliance management including operational risk, policy and compliance management, and control management.

Governance describes the general management approach whereby senior managers manage and control the entire organization using a combination of management information and hierarchical management control structures. Risk management is the set of processes by which management identifies analyses and, if necessary, reacts appropriately to risks that may adversely affect the achievement of the organization's business objectives. Compliance is the process by which companies document their procedures and standards and monitor the instigation of legislative policies. It consists in complying with the prescribed requirements. These requirements can be specified in legislation, industry regulations or even in company policies.

3.3   The Proposed Information System Architecture Based on IoT Technologies

As confirmed by a survey in several Swiss hospitals at 2009, 64% of them replied that the healthcare sector is a complex and heterogeneous economic sector and cannot be compared to other industry sectors where Control Objectives for Information and related Technology (CobiT) and other IT governance framework have been successfully applied [27]. Therefore, the solution is to design a flexible and efficient management system that takes in consideration the Ad-hoc nature of health institutions.

We propose an architecture that takes in consideration several factors: efficient collection of information and efficient management of the hospital: patients, medical staff, and material resources. Specific sensors are used to collect comprehensive physiological information and uses gateways to send data to the server on the Cloud for analysing and storage. Information is sent after to medical-staff wirelessly. Our proposition is shown on Fig. 2.

For data collection the use of the IoT solution improves the quality of care through continuous attention and lowers the cost of care by eliminating the need for a medical-staff to actively engage in data collection. In addition the technology can be used for remote monitoring using small, wireless solutions connected to patients through the IoT capabilities. Data is collected from different sources: Wearable devices or from sensors (installed on different equipment).

The Middleware plays the role of a gateway, it intercepts data sent by the various sensors to the software platform located in the cloud to be stored and analysed. The middleware performs an authentication operation to identify the device; it formats data under to specific shape before sending it to the server. The formatting operation facilitates the server work, it minimises the time of data recognition operation.

The IoT Platform Components: In what follows the most important constituents of the server on the Cloud architecture are highlighted. First, the register contains a list

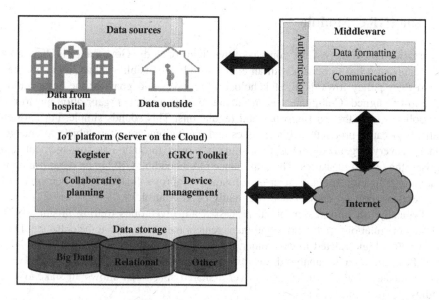

Fig. 2. The proposed architecture

of IoT devices and different equipment that collect data, it used to control and to avoid any external and unwanted attempts to connect to the server or to the gateway.

The Device Management module: is used to manage objects connects to the IoT platform. User can add, remove and configure devices remotely.

Collaborative planning module: this module allows an efficient planning with a collaborative manner. Hence health care task planning process is fundamentally a collaborative task that requires the participation of many health care experts with different skills working simultaneously on same cases. It's based on a collaborative planning approach and it constitutes an evolution of planning environments toward new shared workspaces supporting collaboration [13].

The Data Storage module takes care of the collected data storage either inside or outside the hospital. It uses relational databases as well as big data techniques or any data storage technology. This section provides the user a fast, secure and efficient access to all patient, medical and other resources information.

Finally **the tGRC module** enables the health institution to manage risk and regulatory issues across the organization. It provides a set of essential services and functional components that encompass various areas of risk and compliance management. **The tGRC solution legal register** offers access to the legal universe for each act. Fully searchable, tGRC solution gives the needed law easily and rapidly. The stakeholders can give feedback on the published information. This feedback is sent to the rules database. Finally, the rules administrator can improve and communicate about this information.

This module is detailed in the next section.

4 The tGRC Module

As presented previously, GRC consists of tree fields of study; Governance is about how an organization has to bé run with an efficient and responsible manner, and how they report their policy towards all stakeholders. Processes and goals of the organization have to be aligned. Compliancy is an integral part of this; the organization has to run her policy within the existing rules and regulations. This sounds simple, but is often difficult, because products, services, rules and regulations are often subject to change. Finally, every organization has to identify all risks through risk management and register the related measures. The importance of embedding GRC in an organization is that an organization wants to steer performances, improve the quality of their products and services, prevent damage and eventually be in control.

Typically, all information about processes are inventories (during in-situ work), rules and regulations, policy, risk and management measures, data to be collected. Data are structured and related to each other.

Afterward, data are analysed, quantified and reported, the IoT platform is used to communicate about this information over a shared space that allows all stakeholders finding pertinent information.

Every activity can be detailed and visualised for example, which personal are involved in the process, which applications, things… are used, which risks could occur and which norms are used.

A short description of the risk, effects, and impact and management measures are provided, user can visualize those processes as a chart.

The creation of processes is done in a collaborative manner for several reasons, indeed the most of the medical activities are group-based, and the principal problems in patients monitoring precisely arose from the lack of coordination between the various members of the involved medical team. The collaboration constitutes a key factor as it has been confirmed in several studies carried out on this issue [14]. Using a collaborative way allows decision-makers working together and remotely for hospital policies. This decreases with in significant manner coordination breakdowns.

As we have seen, processes, risks and management measurement, underlying rules and regulations are connected to each other, this gives a possibility to create several extensive management reports in a dashboard, and this gives an insight which risks related to each process. It provides also an overview of the identified risks within the organisation. If a risk or an anomaly occurred, an alert is triggered and notified to all the concerned staff for an immediate intervention.

4.1 Formalization of the tGRC Concepts (First Tentative)

In the beginning we recall the definition of the GRC for the topics involved, and adopted in the seminal work [7].

Definition: GRC is an integrated, holistic approach to organisation-wide governance risk and compliance ensuring that an organization acts ethically correct and in accordance with its risk appetite, internal policies and external regulations through the alignment of strategy, processes, technology and people, thereby improving efficiency and effectiveness [7].

Based on this definition a general structure of reference is proposed for an integrated GRC is presented in on Fig. 3.

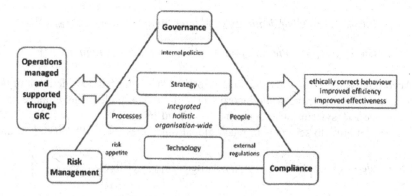

Fig. 3. A structure for integrated GRC

Services in the Cloud are exposed to a high degree of risks that result from technical issues or data access issues. In this section we will pose a formalization bases and state the three most common IoT security objectives: confidentiality, integrity and availability. Different research fields adopt different definitions of risk, depending on their particular research objects. Management theory assumes that the Risk consists in the loss probability and the volume of loss to be known prior to decision-making.

In this paper we introduce a formal model for governance in Cloud Computing that relates compliance and risk factors introduced by the internet of things technologies.

In the considered Governance, Risk management and Compliance model, let GRC_{Sub} be a set of subjects used in the field of the integrated tGRC.

Formally:

$$tGRC_{Sub} = \{tGovernance_{dicision}, tRisk_{management}, tCompliance_{assessment}\}$$

The tGRC subjects are based on four concepts:

$$tGRC_{Conpt} = \{STrategy, PRocesses, Users, TEchnology\}$$

The tGRC subjects depend on two kinds of factors:

$$tGRC_{fact} = \{tRisk_{factors}, tCompliance_{factors}\}$$

The availability of Cloud Computing services is one of the major security issues. The unavailability of data has the same effect as a system failure, because it significantly blocks all processes affected. The integrity of the data also raises questions, as they go across other systems. The fact that the information could be changed in any way is a risk. Finally, each IoT service has an inherent security requirement and level.

Hence, different data protection measures are required in Cloud Computing, the Cloud needs to have multiple and concentric levels of data protection.

In the model we make a basic distinction between a compliance factors (internal policies, norms and external regulations) and a risk factors (confidentiality, integrity and availability). So the tGRC observes the following rules:

$$tGRC_{Ris\_ru} = \{Confidentiality_{threats}, integrity_{threats}, Availibality_{threats}\}$$

$$tGRC_{Conf\_ru} = \{Internal\_policies, Normes, External\_regulations\}$$

Accordingly, the proposed modelling step aims at a balanced consideration of both compliance and risk factors while incorporating the risk attitude of governance maker regarding the IoT systems specificity and the Cloud offers.

The model aims to set goals to reach global objectives. Formally objectives are:

$$tObjectives = \left\{ Ethical_{cor-decision}, Efficiency_{improv}, Effectiveness_{improv} \right\}$$

These three objectives for IoT systems based on tGRC concepts form a solid basis for evaluating the IoT systems and Cloud offers solution which could be extended in practice by more detailed and specific objectives. For example the security objectives have to be detailed by authentication, authorization, accounting, etc.

The model developed here is meant to act as a risk minimization and compliance maximization tool, that is, it is supposed to identify the Cloud Computing service or the combination of services which causes the optimal cost for an organization by taking risk and compliance issues into account.

In conclusion, the constituents of tGRC work together to ensure that the IoT system operations remain sustainable and that business operations are conducted in a legal and ethical manner.

5 Some Implementation Aspects

The development of the proposed architecture requires the use of advanced tools such as: Amazon Web Services Internet of Things (AWS IoT) [36], Windows Azure Cloud platform [34], Windows Communication Foundation [16], and SQL Server Reporting Services [31].

Indeed, AWS IoT is a managed Cloud platform that lets connected devices securely interact with Cloud applications and other devices. It supports Message Queue Telemetry Transport (MQTT) and provides authentication and end-to-end encryption. Since our architecture is based on geographically distributed systems where each system manages its own infrastructures and devices, we need an integrated IoT platform that can support this distribution. AWS IoT makes it easy to use other AWS services in a distributed and integrated manner, so we can build value-added IoT applications that gather process, analyze and act on data which are generated by connected devices from many sources, without having to manage any infrastructure.

Windows Azure Platform is a Cloud platform which provides a wide range of Internet Services. It is a Windows based Cloud services operating system providing users with on demand compute service for running applications, and storage services for data storing (in Microsoft data centers). In our case, we can deploy the server application container as instances of Windows Azure Worker role which gets access to protocols repository on the Windows Azure environment via the Windows Azure Managed Library.

The development of our solution has to enable non-technical users to create sophisticate solutions quickly and easily. When the IoT platform is running, users can add dynamically a risk with its characteristics (category, description, area, type…), he can also add new characteristics for a risk, because risks in health institution have a stochastic nature. Every user have an access to a dashboard, the integrated dashboards provide an overview of risk areas, trend analysis and areas of non-conformance. These dashboards reflect the health of patients and the state of whole health institution in real time, due to combination of IoT and GRC capabilities.

Also the tool must to support maintaining data consistency, concurrent accesses, group interaction, and coordination. The used groupware concepts help users to effectively reduce these problems, such as group awareness that allows experts to be aware of the others work and be warned about events that may arise within the hospital and within the shared workspace on the common handled artefacts.

6 Related Works

IBM utilized RFID technology at one of OhioHealth's hospitals to trace hand washing after checking each patient [17]. That operation could be used to avoid infections that cause about 90,000 deaths and losing about $30 billion annually. In [2], authors are interested in collecting the patients' vital sign measurements and delivering it to multiple nursing stations. Authors are also interested in deploying a light sensor and a door sensor to monitor the activity level of the patients and potentially identify the ones suffering from depression. In order to allow doctors to access the collected data remotely, a mobile application is used.

In [3] Rolim et al. propose a solution to automate patients' vital data collection process by using a sensors attached to existing medical equipment that are inter-connected to exchange service. The proposal is based on the concepts of utility computing and wireless sensor networks. The information becomes available in the cloud from where it can be processed by expert systems and/or distributed to medical staff. [37] presents a platform based on Cloud Computing for management of mobile and wearable healthcare sensors, in this work the IoT paradigm was applied on pervasive healthcare. Gill et al. [38] suggest a novel IoT-enabled information architecture driven approach, which is called "Resalert". Resalert is used to address the challenge of emergency information notification delivery to elderly people. This is accomplished through the IoT- enabled emergency information supply chain architecture pattern views, IoT device and system architecture. The Resalert approach provides the end-to-end information flow or algorithm-source (a disaster-warning originator) to the affected residents (elderly people). The scope of the Resalert is limited to the delivery and presentation of emergency information to elderly people. The items such as information generation, processing, analysis or measurement of the information itself are beyond the scope of this research paper.

Another study [30] proposes a remote Android platform IoT home community health care wireless network. This is an interdisciplinary study of Android platform IoT home community health care system implementation. This system maintains patient identity, signal processing and results collection and analysis via cloud computing. Results are transmitted to the medical host for diagnosis. The work presented in [19] proposes an architecture that considers the use of different types of health managers and gateways, but keeping interoperability by the use of widely adopted standards. The main contribution of this work is the distribution of health managers in different locations, such as mobile devices and cloud applications, enabling the use of a single health service for different types of Personal Health Devices.

EcoHealth [20] (Ecosystem of Health Care Devices), is a Web middleware platform for connecting doctors and patients using attached body sensors, thus aiming to provide improved health monitoring and diagnosis for patients. This platform is able to integrate information obtained from heterogeneous sensors in order to provide mechanisms to monitor, process, visualize, store, and send notifications regarding patients' conditions and vital signs at real-time by using Internet standards. An Android application presented in [23] called SapoMed, users can use this application for registration medication schedule of patients. A web service is used to display prescription information about each registered medication.

In [24], the authors propose a novel IoT-based mobile gateway solution for mobile health (m-Health) scenarios. This gateway autonomously collects information about the user/patient location, heart rate, and possible fall detection. Moreover, it forwards the collected information to a caretaker IPA in real time that will manage a set of actions and alarms appropriately. The algorithms used for each mobile gateway service, and the scenarios where the mobile gateway acts as a communication channel or a smart object are also addressed on this paper. The aim of the work proposed in [26] is to develop an architecture based on ontology capable of monitoring the health and workout routine recommendations to patients with chronic diseases.

7   Conclusion

In this study, we claim that health institution management breakdowns could be solved by using the adequate communication technologies such as IoT and the efficient management processes like GRC. We proposed an architecture that uses a novel concept we called tGRC and we have discussed its basic design. We used IoT for a better data collection inside health institution. We have also showed that it enables collaboration between several participants within a shared workspace and allows users' individual and collective actions on a common patient case as the care planning elaboration.

Being conscious of the great interest of our approach experimentation in effective context situations, we plan in the next step of our research work to collect more information about our targeted context. This represents a double objective; First, we can validate or forsake some technical choices among those we made during the implementation. Second, we will be able to determine with more precisions the appropriated adaptations we should apply to the supports provided in our tGRC approach. To this end, such as any software project we designed modular and extendable software architecture, in the sense that it allows design and integration of new components through an incremental way.

References

1. Vermesan, O., Friess, P. (eds.): Internet of Things-from Research and Innovation to Market Deployment, pp. 74–75. River Publishers, Aalborg (2014)
2. Al-Fuqaha, A., Guizani, M., Mohammadi, M., Aledhari, M., Ayyash, M.: Internet of Things: a survey on enabling technologies, protocols, and applications. IEEE Commun. Surv. Tutor. 17(4), 2347–2376 (2015)
3. Rolim, C., Koch, F., Westphall, C., Werner, J., Fracalossi, A., Salvador, G.: A cloud computing solution for patient's data collection in health care institutions. In: Second International Conference on eHealth, Telemedicine, and Social Medicine (ETELEMED 2010), February 2010, pp. 95–99 (2010)
4. Benmerzoug, D.: Towards AiP as a service: an agent based approach for outsourcing business processes to cloud computing services. Int. J. Inf. Sys. Serv. Sect. 7(2), 1–17 (2015)
5. Haller, S., Serbanati, A., Bauer, M., Carrez, F.: A domain model for the Internet of Things. In: GreenCom/iThings/CPScom, pp. 411–417 (2013)
6. Bauer, M., et al.: IoT reference model. In: Bassi, A., et al. (eds.) Enabling Things to Talk, pp. 113–162. Springer, Heidelberg (2013). doi:10.1007/978-3-642-40403-0_7
7. Racz, N., Weippl, E., Seufert, A.: A frame of reference for research of integrated governance, risk and compliance (GRC). In: De Decker, B., Schaumüller-Bichl, I. (eds.) CMS 2010. LNCS, vol. 6109, pp. 106–117. Springer, Heidelberg (2010). doi:10.1007/978-3-642-13241-4_11
8. How the Internet of Things will impact health care. http://en.community.dell.com/dell-blogs/direct2dell/b/direct2dell/archive/2015/11/20/how-the-internet-of-things-will-impact-health-care
9. $117 Billion Market for Internet of Things in Healthcare by 2020 (2015). http://www.forbes.com/sites/tjmccue/2015/04/22/117-billion-market-for-internet-of-things-in-healthcare-by-2020/#257e927d2471
10. Zhang, X.M., Zhang, N.: An open, secure and flexible platform based on Internet of Things and cloud computing for ambient aiding living and telemedicine. In: International Conference on Computer and Management (CAMAN). IEEE (2011)
11. Zhang, X.M., Xu, C.: A multimedia telemedicine system in Internet of Things. In: Proceedings of the 2nd International Conference on Information and Multimedia Technology (ICIMT), vol. 3. IEEE (2010)
12. Zhang, X.M., Li, J.: Research on interoperability of Internet of Things' gateway oriented to telehealth and telemedicine. Energy Procedia 13(2011), 8276–8284 (2011)
13. Lezzar, F., Zidani, A., Chorfi, A.: Using a mobile collaborative approach to improve healthcare tasks planning. Int. J. Multimed. Ubiquitous Eng. 8(3), 407–420 (2013)
14. Kuziemsky, C.E., Varpio, L.: A model of awareness to enhance our understanding of interprofessional collaborative care delivery and health information system design to support it. Int. J. Med. Inform. (2011). doi:10.1016/j.ijmedinf.2011.01.009

15. Masimo Corporation: Radical-7 breakthrough measurements. Radical monitor http://www. masimo.com/rainbow/radical7.htm
16. Cibraro, P., Claeys, K., Cozzolino, F., Grabner, J.: Professional WCF 4: Windows Communication Foundation with .NET 4. Wrox Publishing (2010)
17. Jain, S., Mane, S., Lopez, J., Lie, D.Y.C., Dallas, T., Dissanaike, S., Banister, R.E., Griswold, J.: A low-cost custom HF RFID system for hand washing compliance monitoring. In: IEEE 8th International Conference on ASIC (ASICON 2009), pp. 975–978 (2009)
18. World Health Organization Global Health Expenditure database. apps.who.int/nha/database
19. Santos, D.F., Perkusich, A., Almeida, H.O.: Standard-based and distributed health information sharing for mHealth IoT systems. In: IEEE 16th International Conference on e-Health Networking, Applications and Services (Healthcom), pp. 94–98 (2014)
20. Maia, P., Batista, T., Cavalcante, E., Baffa, A., Delicato, F.C., Pires, P.F., Zomaya, A.: A web platform for interconnecting body sensors and improving health care. Procedia Comput. Sci. **40**, 135–142 (2014)
21. Atzori, L., Iera, A., Morabito, G.: The Internet of Things: a survey. Comput. Netw. **54**(15), 2787–2805 (2010)
22. http://www.marketsandmarkets.com/PressReleases/enterprise-governance-risk-compliance. asp
23. Silva, B.M., Lopes, I.M., Marques, M.B., Rodrigues, J.J.P.C., Proença Jr., M.L.,: A mobile health application for out patients medication management. In: Proceedings of the IEEE International Conference on Communications, Budapest, 9–13 June 2013, pp. 4389–4393 (2013)
24. Santos, J., Rodrigues, J.J., Silva, B.M., Casal, J., Saleem, K., Denisov, V.: An IoT-based mobile gateway for intelligent personal assistants on mobile health environments. J. Netw. Comput. Appl. **71**, 194–204 (2016). ISSN 1084-8045
25. Gómez, J., Huete, J.F., Hoyos, O., Perez, L., Grigori, D.: Interaction system based on Internet of Things as support for education. Procedia Comput. Sci. **21**, 132–139 (2013)
26. Gómez, J., Oviedo, B., Zhuma, E.: Patient monitoring system based on Internet of Things. Procedia Comput. Sci. **83**, 90–97 (2016)
27. Krey, M., Harriehausen, B., Knoll, M.: Approach to the classification of information technology governance, risk and compliance frameworks. In: 2011 UKSim 13th International Conference on Computer Modelling and Simulation (UKSim), pp. 350–354. IEEE (2011)
28. Sabooniha, N., Toohey, D., Lee, K.: An evaluation of hospital information systems integration approaches. In: Proceedings of the International Conference on Advances in Computing, Communications and Informatics, pp. 498–504. ACM (2012)
29. Jończyk, J.A.: The impact of human resource management on the innovativeness of public hospitals in Poland. Procedia Soc. Behav. Sci. **213**, 1000–1007 (2015)
30. Sung, W.T., Chang, K.Y.: Evidence-based multi-sensor information fusion for remote health care systems. Sens. Actuators A Phys. **204**, 1–19 (2013)
31. Microsoft Docs (2017). https://docs.microsoft.com/
32. Pocztowski, A.: Adding value from human resource development in international assignment. Argumenta Oeconomica Cracoviensia (09), 9–28 (2013)
33. Tan, C.L., Nasurdin, A.M.: Human resource management practices and organizational innovativeness: an empirical study in Malaysia. J. Appl. Bus. Res. **2**, 105–115 (2010)
34. Mackenzie, N.: Microsoft Windows Azure Development Cookbook. Packt Publishing (2011)
35. Manyika, J., Chui, M., Bughin, J., Dobbs, R., Bisson, P., Marrs, A.: Disruptive Technologies: Advances that Will Transform Life, Business, and the Global Economy. McKinsey Global Institute, San Francisco (2013)

36. Amazon WS-IoT. https://aws.amazon.com/iot/2017
37. Doukas, C., Maglogiannis, I.: Bringing IoT and cloud computing towards pervasive healthcare. In: 2012 Sixth International Conference on Innovative Mobile and Internet Services in Ubiquitous Computing (IMIS), pp. 922–926. IEEE (2012)
38. Gill, A.Q., Phennel, N., Lane, D., Phung, V.L.: IoT-enabled emergency information supply chain architecture for elderly people: the Australian context. Inf. Syst. **58**, 75–86 (2016)

Energy Consumption Estimation for Energy-Aware, Adaptive Sensing Applications

Nattachart Tamkittikhun[✉], Amen Hussain[✉],
and Frank Alexander Kraemer[✉]

Department of Information Security and Communication Technology,
Norwegian University of Science and Technology (NTNU), Trondheim, Norway
{nattacht,kraemer}@ntnu.no, amenh@stud.ntnu.no

Abstract. We propose and evaluate an approach for the estimation of the energy consumption of sensor nodes in IoT sensing applications. The approach is based on the identification of distinct activity phases that sensor nodes repeatedly execute. The power consumption of these activity phases is measured before the nodes are deployed. The total energy consumption at runtime is then estimated by combining the measured values with timestamps captured at runtime. Therefore, the approach can take runtime adaptations of the application behavior, as necessary for adaptive sensing, into account, but without involving complex hardware measurements of power consumption at runtime. We show that the error of the estimation for selected applications is low (max. observed was 2.438%), which makes the approach very suitable for energy-aware, adaptive sensing.

1 Introduction

For many sensing applications within the Internet of Things (IoT), the energy available at the wireless nodes is the most scarce resource. The energy budget limits how much processing can be done at the nodes, how sensors can operate, and how much data can be transmitted. Also the quality of measurements is energy-dependent. More energy allows to measure several times and reduce errors, additional processing can increase data quality, and for some sensors the sensing quality can be increased with prolonged sensing time.

An additional challenge within the IoT is that nodes are subject to heterogeneous and non-stationary environments [5]. When nodes are powered by solar energy, for instance, their energy budget depends on the current weather conditions. This makes it difficult or impossible to optimize a node's operation at design time, for instance by selecting constant values for all durations and application parameters.

Instead, optimization must happen at runtime and continuously. Durations and parameters that influence sensing quality and energy consumption can then be selected according to the energy budget, also taking forecasts into account. This can prevent nodes from suddenly running out of energy. Similarly, it can

S. Bouzefrane et al. (Eds.): MSPN 2017, LNCS 10566, pp. 222–235, 2017.
DOI: 10.1007/978-3-319-67807-8_17

prevent nodes from selecting a too conservative sensing strategy that leads to a fully charged battery, although plenty of solar energy is available. With such a decision, the node misses an opportunity to provide the best possible data quality or quantity, given available yet non-harvested solar energy [9]. Energy-aware planning can also consider the system as a whole, across several nodes, where sensors with a higher energy level can compensate for sensors with less energy. To support such energy-aware planning, we require detailed data about the energy budget of the nodes.

Obtaining good, instantaneous estimates for the current energy consumption is the subject of an approach presented in the following. One way to acquire such data is by using onboard hardware that samples the energy consumption. However, this comes with increased hardware complexity and also requires interpretation of the samples. On the other side, only measuring the power consumption in a lab setting is not flexible enough, since the applications will be adapted by an energy-aware planning algorithm. We therefore devise an approach that combines power estimation before deployment with logging at runtime. It is based on experience with a number of applications and the insight that most sensing applications decompose into a periodic sequence of activity phases. We found that it is relatively simple to obtain an accurate estimate of the power consumption of such phases once the hardware of the node is built and the application is written. When the system is deployed and running, the average power consumption of the different phases does not change significantly. The phases only execute with different durations and more or less often, based on feedback of energy-aware planning. This can be logged with timestamps at runtime. The power measurements from the lab are combined with the dynamic timestamps captured at runtime to estimate the total energy consumption of a sensing cycle. An evaluation for several applications shows that this estimation matches well with the actual energy consumption, so that it is a valuable input for planning algorithms for adaptive sensing. The benefit of the approach is that it requires little instrumentation, and it does not require any complex hardware for measuring energy consumption at runtime.

The remainder of the paper is structured as follows: We will continue with an overview of related approaches. In Sect. 3, we will introduce energy-aware, periodic sensing applications. We will then introduce the estimation approach in Sect. 4. Section 5 will detail the runtime necessary for the approach, while Sect. 6 will detail the offline preparation and measurement setup at design-time. We will then evaluate our approach in Sect. 7.

2   Related Work

There exist various approaches to obtain the energy consumption of embedded devices. We can roughly categorize them into online and offline approaches, as well as hardware and software approaches. Online approaches acquire the energy consumption of the device at runtime, while offline approaches determine static consumptions in a lab setting. Hardware approaches require additional physical instrumentation to measure the energy consumption. Software approaches do not need any additional hardware, instead, the energy consumption is calculated from a model or can be obtained from a simulation based on a given processor and application. Both hardware and software approaches can also fall into offline or online categories. The energy estimations can be done in different scopes: only at CPU level; a combination of CPU, ADC, memory; only at peripheral devices; or the entire system.

The approach in [7] uses additional hardware including a microcontroller to measure the entire system consumption at runtime, based on realtime measurements of current and voltage. Measurements are stored on an SD card and manually transferred to a computer for analysis. This makes the process quite elaborate and also costs energy.

Shin *et al.* [13] present an approach based on a board that is tightly integrated to a target embedded processor from which the board and associated software gather the energy consumption profile. A program to be measured is run on the target processor on the board, offline in a lab setting.

The board uses the pre-gathered energy profile to estimate the program's energy consumption. The authors used the ARM7TDMI. Even though the concept is applicable to any target processor, it requires hardware modification of the measurement board for different processors.

The energy consumption of a microprocessor can be estimated offline for certain applications by using the energy profile of each assembly-level instruction [2], similar to the previous work. The model considers three types of instruction-level energy costs: the base cost which is the energy consumption of the instruction itself, the switching cost which occurs when switching between instructions, and extra costs to capture cache misses and branch mispredictions. The profiling is a one-time process and can be used to estimate power and energy of all applications run on the same microprocessor. It is appropriate for static code analysis that results in the estimated power and energy consumption of the application. The mean errors of the estimated power and energy are 7% and 14.6% respectively. This approach does not consider energy consumption of peripheral devices and the assembly-level source code corresponding to the high-level language of an application needs to be analyzed. Additionally, profiling the energy consumption of the instruction set of a microprocessor unit (MCU) takes time and has to be worked out whenever a new MCU is to be used.

If only certain types of applications should be analyzed, high-level parametric laws of consumption and performance can be modeled [10,11]. This methodology helps to extract important parameters of the target application and hardware that significantly contribute to the energy consumption and performance. Then example applications with varied parameters are simulated or run on the target platform to gain a set of power and energy consumption values, which will be used for a model deduction by regression. When the model is derived, the energy consumption of the target application on a specific hardware platform with different parameter values can be calculated. The average errors on estimates by the deducted models vary upon different applications and processors. In [10], energy estimates errors are 7.1% and 7.6% for finite impulse response

(FIR) application running on C6701 and C5501 processors respectively. For a
Fast Fourier Transform (FFT) application the estimated energy errors are 4%
and 6.6%, respectively.

Another modeling approach parameterizes applications by processor instructions [4], instead of application-level parameters. Besides instructions, other
instruction-level operations such as the number of shift operations and memory access types are also taken as model parameters. This approach is evaluated
by testing a model of a set of applications from the MiBench benchmark suite [6]
on ARM7TDMI processor against actual measurements. The estimation errors
from the model of all applications range from 1% to 5.77%.

The nominal power consumption according to the specification of related
devices can be used to estimate an embedded system's energy consumption without additional hardware [17]. This work also considers the fact that a variety of
devices connected to a processing module can interfere with each other, resulting in deviated power consumption from the values stated on the data sheet
of each device. Thus, it introduces a technique to compensate this deviation to
reduce errors in the estimation. This approach is only feasible when the power
consumption specifications of all parts are available.

3 Energy Aware Sensing Applications

Let's first consider why we need an energy estimation approach as a tool that
complements our energy-aware sensing applications. The context of our applications is illustrated by the general architecture for an IoT sensing application
in Fig. 1. This architecture can for example realize a city-wide sensing system
for emissions like particles or CO_2, a climate monitoring system for buildings
with fine-grained temperature measurements, or a tracking system for animals
and goods containers. In our setting, the sensor nodes are Multitech mDot
devices [12], based on the STM32F4 microcontroller [16]. To cover various energy
profiles, we consider the following three distinct applications:

- *Temperature sensing*: This application uses a digital thermometer, samples
  it, and sends off the data.
- *Particle sensing*: A particle sensor streams air over an LED and analyzes the
  amount of particles. This type of sensor requires much more energy than the
  thermometer since it uses a motor-driven fan to create the air stream. For
  the measurement to be accurate, the fan must be active for at least 10 s.
- *GPIO*: This application samples the state of an I/O pin. We included this
  simple application to have an example where the energy used for sensing is
  minimal.

All sensor nodes communicate with a cloud backend via LoRaWAN, a communication stack optimized for low energy consumption and long ranges [14]. It
supports a star topology, in which sensor devices communicate directly with a
gateway, which then forwards LoRaWAN packets with the sensor data into a
cloud backend. The cloud backend is responsible for acquiring and analyzing the
sensor data.

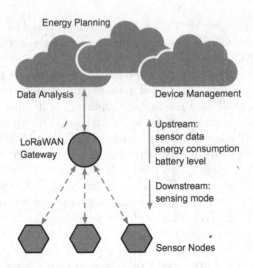

Fig. 1. Sensing system overview

3.1 Sensor Node Logic

Many applications for sensing systems follow a simple logic. First, the node wakes up from its sleep phase. Next, the first step of the active mode is to acquires data from sensors. Thereafter, the data goes through processing tasks. Then, the processed data is transmitted to remote receivers such as remote servers for further processing. Finally, the node returns to the sleep phase for a period of time before going back to the first step in the active mode again.

Some of the logic in a sensor node is entirely determined by the specific sensor and its interface. Still, developers face a lot of choices and degrees of freedom when designing the application. One of the choices is the duty cycle which determines how long the sensing logic goes into the sleep phase, i.e., the time between distinct sensing cycles. Within a sensing cycle, the sensor can be activated more than once to take an average over several measurements. Some sensors also offer choices over more specific parameters. CO_2 sensors, for instance, require a warm-up period for heating, and the particle sensor introduced above needs to activate its fan for a specific time. All of these parameters are not only flexible and have an influence on the quality and amount of acquired data, but also influence the energy consumption. Based on experience with a smart city sensing system [3], we have observed how difficult it is to just determine the proper duty cycle and sensing time at design time, even for domain experts. Instead, parameters need to be adjusted after the system is deployed and data about its operation and specific environment is available.

As a practical simplification, we define a set of discrete *sensing modes* for the example applications that combine several of the parameters from above. For the temperature application, there are two distinct sensing modes:

- Mode T1: Take one temperature sample, send it and sleep for 2 s.
- Mode T2: Take two temperature samples separated by 0.1 s, calculate their average and standard error, send the result, and sleep for 2 s.

There are two distinct sensing modes for the particle sensor:

- Mode P1: Take one dust sample, send the result, and sleep for 60 s.
- Mode P2: Take two dust samples, calculate their average and standard error, send, and sleep for 120 s.

The data quality of T2 and P2 are better since they are based on more measurements. We will later see that the sensing modes also lead to different energy profiles of the applications. (We use only two modes here for brevity. Other applications may require more to cover a wider variety for optimal operation.)

3.2 Energy-Aware Planning

The sensing modes from above exemplify a typical tradeoff: With plenty of energy available, the sensor node can choose to use a sensing mode that leads to higher data accuracy or more data. When the available energy is low, it may instead opt to only sense in a cheaper mode to at least stay alive and provide some data. Energy-aware planning can be based on simple policies or heuristics, but it can also involve more complex techniques, like reinforcement learning [5]. Planning may for instance take the weather forecast into account, or decide dynamically which level of sensor precision is necessary, based on the state of other nodes in the system. Sensing modes may also depend on events, for example, when sudden changes of temperature should be captured with a higher sensing rate than periods with only little changes. For these reasons, planning may also be performed by the cloud backend as part of the device management. The detailed implementations, however, are not subject of this paper. Whenever the backend detects the need for changing the current sensing mode, it sends messages to the sensor devices. LoRaWAN allows this kind of communication by pushing messages out to gateways which then forward them to the sensor nodes.

To aid the planning algorithm in the cloud, the sensor nodes do not only send the actual domain data but also metadata about their operation, including their current battery level, derived from the voltage at the battery. Observing the battery level can lead to insights about the energy consumption of the current application and sensing mode. However, we found that it requires a long observation time to get a precise enough estimate of the energy consumption, since the battery usually depletes over a long time period and is subject to noise. To provide a better input for the planning, we want the sensor node to also send more instantaneous estimates of the energy consumption of the current sensing modes into the backend. This is where the online estimation of energy consumption comes into play.

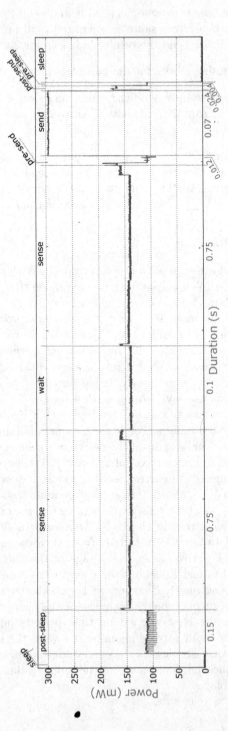

Fig. 2. Power consumption of one cycle of a sensing application. some phases are shortened on the x-axis, to save space. The labels reveal the actual duration.

4   Simple Sampling Approach

Figure 2 shows the power consumption of a sensor node, measured with the setup described in Sect. 5. The vertical axis shows the power consumption. The graph reveals different phases of the application, which can be identified by comparing the graph with timestamps in the application [8]. In the *sleep* phase, the sensor node consumes $\approx$1.2 mW. When waking up, we see a *post-sleep* phase that takes $\approx$0.15 s and consumes $\approx$110 mW. Thereafter, the temperature is sensed twice in the *sense* phases, with a *wait* phase of $\approx$0.1 s in between both measurements, which consumes the power of $\approx$80 mW. The averaged power consumption of the *sense* phase is $\approx$86 mW and has a duration of $\approx$0.75 s. The following *pre-send* phase lasts for $\approx$0.012 s and consumes $\approx$75 mW. The *send* phase consumes the power of $\approx$280 mW and takes $\approx$0.07 s. After the *send* phase is the *post-send* phase which takes $\approx$0.024 s and needs the power of $\approx$170 mW. Before the application enters the *sleep* phase, there is a short *pre-sleep* phase of $\approx$0.004 s that consumes $\approx$100 mW. Figure 3 illustrates an abstraction of a sensing cycle with the different phases. The shaded boxes represent pre and post phases with constant durations are related to sleep and transmit operations that we consistently observed [8].

The rather distinct phases during a sensing cycle motivate the estimation approach. Instead of sampling an entire sensing cycle, we base the estimation on the distinct activity phases, with their individual durations and power consumptions:

- During a sensing phase, the power consumption depends on the specific sensor used. Some sensors (like temperature) only require little power. The particle sensor, in contrast, needs lots of power due to its fan driven by a motor as well as the internal LED. A CO_2 sensor also draws a lot of power since it requires to heat up, so that the gas concentration can be measured properly. Similarly, the sensing duration can vary considerably. While some sensors deliver almost instant readings, the particle sensor should be active for at least 10 s, CO_2 sensors for up to 2 min.
- During the sleeping phase, most platforms have a very low power consumption. The duration depends on the duty cycle of the sensing application, i.e., how many sensing cycles it should perform per hour.
- The power consumption during transmission is a function of the signal strength of the radio. The duration is a function of the amount of data to send, usually quantized by the discrete packet lengths.
- We observed that the power consumption during the *compute* phase is approximately the same, irrespective of the computed tasks. Its energy consumption therefore only depends on the duration of the task. However, computational tasks that make use of specific hardware support, such as for instance Fast Fourier Transformations can yield different power consumptions [15]. These, must be modelled as distinct phases and measured separately.

The total energy consumption of a sensing cycle is then calculated by the sum of contributions from all activity phases:

$$E = \sum_{i=1}^{I} P_i \Delta t_i \qquad (1)$$

where E is the total energy of a sensing cycle, P_i is the power consumption of a phase i, and Δt_i is the duration taken by the phase i. I is the total number of phases in a sensing cycle, including the *send* phase. Crucial for our approach, the values P_i and Δt_i are acquired at different times:

- The power consumptions P_i of the different phases are constant for a given hardware configuration of processing platform and peripheral devices such as sensors. They are measured at design time, when the hardware is built or subject to power profiling described in Sect. 5.
- The durations of activity phases Δt_i are measured at runtime. This is important, since the length and the occurrence of activity phases change dynamically based on planning, as described in Sect. 3.

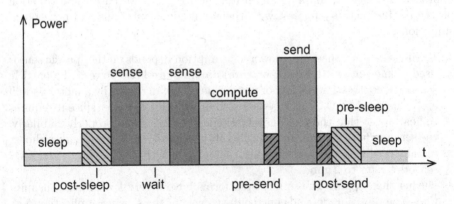

Fig. 3. An abstract model of the energy consumption, with focus on the different activity phases. power and time axis are not to scale.

5   Measuring Power Consumption of Phases

This section describes components and setup used to profile power consumptions of the different activity phases. This profiling is a one-time process for a distinct platform including peripheral devices such as sensors. The microprocessor platform used in our experiments is a Multitech mDot [12], which has a built-in LoRaWAN radio transmission module. In addition, we use the DS18b20 temperature and the DN7C3CA006 particle sensors for the temperature and particle applications. The supplied voltage is connected to a current shunt resistor of 10 Ω in series with the hardware platform. The current consumption i can be derived via $i = v/R$, where v is a measured voltage dropped over the 10 Ω shunt resistor R. The instantaneous power consumption p is then derived by $p = Vi$, where i is the obtained current consumption and V is the mDot's Vcc of 5 V.

To start profiling, the voltage at the shunt resistor is captured by the oscilloscope automated by a Python script. The periods of each phase in mDot's application is synchronized with the oscilloscope by a trigger every time the phase starts and ends. This boundary data is also logged to confine sets of measured voltages of each phase. The voltage data of phases in the files are converted into power, which are then averaged, and the profiling process finishes. These values are then used as representative power consumptions of the phases, in any application running on this hardware configuration to estimate their energy consumption.

Algorithm 1. General Application with Energy Estimation

1: *Init the array P of size $I - 1$ with all pre-measured P_is.*
2: $ES_{send} \leftarrow$ *pre-measured energy of pre- and post-send phases*
3: *Initialize array ES with pre-measured energy of any pre- and post- phases*
4: $P_{send} \leftarrow$ *The pre-measured power cons. of the send phase*
5: $E_{n-1} \leftarrow 0$ $\triangleright$ Let n represent cycle n.
6: **loop**
7:     $E_n \leftarrow 0$
8:     $i \leftarrow 1$
9:     **while** $i \leq I - 1$ **do**
10:         $t_{start} \leftarrow timestamp()$
11:         *Execute phase i*
12:         $t_{end} \leftarrow timestamp()$
13:         $\Delta t_i \leftarrow t_{end} - t_{start}$
14:         $E_n \leftarrow E_n + P_i \Delta t_i + ES_i$
15:         $i \leftarrow i + 1$
16:     **end while**
17:     $t_{start} \leftarrow timestamp()$
18:     *Send the data and energy of the previous cycle E_{n-1}*
19:     $t_{end} \leftarrow timestamp()$
20:     $\Delta t_I \leftarrow t_{end} - t_{start}$
21:     $E_{n-1} \leftarrow E_n + P_{send} \Delta t_I + ES_{send}$
22: **end loop**

---

6   Runtime Logic for Energy Estimation

At runtime, we only log the duration Δt_i of the different activity phases. Here, we use the *timer.h* library provided from *mbed* [1] to compute Δt_i for each phase. The timestamps before and after a specific phase are recorded as shown in Algorithm 1 at lines 10 and 12. The $\varDelta t_i$ of phase i is calculated at line 13. The *sleep* phase is encoded as phase 1; hence the first phase of the sensing cycle. The summation according to Eq. 1 is implemented in line 14.

The static pre-and post-phases (shaded in Fig. 3) are initialized in lines 2 and 3, and added as constants in lines 14 and 21. (For the phases without pre- and post-phases, the corresponding value is simply set to 0).

To enable energy-aware planning in the cloud backend, the sensing application includes the energy consumption estimate in the LoRaWAN packet sent out as part of the sending activity. Since, the duration of the transmission is only known after it has been executed. Therefore, the algorithm sends the power estimation of cycle $n-1$ as part of the sending activity of cycle n, i.e., one cycle later. The planning algorithm in the backend can take this into consideration.

7   Evaluation and Discussion

To evaluate the accuracy of the proposed estimation approach, we compared the estimated energy consumption of the example applications from Sect. 3, with actual measurements with a similar setup as explained in Sect. 5. The applications have different energy profiles, summarized in Fig. 4. It shows that the different activity phases consume different shares of the energy budget. The processing cost in all applications is negligible because its duration is very short. In Particle Mode P1 and P2, the energy consumption of the send phase is close

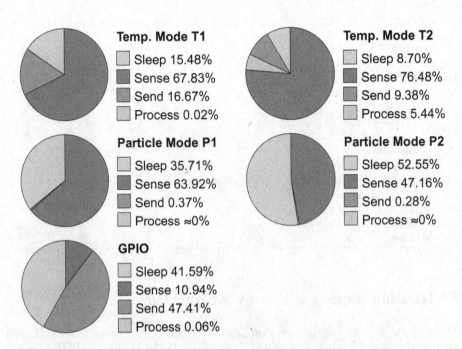

Fig. 4. Energy profiles of the applications in their different sensing modes.

to zero percent because the particle sensor, when sensing, consumes relatively large amount of energy comparing to sending.

Table 1 presents the comparison between the estimated energy consumption by the presented approach and the actual measurements. The estimation was performed at runtime, as explained by Algorithm 1. All results were acquired 10 times for combination of each application and sensing mode. The standard deviations of estimated and measured data are presented in columns $\sigma_{estimated}$ and $\sigma_{measured}$ respectively. The difference between estimated and the actual energy consumption ranges between 0.469% and 2.438%. Given the context of the planning algorithm that includes other models such as weather forecasts to predict solar intake (see Sect. 3), we consider this accuracy to be sufficient, especially when compared to other estimation methods based on the long-term observation of the battery level. The approach also scores well compared to those presented in the literatures, in Sect. 2.

Table 1. Comparison of estimated and measured energy consumption

Application	Estimated energy (J)	$\sigma_{estimated}$ $(\times 10^{-5}$ J)	Measured energy (J)	$\sigma_{measured}$ $(\times 10^{-5}$ J)	Error (%)
Temp. (Mode T1)	0.159	14.9	0.158	6.9	0.469
Temp. (Mode T2)	0.282	13.0	0.284	22.0	0.809
Particle (Mode P1)	7.720	143.1	7.665	503.5	0.810
Particle (Mode P2)	10.464	9.8	10.384	198.4	0.764
GPIO	0.056	15.9	0.058	8.2	2.438

The computational complexity of the approach is negligible for the applications presented. The energy model in Eq. 1 is implemented as part of the application logic, and the estimated value is sent as metadata with each transmission. For the given applications, the computational effort used for the estimation and the acquisition of the timestamps is negligible. Since the estimated energy consumption is sent as metadata and takes 8 bytes, the corresponding LoRaWAN frames are slightly larger, which adds to the energy consumption. However, this overhead is negligible in the given applications. The retransmission of LoRaWAN frames are managed by the protocol itself [14], and therefore the captured transmission duration in the application also includes retransmissions when occuring.

8 Conclusion

We presented an approach for the estimation of energy consumption of wireless sensor nodes. The approach is based on measurements of the power consumption of different activity phases during design time, and complemented by runtime measurements. These runtime measurements of the duration of the different phases take the dynamics of applications into account, to capture optimizations performed for instance by an energy-aware backend planning system. Thanks to this division of measurements, the approach does not require the sensor nodes to have any additional hardware for energy measurements when they are deployed, but can still capture the variations and adaptations as required by the adaptive sensing approaches. The accuracy of the approach is sufficient to support the planning algorithms. The results can either be used for reasoning within the sensor, or by a planning algorithm located in a cloud backend.

We currently consider how the presented approach to instantaneously estimate energy can be combined with the more long-term methods based on the observation of the battery level. The instantaneous estimation can predict the effect of changes in the sensing mode quickly, while the long-term observation of the battery captures key indicators regarding the battery health.

In the context of adaptive IoT sensing applications, this approach is a valuable contribution to enable optimal, energy-aware operation of constrained nodes, where both hardware and software instrumentation must be kept to a minimum.

References

1. ARMmbed timer. https://developer.mbed.org/handbook/Timer. Accessed 30 Mar 2017
2. Acevedo-Patio, O., Jimnez, M., Cruz-Ayoroa, A.J.: Static simulation: a method for power and energy estimation in embedded microprocessors. In: 2010 53rd IEEE International Midwest Symposium on Circuits and Systems, pp. 41–44, August 2010
3. Ahlers, D., Driscoll, P., Kraemer, F.A., Anthonisen, F., Krogstie, J.: A measurement-driven approach to understand urban greenhouse gas emissions in nordic cities. NIK Norsk Informatikkonferanse, pp. 1–12, November 2016
4. Bazzaz, M., Salehi, M., Ejlali, A.: An accurate instruction-level energy estimation model and tool for embedded systems. IEEE Trans. Instrum. Meas. 62(7), 1927–1934 (2013)
5. Ditzler, G., Roveri, M., Alippi, C., Polikar, R.: Learning in nonstationary environments: a survey. IEEE Comput. Intell. Mag. 10(4), 12–25 (2015)
6. Guthaus, M.R., Ringenberg, J.S., Ernst, D., Austin, T.M., Mudge, T., Brown, R.B.: Mibench: a free, commercially representative embedded benchmark suite. In: Proceedings of the Fourth Annual IEEE International Workshop on Workload Characterization. WWC-4 (Cat. No. 01EX538), pp. 3–14, December 2001
7. Homb, G.R.: Adaptive store and forward. master's thesis, Norwegian University of Science and Technology, NTNU, June 2016
8. Hussain, A.: Energy consumption of wireless IoT nodes. master's thesis, Norwegian University of Science and Technology, NTNU, June 2017
9. Kansal, A., Hsu, J., Zahedi, S., Srivastava, M.B.: Power management in energy harvesting sensor networks. ACM Trans. Embed. Comput. Syst. 6(4), 32–38 (2007)
10. Ktari, J., Abid, M.: System level power and energy modeling for signal processing applications. In: 2007 2nd International Design and Test Workshop, pp. 218–221, December 2007

11. Laurent, J., Julien, N., Senn, E., Martin, E.: Functional level power analysis: an efficient approach for modeling the power consumption of complex processors. In: Proceedings of the Conference on Design, Automation and Test in Europe, DATE 2004, vol. 1, p. 10666. IEEE Computer Society, Washington, DC(2004). http://dl. acm.org/citation.cfm?id=968878.968987

12. Multi-tech systems Inc., 2205 woodale drive, mounds view, MN 55112: multiconnect mDot: MTDOT developer guide, 3 edn. (2016)

13. Shin, D., Shim, H., Joo, Y., Yun, H.S., Kim, J., Chang, N.: Energy-monitoring tool for low-power embedded programs. IEEE Des. Test Comput. **19**(4), 7–17 (2002)

14. Sornin, N., Luis, M., Eirich, T., Kramp, T., Hersent, O.: LoRaWAN specification. LoRa alliance, 1 edn., January 2015

15. STMicroelectronics: AN4841 application note digital signal processing for STM32 microcontrollers using CMSIS, 1 edn., march 2016

16. STMicroelectronics: STM32F411xC STM32F411xE ARM cortex-M4 32b MCU+FPU, 125 DMIPS, 512KB flash, 128KB RAM, USB OTG FS, 11 TIMs, 1 ADC, 13 comm. interfaces, 6 edn., December 2016

17. You, D., Hwang, Y.S., Ahn, Y.H., Chung, K.S.: Energy consumption prediction technique for embedded mobile device by using battery discharging pattern. In: 2010 2nd IEEE International Conference on Network Infrastructure and Digital Content, pp. 907–910, September 2010

Author Index

Afifi, Hossam 63
Ansari, Keyvan 122
Aoudjit, Rachida 63
Astaiza, Evelio 138

Banerjee, Soumya 178
Beck, Michael Till 88
Belzner, Lenz 88
Benmerzoug, Djamel 207
Bermudez, Héctor 138
Bouzefrane, Samia 49, 178
Bouzegza, Wassila 74
Brune, Philipp 155

Cheng, Feng 18
Chin, Won Sang 99

El Kamel, Ali 109
Erritali, Mohammed 195

Feng, Yanming 122
Fonseca, Camilo Isaza 166
Franck, Christian 1

Großschädl, Johann 1

Hahn, Carsten 88
Hoceini, Ouassila 63
Holzner, Stephan 88
Hssina, Badr 195
Hu, Jiawei 34
Hussain, Amen 222

Ilham, Kitouni 207
Ioualalen, Malika 74

Jang, Ju Wook 99
Jung, Moon Yong 99

Khemissa, Hamza 49
Kim, Hong Jin 99
Kraemer, Frank Alexander 222

Lamkhantar, Soukaina 195
Lezzar, Fouzi 207
Li, Hui 34

Madani, Youness 195
Majdoub, Manel 109
Meinel, Christoph 18
Merbouha, Abdelkrim 195
Mühlethaler, Paul 178

Naghavi, Hannaneh Sadat 122

Osmani, Aomar 207
Ouroua, Naouel 74

Reyes Daza, Brayan S. 166

Salcedo Parra, Octavio J. 138, 166
Schedel, Angela 155

Tamkittikhun, Nattachart 222
Tandjaoui, Djamel 49
Tian, Yu-Chu 122

Ussath, Martin 18

Wang, Yunmin 34

Xu, Li 34

Youssef, Habib 109

Zhang, Huayu 34

Printed in the United States
By Bookmasters

Printed in the United States
by Bookmasters